Social Work

Introducing Professional Practice

Patricia Higham

SAGE Publications

London ● Thousand Oaks ● New Delhi

SAGE Publications Ltd
1 Oliver's Yard
55 City Road
London EC1Y 1SP

SAGE Publications Inc.
2455 Teller Road
Thousand Oaks, California 91320

SAGE Publications India Pvt Ltd
B-42, Panchsheel Enclave
Post Box 4109
New Delhi 110 017

British Library Cataloguing in Publication data

A catalogue record for this book is available from the British Library

ISBN 1-4129-0856-6   ISBN 978-1-4129-0856-6
ISBN 1-4129-0857-4   ISBN 978-1-4129-0857-3 (pbk)

Library of Congress Control Number: 2005928153

Typeset by C&M Digitals (P) Ltd., Chennai, India
Printed on paper from sustainable resources
Printed in Great Britain by The Alden Press, Oxford

CONTENTS

ACKNOWLEDGEMENTS

The book has benefited from the encouragement of colleagues, professional associates, practitioners, carers, and service users who responded to my ideas with helpful comments, especially: Professor Pete Alcock (University of Birmingham); Professor Suzy Braye (University of Sussex); Jack Higham (Canon Emeritus, Peterborough Cathedral); Dr Ray Jones (Chair of the Assembly for Social Work and Social Care Education Training and Research, and Director of Adult and Community Services, Wiltshire County Council); Siobhan Laird (University of Sheffield); Professor Joyce Lishman (Robert Gordon University); Jackie Powell (University of Southampton); Professor Michael Preston-Shoot (University of Luton); Mavis Sharp (Skills for Care East Midlands Practice Learning Centre Network and Lincolnshire Social Services Department); Dr Roger Smith (University of Leicester); Sandra Vanner and members of the Carers Council (Allies in Adult Mental Health Nottinghamshire); and Angela Washington (Independent Care Manager for Brain Injury).

FOREWORD

Social workers have a powerful and persuasive tale to tell of how they and their craft have been at the cutting edge of social policy development and delivery for over 50 years. Before 'social inclusion' became a part of political-speak, it was social workers who valued people who were experiencing exclusion. It was, and is, social workers who stayed alongside people who were distressed while others withdrew their gaze and looked elsewhere, with their backward glances stigmatising, stereotyping, and segregating people who were poor, disabled, or who had been abused and exploited. Social work itself has also sometimes been marginalised.

But now, as Higham notes, the requirement for social workers to be registered and regulated, to be educated and trained to at least graduate level, and with the title of 'social worker' at last protected, gives social work a platform of professional credibility alongside other 'caring professions'.

It is for these reasons that this text is topical and timely. The story told traces social work's history and development and discusses and debates its dilemmas, but it ultimately portrays social workers basing their practice on a strong foundation of values, informed by evidence, and with social workers as competent and skilled professional craftsmen and women. A noble profession indeed.

Dr Ray Jones

Director of Adult and Community Services,
Wiltshire County Council
Chair, Assembly for Social Care and Social Work Education, Training and Research
Deputy Chair, British Association of Social Workers

INTRODUCTION

Purpose: the Development of Social Workers

This book was written to engage you, the reader, in questioning and reflecting on social work and social care, and your own emergent role in relation to changes taking place in professional social work. In March 2004 the Parliamentary Under Secretary of State for Community announced that 'social work' was a protected title in the UK. Significantly, the Under Secretary announced that he welcomed hearing from the voice of the profession. At last, the profession of social work seemingly had won official recognition, although many social workers would argue that social work had already demonstrated that it was a profession. No longer would just anyone be able to call himself or herself a social worker. Intending social workers are now required to complete successfully the qualifying social work degree (introduced from 2003); to register with a care council; and to undertake continuing professional development.

However, contemporary changes in policy and practice range more widely than just winning professional status for social work:

- The new opportunities given to the social work profession are linked to modernisation of service delivery that seeks to drive up standards.
- New ways of thinking about social work practice require social workers to share power with the people who use their services and their carers.
- The nature of 'caring' roles is being redefined, with new roles either seemingly usurping social work's place, or alternatively prompting social work to embrace wider definitions of its own purpose.

Therefore this book was written to do more than state the requirements of the qualifying degree – it tries to capture the essence of the changes sweeping through social work, social care, and children's services and to engage you in the debate.

The book's main purpose is to assist the development of future professional social workers in the UK from when they first begin to consider social work as a career, as they progress through the qualifying social work degree, and as they begin their practice as newly qualified workers seeking to consolidate their learning. The book's first specific aim is to enable readers to gain an initial understanding of the knowledge, value, and skill requirements of professional social work.

Second Purpose: Reaching a Wider Audience

The book's second purpose is to address changes in the nature and context of social work practice in the UK. This will be of interest to social work students and practitioners but also to others working in vocational and professional areas of the caring services. The book will discuss the relationship of social work to new organisational arrangements for services to children and young people, new support roles in health and social care, multi-professional practice, and international models of social work. Practitioners undertaking foundation degrees and qualifications in health and social care or children's services can use the book to develop an understanding of professional social work. They will benefit from considering important themes that are shared within multi-professional practice.

Professionals from other disciplines who work alongside social workers in multi-professional teams will find the book helpful in debating the nature of social work. Experienced social workers whose qualifications pre-date the social work degree can use the book to update their knowledge of contemporary themes – useful for supporting their post qualification studies. Practitioners located outside the UK will find the content relevant to issues that affect social work practice across and beyond national boundaries.

Rationale

The book uses the Benchmark Statement for honours degrees in Social Work (QAA, 2000) as its basis for discussion. A group of 10 UK based academics, including the author, developed the Benchmark Statement for the Quality Assurance Agency for Higher Education. The Statement provides a template of the knowledge, understanding, skills, and standards that might be expected of a graduate in social work. Since its publication, the Benchmark Statement has informed generally the curriculum of the social work degree. QAA intends to review the Statement for its ongoing relevance – a likely change may place more emphasis on multi-professional practice, which this book has taken into account.

In addition, the care councils require that social work degrees incorporate the National Occupational Standards for Social Work (Topss UK Partnership, 2002). In Scotland, the Standards in Social Work Education (SiSWE, Scottish Executive [SE], 2003) bring together key elements of the Benchmark Statement and the Occupational Standards. Because the Benchmark Statement was developed by academics, it does not cover the specific social work practice requirements. National Occupational Standards (developed through a process of consultancies with social workers, people who use services, carers, students, academics, professional bodies, and employers) provide the basis of assessing students' competence in practice to a recognised standard before they are awarded the degree. The Standards state specifically what social work students must be able to demonstrate in practice, and these are discussed throughout the book.

Within the UK, each country's requirements for social work training (Department of Health [DH], 2002b; SE, 2003; Care Council for Wales [CCW], 2004; Northern Ireland Social Care Council [NISCC], 2003, 2004) place the National Occupational Standards at the centre of the new degree, and state additionally their particular requirements for standards, training and assessment, entry, teaching, learning and assessment (including days in practice). These documents provided the basis for universities to plan the degree. Universities offering the degree present their particular country's requirements in different ways, but by the end of each degree programme, all social work students will have gained ample opportunity to attain the qualifying requirements. Students achieve a national award but one that is specific to their particular country within the UK. They are also able to undertake some customised regional and local learning that is particular to the university at which they enrol.

Content and Structure

The book comprises seven chapters:

- Chapter 1 'What Is Social Work?' explores contrasting definitions of social work that are rooted in different historical traditions and international contexts, the concepts of professionalism, the mechanisms for promoting the UK emphasis on regulation and standard setting, and the quest for a collective voice for professional social work.
- Chapter 2 'Focus on Practice' suggests strategies for developing and sustaining good practice within and beyond the requirements of the degree, arguing that transferable key skills provide an essential toolkit for future development. The point is made that social workers need to balance empowerment of people who use services with protection of vulnerable people, thus posing potential dilemmas for practice.
- Chapter 3 'Different Contexts for Practice' explores the social policy contexts of practice, including: the history of the welfare state and its transformation to a welfare mix; the rise of social care; and the impact of themes of citizenship and social exclusion, resources for social policy, and international policies and practice. The chapter argues that the history and strategies of social policy and social work are intertwined, and that contemporary British social work is beginning to resemble international social welfare models by adopting social pedagogy and delivering services on a subsidiarity basis.
- Chapter 4 'Social Work Roles' provides accounts of the different roles that social workers select, and explores the dilemma of balancing empowerment of individuals with protection of them.
- Chapter 5 'Values for Practice' sets out the change in understanding of the values required by professional practice, arguing that social work has adopted and owned values from other sources. The values dilemmas that can occur within practice are part of the realities of practice.
- Chapter 6 'Knowledge for Professional Practice' explores different contexts of knowledge, with a particular emphasis on human growth and development, the social model of disability, and the contribution of research to practice.
- Chapter 7 'Skills for Practice and Continuing Professional Development' discusses skills, assessment processes, and theoretical approaches to practice. The chapter explores how social workers can continue to develop their practice beyond the point of qualification through reflection and continuing professional development.

How to Use the Book

Each chapter contains topic headings, case study examples of practice, questions for reflection, and suggestions for further reading. You can read the book chronologically, or else refer to the headings in each chapter for a more random selection of topics. Questions placed within each chapter can be used for discussion. Some of the textual details will change, but the central issues will remain open to debate. Further acquisition of knowledge and experience, and then reflection on what is learned must follow this introduction to professional social work.

1 WHAT IS PROFESSIONAL SOCIAL WORK?

Contemporary definitions of social work as a degree subject reflect its origins in a range of different academic and practice traditions. The precise nature and scope of [social work] is itself a matter for legitimate study and critical debate. (Quality Assurance Agency [QAA], 2000: §2.2)

Introduction

What is the most appropriate definition of contemporary social work? Competing definitions of social work vie for acceptance. This chapter provides an initial understanding of what social work aspires to be, how the British social work degree is constructed, and why the caring services need professional social work. Social work changes and adapts to new social concerns and organisational structures, so that contemporary social work is characterised by its changing nature, rather than its agreement on a specific definition.

Social work's search for a definition was prompted by its quest to attain professional status. Leading figures in the development of British social work after the Second World War asked:

- What is social work?
- Is social work a profession?

The answer to the second question is now more evidently 'yes', but the search for professional status is not yet concluded. Higher expectations of social work pose a challenge for social workers. Social work practitioners themselves will validate social work's claim to be a profession as they develop their professional practice to the high standards required by the social work degree and by their post qualification studies. Whether you, the reader, are a social work student on a degree programme or an experienced practitioner, you will be (or will become) familiar with the climate of change that challenges social work's ability to respond. Social workers have to grapple with new social issues and dilemmas that affect the lives of people seeking help. To function at that level of practice, they have to be well informed and confident in their professional ability to exercise appropriate judgements.

Chapter Structure

The chapter is based on four main themes:

1. The problems of defining social work because of its changing nature. Social work is located in the context of the helping professions, the caring services, and the history of the British welfare state. Comparing different definitions of social work from North American, British, European, and international perspectives provides some understanding of how and why social work became recognised as a profession.
2. The role of social work in wider contexts and in the context of contemporary developments. Social work is influenced by the modernising efforts of organisations that regulate social work practice and education, and is characterised by an emergent partnership and alliance between social work and social care.
3. History and origins. Social work is influenced by the contributions of casework, social inequality, and social inclusion models.
4. Considering the future of social work. Differing views of the nature and role of social work can lead to fragmentation, so there is a case to be made for recognition of 'Allied Caring Professions' and a collective non-governmental voice for social work and social care. Recent attempts to define social work have led to broad agreement on an international definition and a new kind of professionalism that calls for a broader remit but recognises further challenges to defining social work.

Social Work, Helping Professions, Caring Services and the Welfare State

Social work is located within a network of *caring services* or *personal social services* staffed by members of the *helping professions*. The term *helping profession* is self-explanatory. Social work is not the only helping profession (Heraud, 1970). Other helping professions include the well-accepted roles of nursing, teaching, and medicine.

Social workers practise alongside other professional and vocational workers in a range of service provision designated as the *caring services*. The term 'caring services' is an imperfect description of the service provision delivered by different organisational structures (Tossell and Webb, 1994). Not all of these organisations are overtly 'caring'. History determines their inclusion on the list. Current networks of services developed after the founding of the British welfare state in 1948 (Jones, 1994), for which the Beveridge Report (1942) supplied a blueprint. Beveridge identified five *giants* (want, ignorance, idleness, disease, and squalor) that had to be overcome through establishment of the range of comprehensive services that are known as the welfare state. For the purposes of this book, the term *caring services* is used to refer to the following areas of provision:

- Advice, guidance, and information
- Benefits and pensions agencies
- Carer organisations
- Children's and young persons services
- Community development and regeneration
- Education
- Health
- Housing
- Service user organisations

- Social care
- Social work
- Social workers in the justice field, youth justice workers, and probation officers
- Support roles in education, including education welfare, learning mentors, and in England, Connexions personal advisers
- Welfare rights
- Youth work

The organisational structures of the caring services vary according to location within the UK. Each broad service category may comprise statutory organisations based in local authorities, nationally based organisations with regional structures, regional organisations, and large and small independent organisations that are charities or private organisations. Munday (1990: 48) helps us to understand what is usually meant by *caring services* in contemporary contexts.

Caring services comprise:

- work undertaken by social workers, but also other occupational groups, and possibly volunteers;
- services provided for particular groups including elderly people, people with physical and/or mental disabilities or mental health problems, children and families, and sometimes young and adult offenders;
- services provided through fieldwork and in domiciliary, day care or residential settings, with some trend towards 'community care';
- a selective rather than universal service aimed at individuals, clients or users with particular needs;
- work aimed at achieving change (whether in human relationships and/or social environment); providing social support and/or control; and protecting civil rights.

Caring Services and Multi-professional Teams

The organisational context for social work practice requires social workers to work with different professionals in multi-professional teams, for example, in primary health care trusts, children's services, and youth offending teams. For example, in England and Wales the Youth Justice Board (YJB) promotes multi-professional Youth Offending Teams (Yots) as key components of the youth justice system. The Crime and Disorder Act 1998 established Yots in April 2000 to bring together services that work with young people and prevent crime, including the police, probation, social services, workers in the field of drug and alcohol misuse, housing officers, health, and education. Each local authority in England and Wales has a Yot whose work is coordinated by a manager. The YJB argues that the multi-professional nature of the Yot provides a more appropriate response to the needs of young offenders. Yots use a national assessment tool to assess young offenders' needs, the particular problems that led to offending behaviour, and the risks posed to others. The Yot then identifies programmes that address the needs identified to prevent further offences taking place.

A Yot Inspection Report (September 2004), published by the Audit Commission, the Commission for Social Care Inspection and the education inspectorate Ofsted, points to examples of good partnerships in Yots. Inspectors commented positively on the team members' hard work, positive engagement with children and young people, enthusiasm and commitment (YJB, 2004).

⬚ Case Study 1.1 – Multi-professional Practice

Jonathan Allen is an experienced social worker who was seconded by his local authority into the Yot when it was first established. At first he found it difficult to communicate effectively with his new colleagues, none of whom were social workers. He noted the different practice cultures. For example, the police were used to quick action while the social workers were accustomed to more reflection before deciding what to do. He had never worked in a team with a teacher or a nurse, and at first he expressed some stereotyped views of their contributions. The Yot set a short time frame for responding to referrals. He felt under pressure. His line manager was not a social worker. Jonathan was the sole representative of social work, working in an environment where a shared understanding of social work was missing. At first this was daunting, but over time he and his new colleagues built a team relationship. Their uniting concern was their wish to work with young offenders in a constructive way to prevent re-offending and meet individual needs. The team's use of a shared assessment provided a way forward that in its ideal form resulted in complementary pooling of knowledge and skills. At times, Jonathan thought that his perspective and values were entirely different from those of his non-social worker team members. The importance of communication and working with shared goals provided a bridge across potential professional divides and helped Jonathan to appreciate the values and skills of his colleagues.

Social workers comprise an important part of Yots. As the example in Case Study 1.1 shows, when social workers first joined Yots, they were likely to find the working environment different from their experiences when working alongside other social workers. Similar multi-professional models of practice are being developed at accelerating rates in other service areas and in other countries of the UK. Part of the art of being a social worker in contemporary practice is to become acquainted with the professional and vocational workers employed in the myriad of allied service delivery organisations – they are colleagues on whose collaborative efforts social workers will depend to deliver the best possible services to people who use services. Instead of working across the divide of agency boundaries, social workers increasingly will work with these multi-professional colleagues in the same team.

The example in Case Study 1.1 illustrates the changing nature of social work practice. Over the years, different definitions of social work have tried to capture social work's essential nature.

Definitions of Social Work

The lack of an entirely satisfactory or agreed definition of social work makes it more logical to take a comparative critical view rather than argue a particular definition. The Benchmark Statement suggests that 'contemporary definitions of social work as a degree subject reflect its origins in a range of different academic and practice traditions' (QAA, 2000: §2.2). These include:

- North American traditions of social work
- UK traditions of social work
- European and international traditions of social work

The Benchmark Statement identifies three main issues for defining social work: its location in different welfare contexts in different countries; 'competing views' (QAA, 2000: §2.2.2) about the nature, place, and purpose of social work; and the changing nature of social work as it responds to external challenges and demands (QAA, 2000: §2.2.3). In order to understand the social work profession of today and where it might be heading in the future, one should consider the historical attempts to define social work.

North American Definitions of Social Work

American perspectives of social work dominated the early search for a definition because the professionalisation of social work proceeded more rapidly in the USA than in the UK. Kenneth Pray (1949: 33–4), an American academic, suggested that social work was:

> a normal constructive social instrument … a necessary part of the structure of a civilized, well-planned society because it is directed to helping individuals meet the problems of their constantly shifting relations with one another and with the whole society, and to helping the whole society, at the same time, adjust its demands upon its members and its services to them in accordance with the real needs of the individuals that compose and determine its life.

This definition emphasised social work's benevolent change agent role in the interaction between the individual and society, affirming that social work's role was caring about and promoting the 'real needs' of individuals.

Almost a decade later in 1958, the National Association of Social Workers (CSWP NASW, 1958: 15–16) in the USA defined social work as 'a constellation of values, purpose, sanction, knowledge, and method'. The three purposes of social work were:

1. To assist individuals and groups to identify and resolve or minimize problems arising out of disequilibrium between themselves and the environment.
2. To identify potential areas of disequilibrium between individuals or groups and the environment in order to prevent the occurrence of disequilibrium.
3. In addition to these curative and preventive aims, to seek out, identify, and strengthen the maximum potential in individuals, groups, and communities. (CSWP NASW, 1958: 5–6).

The NASW definition moves beyond the individual to include groups and communities as a focus of concern for social work intervention. The emphasis on 'equilibrium' suggests that the relationship between the individual, the group, the community, and the 'environment' was a matter of achieving the correct balance – but social work's use of power was not defined, except to suggest its responsibility to maximise others' potential.

These definitions imply a general trust in governmental institutions and social work's benevolent power, rather than awareness of the potentially oppressive use of social work power with user groups. Their stance on power can be understood to derive from the post-Second World War years, when the concern in the USA was to build a world of democratic institutions after the defeat of fascism. European intellectuals who had escaped Hitler influenced the direction of social institutions in their adopted country. For example Erikson (1968), who practised psychology at Harvard, and at the Austen Riggs Center in Stockbridge Massachusetts that pioneered community mental health, developed a view of human growth and development that influenced social work practice.

Karl de Schweinitz (1962: 4), another American social work academic, suggested that social work comprised 'the body of knowledge, skills and ethics, professionally employed in the administration of the social services and in the development of programs for social welfare'– a statement consonant with current interpretations of professional knowledge, skills, and ethics with which a social worker both administers services and develops professional activities. However, there is more about the nature of social work than this definition tells us. Pincus and Minahan (1973: 9) argued that:

> Social work is concerned with the interactions between people and their social environment which affect the ability of people to accomplish their life tasks, alleviate distress, and realize their aspirations and values. The purpose of social work therefore is to (1) enhance the problem-solving and coping capacities of people, (2) link people with systems that provide them with resources, services, and opportunities, (3) promote the effective and humane operation of these systems, and (4) contribute to the development and improvement of social policy.

They saw social work as an interaction between individuals and the environment with an increased emphasis being placed on interaction with systems to bring about change, for example the locus of change is not always the user of services. They portrayed social work as an influence on social policy, not simply intervening with individuals.

The *Code of Ethics* of the NASW (1999: 1) expresses a more contemporary definition that attempts to bring together different elements of social work practice – values, individual interactions, and also goals to change societal institutions:

> The primary mission of the social work profession is to enhance human well-being and help to meet the basic human needs of all people, with particular attention to the needs and empowerment of people who are vulnerable, oppressed, and living in poverty … . Social workers promote social justice and social change with and on behalf of … individuals, families, groups, organizations, and communities. Social workers are sensitive to cultural and ethnic diversity and strive to end discrimination, oppression, poverty, and other forms of social injustice. These activities may be in the form of direct practice, community organizing, supervision, consultation, administration, advocacy, social and political action, policy development and implementation, education, and research and evaluation. Social workers seek to enhance the capacity of people to address their own needs. Social workers also seek to promote the responsiveness of organizations, communities, and other social institutions to individuals' needs and social problems. The mission of the social work profession is rooted in a set of core values … service, social justice, dignity and worth of the person, importance of human relationships, integrity, and competence.

The conclusion is that social work is a broad endeavour embracing many different aspects and purposes, not all of which can always be easily reconciled with each other. The ascendancy of one kind of social work practice over another is influenced by the purpose and policies of the organisations that employ social workers. Social workers have some choice about how they practise. The obligations of assuming professional status require social workers' allegiance to wider sets of professional goals than are expressed by employers' mission statements. The wider allegiances may at times lead to potential conflict with organisational policies – a dilemma that has troubled social workers in the past and which continues to pose problems.

UK Definitions of Social Work

Payne (1996: 2) provided an overview of British attempts to define social work and professionalism. Looking at the historic attempts to construct the nature of social work and how and whether it might be considered a profession, he identified three perspectives 'around which visions of social work coalesce'. Each perspective suggests a different use of social work power. The three perspectives (1996: 2) are:

- *Individual reformist*, in which social work is a part of welfare services, meeting individual needs, but also improving services.
- *Socialist collectivist*, in which social work is part of a system that promotes co-operative and mutual support to empower oppressed people, and to create an alternative society marked by more egalitarian relationships.
- *Reflexive therapeutic*, in which social work tries to attain well-being for individuals, groups and communities by promoting their growth and self realisation, helping them to gain control over their lives.

The early definitions of social work in the USA were built on the perspective of the *individual reformism* approach, but gradually moved to incorporate more of the ethos of the *socialist collectivist* and *reflexive therapeutic* perspectives. The British definitions of social work tended to pattern themselves on American definitions, but they too changed over time to reflect changing views of social work's purpose and use of power. Within a context of competing ideas about social work, some British academics avoided the dilemma of definition and instead sought to explain what social workers did. For example, the Barclay Committee (1982) analysed British social workers' roles and tasks instead of defining social work as a profession. Payne (1996) analysed social work of the 1990s as a professional 'occupation' in apparent acknowledgement of its semi-professional status. Contemporary social work academics (Parton and O'Byrne, 2000) acknowledge the ambiguous and disputed purpose of British social work, echoed by the Benchmark Statement's emphasis on social work graduates being: 'Equipped both to understand, and to work within, this contested debate about nature, scope and purpose [of social work]' (QAA, 2000: §2.2.4).

European and International Definitions of Social Work

Social work in Europe and in other areas of the world uses approaches that resemble the UK and North American definitions but contain a broader range of roles. The European Association of Schools of Social Work and the International Association of Schools of Social Work are unifying organisations, communicating ideas and strategies that are appropriate for the particular contexts in which social work is practised. In some European countries the role of *social pedagogue* (discussed in Chapter 3) is recognised as a popular form of social work intervention, but is largely unrecognised in the UK (Higham, 2001). Social pedagogy adopts a developmental model of practice rather than a welfare model.

Social Work as a Profession: Making a Case

Early attempts to define social work tried to address the question: what makes a profession? Preoccupied with establishing its identity, social work in the USA and the UK considered this question to the point of obsession. As early as 1915, Flexner began to consider whether social work in the USA was a profession. Greenwood's (1966) study of the elements of professionalisation suggests five attributes: (1) a body of systematic theory; (2) recognised authority; (3) community approval of the authority; (4) a code of ethics; and (5) a professional culture with formal professional organisations.

Heraud (1970: 221) defines professionalisation as 'the process by which occupations change in the direction of the elements represented ... [by the ideal type or model]'. He suggests that occupations can be grouped on a continuum with established professions at one end and 'less skilled and prestigious occupations' at the other end. Compton and Galaway (1984) argued that a profession contains *inter alia* the traits listed in Box 1.1.

**Box 1.1: Traits of a Profession (adapted from
Compton and Galaway, 1984)**

1. a distinctive body of knowledge;
2. a code of ethics;
3. recognised practice expertise;
4. restricted entry through qualifications.

By the end of the 20th century, social work in the UK had provided considerable evidence for recognition as a profession based on these criteria and guidelines.

Social Work Developed a Distinctive Body of Research Based Knowledge

Most British universities that offer social work education have appointed professors of social work who contribute to social work research activity and publications. In 1999/2000, the Economics and Social Research Council funded a six seminar series for social work academics, Theorising Social Work Research (TSWR), followed by a conference in December 2000 to explore the distinctive contributions of social work research to social science research activity with the intention of raising social work's profile as a research discipline in its own right. The organising group, drawn from the Joint University Council (JUC) Social Work Education Committee (SWEC), the National Institute for Social Work and the Association of University Professors of Social Work, argued that social work research's importance was enhanced through the demand for evidence-informed and research-minded practice. The seminars identified social work research's promotion of social inclusion through research and innovative involvement of research stakeholders, including the voices of usually silent groups in research activities (TSWR, 2000).

Payne (1991) portrayed social work theory as socially constructed and part of the social construction of social work's activities. Howe (1987: 3), arguing that particular theories determine the characteristics of individual practice at its different stages, classified social work theories into four paradigms that drew on Burrell and Morgan's classification of theory (1979):

- raisers of consciousness;
- revolutionists;
- seekers after meaning; and
- fixers.

Social Workers accept the British Association of Social Workers (BASW) *Code of Ethics*

A widely agreed perception is that social work practitioners identify values and ethics as important motivators for their practice. The BASW *Code of Ethics* has a much wider level of acceptance among social workers than its actual membership numbers indicate, and social work education has traditionally given a prominent place in its curricula to social work values.

Social Work Has a Recognised Practice Expertise

Since 1991, well-established post-qualification programmes, including the Practice Teaching Award, the Post Qualifying Award in Child Care, and the Mental Health Social Worker Award (General Social Care Council [GSCC], 2001), demonstrate achievement of recognised practice expertise. Post-qualification study following the degree in social work will enhance social workers' skills and specialist expertise.

Social Work Has Restricted Entry through Qualifications

Universities and colleges offering social work education have a tradition of requiring qualifications for entry, including *non-standard* qualifications of previous life experience, experience in social care, and access to higher education courses as well as conventional academic qualifications. Social work education traditionally has interviewed applicants to ensure a sound selection for the profession.

Becoming a Profession: from Despair to Recognition

Official recognition of social work as a profession was slow to arrive. From a European perspective, Etzioni (1969) argued that certain occupations such as social work, teaching, and nursing, where the majority of employees are women, are semi-professions because their practitioners work for the most part within hierarchical public organisational structures and therefore lack autonomy. This kind of employment was typical of the UK, where social workers worked mainly in large social services or social work departments, but now social workers in the UK are working in a wider range of organisations, including independent agencies, regeneration projects, health care trusts, and children's services that create different identity problems for social workers.

Social work educators and practitioners in the UK mounted considerable evidence to prove that social work met most of the criteria of a profession. The social work community did not all support the argument because of fears of elitism. Bamford (1990) argued that British social work had failed to establish its independent professional status, and had lost public esteem. He portrayed a situation where social workers' employment contexts were marked by managerial control, high turnover of staff, absence of clearly identified personal responsibility, and lack of a practitioner career structure. Professionalism was circumscribed by managerialism (1990: 1). There was no self-regulation of the profession in training or in disciplinary action. This despairing view was widely held in 1990, but the situation changed, triggering the questions:

- What led to social work's recognition as a profession in 2004?
- What changed the negative views of social work?

Key factors in the winning of official recognition for social work as a profession were:

- Social work's own expectations of professional practice.
- The drive to modernise policy and practice in order to raise standards (DH, 1998).
- The UK's emphasis on regulation and standard setting.

Modernisation: Raising Standards in Social Work and Social Care

Both carers and people who use services sought more community-based services from social workers and social care workers. In response to these demands, the government introduced the

Modernising Social Services agenda (DH, 1998) to improve the quality of service outcomes through a range of programmes. The modernising agenda sets concrete targets and monitors whether they are achieved. As part of modernisation, the government wanted joined-up 'best value' services, characterised by accountability and efficiency. Modernisation strives to provide better multi-professional working, and requires social care and social work to provide excellent quality through working with the National Health Service (NHS), education, and other organisations to integrate care across professional boundaries. Modernisation triggered events culminating in the official recognition of social work as a profession. These events are listed in Box 1.2:

Box 1.2: Factors Leading to Official Recognition of the Social Work Profession

- The protected title status granted to social work in 2003, so that only qualified social work practitioners may call themselves social workers.
- Compulsory registration of social workers on a social care register from 2005.
- The introduction of the social work degree from 2003.

New Regulatory Frameworks and Organisational Structures

The UK government believes that standards can be raised through regulation of the three inter-related components of services, staff, and training. The DH's (2002a) quality framework sets standards and regulates social care's provision of services (including professional social work). Care councils in Scotland, Northern Ireland, and Wales carry out combined regulatory functions for social work and social care. In England, the situation is more complex: four organisational structures have been set up to take responsibility for the regulatory and information functions relating to social care and professional social work. The English 'Big Four' include:

- The Social Care Institute for Excellence (SCIE) that identifies and promotes best practice based on evidence from research and other sources, produces guidance, promotes learning networks, and feeds into work on developing occupational standards. SCIE's remit extends to policy makers and government departments in England, Wales, Northern Ireland, and Scotland. Its scope of responsibility has been under discussion by the DH and there are concerns that SCIE may not be able to avoid organisational change.
- The Commission for Social Care Inspection (CSCI) (formerly the National Care Standards Commission), an independent watchdog that ensures high standards of care, inspects homes, provides public reports and user advice, reports annually on agency performance in relation to Care Standards and Service Frameworks, and protects vulnerable adults. The 2005 Budget announced the intended merger of CSCI and the Healthcare Commission and the dispersal of its responsibilities to other bodies.

- The GSCC (2003) regulates staff in England by maintaining a register of staff fit to practise and taking action where staff breach standards. Codes of practice (developed UK-wide) provide guidance to social care workers. Individual social workers on the Social Care Register may be struck off if they are found to have practised in a manner that is contrary to the ethics and standards required for registration.
- Skills for Care is a sector skills council formerly known as Topss (the Training Organisation for Social Care). Skills for Care regulates training by undertaking workforce planning, linking qualifications to posts, assessing and responding to the social care sector's training needs, setting targets for training, developing qualifications, and promoting equal opportunities and social inclusion. A UK partnership ensures that qualifications are accepted on a UK-wide basis. In England its responsibilities are limited to adult care. A separate body takes responsibility in England for work force planning and developing qualifications for workers in services to children, young people and families.

Concerns have been expressed about how and whether the regulatory bodies in England will achieve their goals, given the pressure for rapid change and their own organisational turbulence. All of these regulatory bodies have experienced changes of function and growth in a short space of time. Social care education and training particularly in England may experience some gaps and discontinuity in policy and expectations as a result, but Scotland, Wales, and Northern Ireland may be able to avert some of the discontinuity.

Social Work's Relationship to Social Care

A historical impediment to recognition of social work as a profession was a misguided use of the term *social work* to describe activities now defined as *social care*. Along with considering definitions of social work, this chapter also considers a definition of social care. Social care workers provide personal care and support services to individuals, families, and communities (NISCC, 2005) to meet their common human needs, give them quality of life (Social Care Association [SCA], 2005) and enhance capabilities to help people become as independent as possible (Wing, 1978). One of the first times the term social care was used was probably at a seminar on social care research held at Downing College, Cambridge in July 1977 by the Centre for Studies in Social Policy with the Department of Health and Social Security (DHSS). The concept of social care was 'selected as a prism through which to order the questions for discussion … [meaning] the social as distinct from the economic ways in which people look after each other directly or indirectly … [and] the ways in which they can be helped to do so by or through official or unofficial caring agencies' (Barnes and Connelly, 1978: iii). The social care concept was used because 'it straddles established administrative, professional, and academic boundaries … [such as] the responsibilities of the DHSS and the local authorities for the personal social services, the professional practice of social work and the social rather than the medical and operational sciences' [which are] the dominant fields' (1978: iii).

The seminar pursued the idea of social care as an entity distinct from medical care, thinking outside the perceived existing boundaries of policy and practice and agreeing on the desirability of multi-professional interventions that could extend care beyond the scope of social services offered by local authorities and voluntary organisations (Barnes and Connelly, 1978: 147). Wing (1978) viewed social care not simply as routine activities that involved looking after people's physical needs but also the enhancement of independence. Social care, he concluded, should be offered when people's problems result in social disablement – where people are unable to perform satisfactorily their expected social and occupational roles. The seminar sowed the seeds of future social policy – the importance of promoting independence through integrated services in the broad context of social care.

Parker (1981) defined social care in a more matter of fact way as 'tending' activities – dressing, washing, cleaning, toileting, feeding tasks. As such, social care was destined to have a lowly image and to be the Cinderella of service provision. The social work profession did not take up the cause of social care, because it viewed social care's remit for physical care as distinct from social work. This was during the period when social work searched for its own defini- tion. (In contrast, the professions of nursing, physiotherapy, and occupational therapy com- bined aspects of physical care giving with professional level tasks such as assessment of need.) Instead of valuing hands-on care, professional social work adopted a casework/counselling role involving assessment of needs rather than a social care role of providing ongoing care and rehabilitation (Higham, 1998).

Social care staff who worked in residential homes and day centres were mainly unqualified part-time female workers. The Central Council for Education and Training in Social Work (CCETSW, the predecessor to the care councils) made some attempts in the 1970s to train social care staff through various certificated courses, which contained valuable learning, but were not part of a qualifications framework or a logical career progression, perhaps because it was feared that demand would exceed available training resources if too many social care staff aspired to become social workers. One of the courses, the Certificate in Social Services (CSS), was deemed a success, but eventually the government declared CSS to be the equivalent of a social work qualification, with the result that workers with a CSS qualification took jobs as social workers, leaving social care much as it was. Social work's early attempt to build a shared understanding of its professional role with social care ended with the demise of CSS in 1992.

The introduction of work-based vocational qualifications in the mid-1980s re-awakened interest in training social care staff, culminating in strategic policies for improving their qual- ifications. Training has been a hitherto neglected aspect of social care, and the majority of social care workers have had few opportunities for gaining qualifications related to the work that they do. Modernisation attempts to address this shortfall through the establishment of a regulatory system and provision of qualifications for the entire social care workforce, includ- ing professional social work. For example, of the approximately one million people in the social care workforce in England (comprising 5% of the English workforce), there have been no recognised qualifications either for managers in social care or for the workforce; and in 2000 around 80% of the workforce had no qualifications or had qualifications unsuitable for their current work (Topss England, 2000: 1). A similar situation exists in the other countries of the UK. Skills for Care's (2005) Workforce Intelligence Report estimated that training targets set in England of having 50% of staff achieve at least NVQ2 had not been met, but significantly, full information was lacking about the levels and qualifications in the workforce as a whole, and concerning the social care workforce in the independent sector, day care organisations, partnership bodies, the NHS, and new types of care providers, thus casting doubt on the accuracy of information.

What does this history of social care mean for the profession of social work? Social care has now gained the attention it merits. Social care is recognised as an overarching domain of activity that promotes people's well-being and quality of life and seeks to overcome the social barriers that impede meaningful choices. Instead of social care being part of social work, British social work is now seen as part of social care, although the dominance of social care is disputed internationally. Social work and social care benefit from their alliance with each other.

Case Study 1.2 – The Alliance of Social Work and Social Care

Jane Clark is a social worker working as a care manager in an Adult Services team. She undertakes needs assessments of older people who need support. Following her assessment, Jane arranges appropriate 'packages of care' for people who use services, to be delivered by social care staff.

Jane assessed Mrs Elsie Green, aged 87, a widow living on her own, whose son lives abroad. Because of arthritis and increasing forgetfulness, Mrs Green had become housebound and isolated. She found the day-to-day tasks of looking after herself and her home very difficult. Consequently, she became depressed and self-neglecting. Mrs Green was reluctant to seek help, fearing that she would be put into a residential home.

Jane Clark's assessment of need recommended a referral for determining Mrs Green's mental health needs; a visit from an occupational therapist to consider adaptations to the home to make daily living tasks easier; attendance at a day centre two days a week; a personal alarm system; and home care support several days a week. The continuous presence in Mrs Green's life that offered some respite from isolation and monitored her well-being was the social care staff that worked at the day centre, and the social care staff that visited her at home. Mrs Green developed a trusting relationship with Denise Michael, a woman in her 40s who was her home care worker. Denise had recently completed a level 2 vocational qualification in care, the first qualification she had ever attained. Denise felt that her vocational qualification helped her to do a better job in social care and to feel more valued. When Jane, the social worker, reviewed the care package of Mrs Green, Denise the social care worker was knowledgeable and informative about Mrs Green's progress.

The example of Case Study 1.2 affirms that professional social workers practise in alliance with their social care colleagues, who probably will have attained a vocational qualification for the occupational standards required to perform their roles, and suggests that the relationship with the social care worker is important for the service user and is part of good practice. However, the drive for efficiency combined with the difficulty of finding staff sometimes makes continuity of relationships difficult to achieve.

📝 Case Study 1.3 – How Important Are Relationships?

After Mrs Green had developed trust and confidence in Denise Michael, her home care worker, she was dismayed to learn that Denise would no longer be calling on her. The agency supplying home care was very short staffed. Denise was reassigned to another area. Mrs Green tried to get used to a succession of temporary workers from other care agencies, none of whom she felt she got to know. She felt uneasy about the number of strangers coming into her home and wondered whether making the effort to maintain her independence in the community was worth the bother. Jane, the social worker, reviewed the situation, and recognising the desirability of continuous care relationships, raised the issue with her line manager to try to get Denise reassigned to Mrs Green. Although it could be argued that the most important outcome was that Mrs Green received her allocated hours of care, the social worker acknowledged the value of the particular relationship with Denise in sustaining Mrs Green's morale.

Clearly, relationships are crucially important within social care practice (Case Study 1.3). Social care is becoming a career in its own right, helped by the introduction of vocational qualification awards. The Registered Managers Award (Topss England, 2004) for managers of social care homes is an example of a higher-level vocational award in social care. Skill-mix teams, where professional workers from different disciplines and vocationally qualified workers work together in one team, will become a more prevalent work situation for social workers and social care workers. Social care workers are important members of the skill-mix team – colleagues to be valued.

Box 1.3: Recognition of Social Care

Rather than feeling threatened by the emphasis on social care, professional social workers who work closely with social care staff might reflect on the issues connected to their colleagues' previous untrained status, and ask themselves whether professional social work, now that it has achieved its own professional status, must acknowledge an ethical and moral requirement to redress the balance of disadvantage. Here is something to consider: social work, as the professional arm of social care, might take some future responsibility for supporting the continuing professional development and practice of their social care colleagues who are now having to gain vocational qualifications.

Attempts to Define the Nature and Tasks of Social Work: Where is Social Care?

As part of the search for a definition of social work, attempts were made to define the nature and tasks of social work but without a corresponding focus on social care. For example,

Butrym's (1976) study of the nature of British social work criticised over-ambitious expectations that social work could meet all the needs and wants placed before it, arguing for the deployment of social workers in skilled interventions rather than in the broader range of work that we now call social care. But Butrym did not define or recognise social care. When Butrym was writing about social work, social care lacked recognition and identity: only 'social work' existed. Definitions of social work struggled with concepts of *lay social work* (e.g. volunteering, or paid work undertaken by unqualified staff) compared to professional social work, which was viewed as more skilled and more professional. Timms and Timms (1977: 219) argued that because there is no one way to do social work, the distinctions between professional and lay social work cannot always be entirely clear, a logic which seems to defeat the claim for professional status.

When Barclay (1982) identified *counselling* and *social care planning* as the two main social work tasks, arguing for neighbourhood based community social work, Professor Robert Pinker from the London School of Economics expressed an alternative view. Pinker (1982) believed that the roles and tasks of social workers should not lose their focus on social casework and its specialisms, nor should they attempt to embrace all the activities demanded by the welfare state. The arguments of Pinker and Butrym tended to be viewed as elitist. The wider social context surrounding social work was seeking to promote equality and tackle oppression, and so the issue of professionalism lost ground. When the concept of social care was introduced in the late 1990s, social work practitioners and some academics initially felt that the rise of social care would signal the demise of professional social work. In fact, the opposite took place.

Now that social care (including children's services) is recognised as the broad domain of interventions operating within community projects, day care, residential care, and home based care organisations, social work has been redefined as the professional arm of social care. The emergence of social care as an entity in its own right has set social work free to become a profession. Instead of having to embrace every kind of intervention, social work can focus on higher level skills, values, and knowledge that are deemed necessary for professional practice. Social workers are expected to undertake complex assessments and interventions, and to take responsibility for significant decisions affecting the life courses of users of services, but they do this in partnership with their social care colleagues who are becoming a skilled and trained workforce in their own right. Social care workers are also expected to work in partnership with people who use services and carers. Far from detracting from the identity of social work, the emergence of social care as a valued entity has assisted in social work's recognition as a profession.

? Question for Reflection

Reflecting on your understanding of social work and its relationship to social care and the 'caring services', can you make a reasonable prediction of how social work practice is likely to change in the future? In responding to this question, you will want to consider the principle of partnership and skill-mix teams as a strategy for meeting the needs of people who use services and their carers.

Using Historical Analysis

Previous attempts to define the social work profession analysed its history (Younghusband, 1951, 1978, 1981) to gain better understanding of how social work developed. Lessons from the past can assist social workers to understand how to make appropriate choices for their future professional practice. A brief overview of the history of social work in the UK follows.

Origins of Social Work: Rise of the Casework Model

Parallel developments took place in the USA and UK because of the strong influence of American social work on British practice. Social work grew out of a religious philanthropic tradition of charity on the one hand (Midgley, 1997), and on the other, the punitive measures of the workhouse as a means of controlling poverty (Longmate, 1974). Soydan (1999) draws attention to two contrasting approaches that vied for dominance both in the USA and in the UK: the *casework* approach (Richmond, 1917) focusing on individual causes of social problems; and the *settlement house* movement (Addams, 1935) that promoted community action and education to address structural rather than individual causes. British and American social work practised both approaches in the late 19th and early 20th centuries (Box 1.4).

**Box 1.4: Two Contrasting Ideas of Social Work
(adapted from Soydan, 1999)**

1. The belief that the origin of (and solution to) social problems lies within the individual, and therefore the helping approach is to change the individual.
2. The belief that the origin of (and solution to) social problems lies with society itself, and therefore the best helping strategy is to attempt to change society.

Casework, explained as one-to-one work that values the use of relationship to bring about change in individuals, initially was not linked to psycho-social interpretations (Richmond, 1917). Casework practice centres on the social work interview conducted by the social worker with the user and/or the family. Caseworkers make an assessment of need, form a plan, and then intervene with the user to address the identified needs. A review of historic texts about social work practice reveals that no one felt a particular need to define casework; everyone understood that it meant the practice of social work. Freudian (1986) analytic theory transformed social work practice during the 1920s and 1930s. Although Richmond (1917) favoured *social diagnosis* as a practical approach, social workers later began to link Freudian analytic theory with casework.

The trend of British social work in the years following the introduction of the post-Second World War welfare state was to expand its casework scope while at the same time restricting recognition as social workers to those with recognised qualifications. By the mid-20th century, Freudian-influenced psycho-social casework became the most popular social work model. Social workers believed that psycho-social casework (Hollis, 1972) provided an effective theoretical base that ensured professional status. Social workers practised long-term psycho-social casework with individual service users, entering into therapeutic relationships based on Freudian analytic concepts. This approach did not address poverty and discrimination directly, but focused on individual malfunction. Then Mayer and Timms' (1970) study of service users' views, which revealed that social workers preferred to analyse adult service users' childhood relationships instead of dealing with problems of poverty, constituted a major criticism of the prevailing model of social work that contributed to the eclipse of psycho-social casework.

The Rise of Para-professionals, Structural Inequality Models and Social Inclusion

During the 1960s, recognition of the complex nature of poverty (Williamson, 1966) led to welfare reform in the USA (Barry, 1966). American social work changed direction to emphasise community development and large-scale welfare programmes that tackled structural causes of poverty. British social work's acknowledgement of structural causes led to a similar change of emphasis. In the mid-1960s, Townsend and Abel-Smith (1965) produced a report that confirmed the continuing existence of wide poverty, and led to the Seebohm Report (1968), the Community Development Programme (Loney, 1983), and radical social work (Corrigan and Leonard, 1978) in the 1970s. By the late 1980s, British social work recognised structural inequalities, discrimination, and oppression, including sectarianism and homophobia, that affected people from ethnic minorities, people with a disability, older people, and people with mental health problems as inequalities that had to be tackled. Social work intervention began to change because of its heightened awareness of the interconnections of poverty, structural inequalities, discrimination, and professional use of power.

Rejection of psycho-social casework led to the rise of *para-professionals* because managers of anti-poverty programmes believed that individuals who previously had experienced the same problems as people who use services and had successfully overcome their problems would be the most effective helpers, rather than qualified social workers whose psycho-social casework ignored structural problems. In the USA, jobs in public welfare agencies were opened to a range of applicants instead of being restricted to qualified social workers (Jacobs et al., 1973). Para-professionals included ex-drug addicts who became drug abuse counsellors; ex-alcoholics who were hired to counsel alcoholics; and abused women who became support workers in women's refuges. Para-professionals injected empathetic realism into assessments of service users' life circumstances (Carkhuff, 1971). They became part of the movement that advocated practical social welfare programmes rather than psycho-social casework (Knight et al., 1979). This was the first challenge to the power of professionals. Now social workers were considered professionals in a pejorative sense because of the (sometimes) oppressive ways they unwittingly wielded power over the people they tried to help. In hindsight, it can be argued that the anti-poverty programmes strengthened the role and identity of social care without conceptualising social care in any significant way. Social work was attacked for being too narrow in focus because it was equated wrongly with the totality of social care.

Social work now recognises the desirability of confronting particular structural oppressions that impede full participation in society. The former notion of professionalism, typified by the unequal use of power over people who use services, is discredited. British social work unfortunately based its initial claim for professional recognition on psycho-social casework, a model of intervention that did not give people who use services sufficient opportunities for partnership in defining and meeting their own needs.

Challenge of Social Inclusion

Social inclusion provides both a challenge and an opportunity for professional social work. The concept of social inclusion is a response to the recognition of the reality of *social exclusion*, which 'can happen when people or places suffer from a series of linked problems such as unemployment, poor skills, low incomes, poor housing, high crime, poor health and family breakdown' (Social Exclusion Unit [SEU], 2004: 1). Social inclusion programmes need to be broadly based, multi-professional, and strategically 'joined-up' to tackle exclusion's seven dimensions (Percy-Smith, 2000: 9):

- Economic – long-term unemployment, income poverty.
- Social – homelessness, crime, and delinquent youth.
- Political – lack of political rights and alienation from or lack of confidence in political processes.
- Neighbourhood – decaying housing and environment.
- Individual – mental and physical health problems and educational underachievement.
- Geographical – concentration or marginalisation of vulnerable groups in particular areas.
- Group – concentration of the characteristics of exclusion in particular groups, for example, disabled people, older people, and people from ethnic minorities.

Social inclusion policy criticises established social organisations, including social services departments that employ the majority of British social workers, for their lack of 'joined up' strategies and consequent fragmented service delivery. Since one of social work's strongest attributes is its ability to co-ordinate service provision in partnership with other services, social workers are well placed to take important roles within social inclusion programmes. (The policy context of social inclusion is discussed in Chapter 3.)

Significantly, the organisational structures of social inclusion programmes like Sure Start and in England, Connexions, personal advisers initially appear to have bypassed British social work. There are three possible explanations:

- Social work's stigmatising image, arising from its focus on statutory child protection activities, impedes more positive perceptions.
- Education or health may be preferred as lead agencies because they, unlike social work, provide universal services that extend to all individuals.
- Social work has either defined itself too narrowly or alternatively, claimed too large a remit that was unachievable.

Potential for 'Allied Caring Professions'

British social work felt uneasy about identifying itself with social care's residential, day care, and home care services, even though social care comprises a far greater part of service provision than social work (Topss England, 2000). Interventions that other European countries might consider 'social work' are viewed in Britain as belonging to other (semi-) professions such as counselling, youth work, or community work. At one time, these other caring roles were more closely related to or were part of social work. The post-Second World War years saw distinct yet related roles break away from British social work to establish their own professionalisms and qualifications, including youth and community workers, counsellors, and careers guidance officers. Their breakaway also meant that the practice of group work and community work that emerged from the settlement movement became more distant from British social work. More recently in the 1990s, probation services in England and Wales separated from social work's training and values to establish their own separate qualification that emphasised evidence based practice and the 'what works' approach (HM Inspectorate of Probation [HMIP], 1998), which some social workers saw as placing less emphasis on the therapeutic relationship skills that had been at the heart of casework.

In Britain, a cluster of professions practising within health (e.g. physiotherapy, occupational therapy, radiography, speech therapy) established an identity as PAMS (Professions Allied to Medicine) or more recently known as Allied Health Professions (AHP) (NHS AHP, 2004). The AHP comprise psychologists, psychotherapists, chiropodists, podiatrists, dieticians, drama therapists, music therapists, physiotherapists, prosthetists and orthotists, radiographers, speech and language therapists, ambulance technicians and paramedics, art therapists, occupational therapists, operating department practitioners, and orthoptists. The distinct helping roles within professions and occupations consonant with a broad definition of social work could form a similar alliance entitled allied caring professions. Social work could be at the heart of the new alliance if it moves from a narrow to a broad understanding of its purpose and values other occupational roles. The alliance could include social workers, but also social care workers; workers employed in services to children, young people and families; probation officers; youth justice workers; youth workers; community workers; counsellors; careers guidance officers; advice workers; education welfare officers; and care managers.

Where Is the Voice of Social Work and Social Care?

Regulatory bodies are government funded. In various ways, they exert control over social work. Although Munro (2004: 1076) considers the GSCC and SCIE in England to be professional organisations, they and their counterparts in the other UK countries are governmentally controlled and therefore cannot represent an independent voice of social work and social care. Munro recognises that both the GSCC and SCIE are subject to growing political and managerial control through audit and inspection. Whether social workers have acquired more autonomy is an open question. Much will depend on the way social work graduates construct their careers, whether they will recognise the importance of supporting BASW as a professional voice for social work, and whether the increasingly skilled cadre of social care workers will support the

SCA as a voice for social care. On a wider scale, there is a need to establish a collective voice for championing the evidence and competence base of both social care and social work.

A Collective Voice for Social Care and Social Work Education, Training, and Research?

The Assembly for Social Care and Social Work Education Training and Research began in 1998 as the UK-wide Co-ordinating Group of Further and Higher Education Interests in Education and Training for the Personal Social Services, convened because the education and research constituency lacked an effective voice at a time when major policy reviews were taking place that would change the structure of social work and social care education and research. Organisations proposed as members included the:

- Association of Care Training and Assessment Networks (ACTAN)
- Association of Teachers of Social Work Education (ATSWE)
- Association of University Professors of Social Work (AUPSW)
- Joint University Council Social Work Education Committee (JUC/SWEC)
- National Association of Training Officers in the Personal Social Services (NATopss)
- National Organisation for Practice Teaching (NOPT)
- Social Services Research Group (SSRG)
- Social Work Research Association (SWRA), and
- UK Standing Conference of DipSW Partnerships (UKSC)

From 1998 to 2004 the Assembly (and its predecessor group, the Co-ordinating Body) provided representation on the board of national bodies such as Topss England (now Skills for Care) and responses to consultations on the Policy Review of Social Work and the Reform of Social Work Education. In 2004, funding was obtained from the Nuffield Foundation for a seminar/forum to debate the future of the Assembly. The constituent organisations, joined by BASW, agreed to support the idea of the Assembly, but the difficulty of finding ongoing funding sufficient to maintain a modest structure may obviate its purpose. The Assembly is intended to be a 'virtual organisation' which could act as an umbrella network to speak collectively for social care and social work education, training and research and to champion, promote and protect the value, knowledge and skills base of social care and social work.

Box 1.5: Assembly Aims

- protect, promote, and develop the values, knowledge, and skills of social care and social work;
- contribute to effective practice and policy that delivers positive outcomes for people who use services;

Box 1.5: *(Continued)*

- network across UK social care and social work education and research representative organisations; and
- foster and maintain interaction between the Assembly and government bodies and key agencies involved in the changing delivery of social care and social work services.

A New Professionalism

The current emphasis on social inclusion, which seeks to break down the barriers between services, suggests that the social work profession might reconsider how it defines its professionalism. A return to claims that social workers should address every social issue is not feasible – a new explanation of professionalism recognises the need for partnerships with other professions and services and with people who use services and those who care for them.

Drawing on Lymbery's discussion of professionalism (2001), five aspects of social work within the degree suggest a new professionalism:

1. Knowledge: Social work's distinctive body of knowledge includes awareness of structural oppression, abuse of power, service user rights and responsibilities, and social inclusion. Curricula for the qualifying social work degree in all four UK countries contain this emphasis in their body of knowledge.
2. Principles: Social work's code of ethics and codes of practice include principles of promoting service users' citizenship, rights and responsibilities. The British Association of Social Workers' *Code of Ethics* (1993) and the UK-wide *Codes of Practice* (GSCC, 2002) address these principles. The social work degree affirms the place of values in the curricula.
3. Practice: Social work's practice expertise embraces strategies for social inclusion, and working within inter-agency, multi-professional structures. The Benchmark Statement and requirements for the degree promote these strategies.
4. Wider access: Entry to the profession should provide opportunities for para-professionals to gain access to the qualification. The requirements for social work training encourage opportunities for wider access by individuals with different experiences and qualifications.
5. Partnership: Social workers work in partnership with people who use services and their carers. The Benchmark Statement, the requirements for the new degree, and the National Occupational Standards all affirm this requirement within the degree.

Developing a Broader Vision of Social Work through New Definitions

The social inclusion agenda with its emphasis on 'joined up' strategies changed the generally accepted purpose of social work, prompting British social work to broaden its conceptualisation of professional social work so that it addresses social inclusion strategies more effectively. The first step is to adopt an appropriate contemporary definition of social work.

The outline of requirements for the two-year sub-degree social work qualification (that was withdrawn when the social work degree began) did not make *inclusion* a priority. British social work was described in 1995 as:

> an accountable professional activity, which enables individuals, families and groups to identify personal social and environmental difficulties adversely affecting them. Social work enables them to manage these difficulties through supportive, rehabilitative, protective or corrective action. Social work promotes social welfare and responds to wider social needs … Social workers are part of a network of welfare, health, criminal justice and penal provision. (Central Council for Education and Training in Social Work [CCETSW], 1995: 8)

Although this description mentions wider aspects of social welfare, it does not go as far as the current emphasis on multi-professional teamwork. The Benchmark Statement (QAA, 2000: §2.2.3–4) is more forward thinking in this respect, stating: 'there are competing views in society at large on the nature of social work and on its place and purpose. Social work … evolves, adapts and changes in response to the social, political and economic challenges and demands of contemporary social welfare policy, practice, and legislation'.

The Statement requires social workers to have knowledge and understanding of 'the social processes that lead to marginalisation, isolation, and exclusion …' (QAA, 2000: §3.1.1). The closest that the Benchmark Statement gets to a definition of social work is to state that 'Social work is characterised by a distinctive focus on practice in complex social situations to promote and protect individual and collective well-being' (2000: §2.1). Other helping professions could adapt this broad characterisation to their own purposes without too much difficulty.

International Definition of Social Work

It may seem as if we are getting nowhere in a search for a definition of social work. However the Topss UK Partnership has adopted the international definition of social work (agreed at the July 2000 Annual Meeting in Montreal of the International Association of Schools of Social Work and later adopted by the European Association of Schools of Social Work) as the Key Purpose of Social Work within the National Occupational Standards in Social Work (Box 1.6). This is the best approximation of a definition suitable for contemporary practice. This definition is valuable to British social work because of its international acceptance, and the way it links together ideas that shape social work. Social work's identity as a profession is strengthened by this definition, which is qualitatively consonant with the future direction of British social work and appropriate for social inclusion initiatives. The definition re-introduces the idea that the origins of social problems lie within society – therefore the approach to working with individuals is to emancipate or liberate them, and achieve social justice, rather than maintain social order. Weiss (2005) studied differences and commonalties in professional ideology among social work students in 10 countries, including the UK, to determine whether there was a common core in their attitudes that transcended cultural contexts. The findings, based on responses from students in a single university in each country, demonstrated 'substantial similarity' (108) in perceptions of poverty being rooted in structural causes, and professional goals of enhancing social justice and individual well-being – thus establishing some limited credence for the notion of a global common core of social work.

Box 1.6: International Definition of Social Work (Topss UK Partnership/Skills for Care, 2002)

Social work is a profession which promotes social change, problem solving in human relationships and the empowerment and liberation of people to enhance well-being. Utilising theories of human behaviour and social systems, social work intervenes at the points where people interact with their environments. Principles of human rights and social justice are fundamental to social work.

British social work has frequently worried about its survival, in part because it has depended on continued governmental support for its existence. This concern has prevented many British social workers from developing a broad vision of what social work can become in the future. Governmental support for the social work degree and its recognition of social work as a profession have opened up new possibilities for social work. The Occupational Standards require standards for practice that *inter alia* will include partnerships with people who use services and carers; empowerment, and multi-professional working. The requirements for a curriculum allow considerable scope for developing particular approaches to practice. The curriculum requirements emphasise the same issues for practice as the Occupational Standards, but (most particularly in England) require a focus on communication and on human development. By adopting new areas of focus, social work in Britain may draw closer to the developmental goals of social inclusion initiatives.

The social work degree provides an opportunity for social work to own this approach that incorporates features of a new professionalism, forges links with other caring professions that are also facing change, and takes note of international models of social work. The history of social work reveals that one of its essential characteristics is the 'competing views on the nature of social work and its place and purpose in relation to social justice, social care, and social order' (QAA, 2000: §2.2.2). The debate about what social work is meant to be and do will probably never cease. Before developing some of these themes in successive chapters, an appropriate task is to ask that the reader reflects on the Benchmark Statement section 2.2.3: 'Social work adapts and changes in response to social, political and economic challenges and the demands of contemporary social welfare policy, practice, and legislation'.

? Questions for reflection

What are the strengths of the current definition of social work? What are its potential contradictions? How will you equip yourself to understand and work within this context of contested debate about social work's nature, scope and purpose?

▶▶ Conclusion

From this chapter you will take forward some understanding of social work's history that led to social work's recognition as a profession in the UK. If you are studying for the degree in social work, employed, or studying in some aspect of the caring services, the discussion should help you orient your own practice towards professional standards. Although social work may best be portrayed by its changing nature rather than by trying to agree a specific definition, the international definition of social work has gained widespread support in the UK. Nothing stands still in social work, and so the definition of social work will change as people who use services and those who care for them are empowered to express their views of what they want from service provision. The concept of professionalism will be challenged and will develop further. You therefore need to become familiar with the current definition of social work, critique it and contribute to its evolution.

📖 Further Reading

Payne, M. (2005) *Social Work Continuity and Change.* Basingstoke: Palgrave Macmillian.
This book traces the origins and development of social work in the context of social policy developments, its professionalisation, crises, and shifts in practice.

Roche, D. and Rankin, J. (2004) *Who Cares? Building the Social Care Workforce.* London: Institute for Public Policy Research (ippr).
This research report, available on ippr's website (www.ippi.org) provides a good analysis of contemporary issues for both social work and social care.

Soydan, H. (1999) *The History of Ideas in Social Work.* Birmingham: Venture Press.
This book discusses the rise of different practice traditions, including St. Simon, Richmond, and Addams.

2 FOCUS ON PRACTICE

As an applied academic subject, social work is characterised by a distinctive focus on practice in complex social situations to promote and protect individual and collective well-being. (QAA, 2000: §2.1)

Introduction: What Do People Who Use Services and Carers Expect from Social Workers?

In 2002 a group of stakeholders undertook consultation with individuals, families, carers, groups, and communities who use services, and with those who care for them. After this consultation a Statement of Expectations of social workers' practice (Topss UK Partnership, 2002) was published, which identified particular aspects of practice that people who use services and carers considered important and captured the voices of recipients of service provision whose views had not been heard until relatively recently. These aspects, which group together under the following headings, set the scene for Chapter 2, which focuses on professional practice:

- communication skills and information sharing;
- good social work practice;
- advocacy;
- working with other professionals;
- knowledge;
- values.

Practice is at the heart of the social work degree. The degree's emphasis on assessed practice (that exceeds the practice requirements of many European social work programmes) is distinctive. In consonance with the Benchmark Statement (QAA, 2000), this chapter takes a broad view of practice:

- Practice begins with transferable skills developed initially in the classroom that later are applied within social care practice learning opportunities.
- The focus on practice includes strategies for developing and sustaining practice within and beyond the requirements of the degree.
- Social workers' practice should balance empowerment of people who use services with protection of vulnerable people, even though maintaining the balance may cause dilemmas for practice.

Chapter Structure

This chapter defines practice and considers its importance to social workers. Service users' and carers' expectations provide templates for students to develop their own practice. The art of practice, the use of self, and the importance of relationships, as well as concepts of competence, professionalism, and expertise, are important themes for students who seek to demonstrate the National Occupational Standards' Key Roles of social work through a staged process of practice learning. Guiding principles include the social model of intervention, group care practice in social care, and the dilemma of balancing empowerment and emancipation with support and development.

Why Is Practice So Important?

The social work degree represents a combination of two traditions: the academic contribution of research and knowledge, and the practical contribution of practice learning. Practice learning is comprised of experiential, action-based activities. Although other undergraduate degrees contain periods of practice learning to develop employability skills, British (and American) social work education has always featured concurrent periods of practice during which the student learns the craft of social work by practising under supervision in caring services' organisations. The period of practice learning was formerly described as a 'placement' but now is known as a 'practice learning opportunity'. Practice learning opportunities in the undergraduate social work degree earn academic credits and are assessed as integral parts of the degree. The contemporary importance of practice traces its roots to Mary Richmond who introduced assessed practice learning into social work education (Soydan, 1999). From 1890 Richmond worked as secretary general of the Baltimore Charity Organisation Society in the USA. During this period, the developing social sciences were interested in studying social problems and applying scientific methods to address social issues. Social workers studied sociology, then considered a suitable preparation for social work.

In 1897 Richmond began to oppose this assumption, arguing instead that social work was a practical activity and so required practical training in separate schools of social work. She wanted practice learning in agencies to take place side by side with academic learning and so established a pattern of social work education in the USA and UK that valued the acquisition of practical skills, with the resulting effect of diminishing social work's historic academic respectability.

Social work is one of many professions that value practice and incorporate practice in their professional training. Nursing combines academic learning with practice learning. Medical training combines academic and practical aspects, and lawyers in the UK first learn legal theory in their undergraduate degree and legal skills training, but begin their practical experience afterwards in a two-year traineeship combined with day-release study. The notions of a 'practice curriculum' and 'practice teaching' (Boswell, 1997) are more highly developed in social work than in other areas of professional education. The Benchmark Statement (QAA, 2000) makes it clear that:

- Practice provides opportunities for [social work] students to improve and demonstrate understanding through the application and testing of knowledge and skills (§2.3.1).
- Learning in practice can include activities such as observation, analysis and research as well as intervention within social work and related organisations (§2.3.4).
- Practice activity is also a source of transferable learning in its own right. Practice learning can transfer both from a practice setting to the 'classroom' and vice versa (§2.3.2).

Classroom activity is not passive learning but active skills development. For example, students may give presentations in class to learn how to communicate to an audience and acquire the skills needed for presentations to court or to multi-professional meetings or improve their communication skills (in 'skills laboratories' where they record their interviewing and listening skills and review their performance). After completing a practice learning opportunity and putting some of these new skills into practice in an organisation, the student returns to the university with skills honed in the realities of the world as it is; these new skills and knowledge then contribute to classroom performance in seminars and debates, helping the student to become more confident in presenting a point of view or effectively arguing a case.

Good Social Work Practice: Service User and Carer Expectations of Social Workers

The expectations of people who use services and carers, published with the National Occupational Standards (Topss UK Partnership, 2002), provide insights for shaping students' practice. For ease of consideration, the expectations are arranged in clusters that cover social workers' *use of time, relationship and communication, assessment skills,* and service users' and carers' wishes for services that promote *independence, recognise their own expertise,* and *forge links to a range of provision.*

Box 2.1: First Cluster of Expectations – Use of Time

Social workers must:

Be good at time keeping.

Give individuals, families, carers, groups, and communities sufficient time to work with them properly.

Ensure that contact is maintained.

Social workers need to turn up on time, give enough time to those they engage with, and maintain contact over time (Box 2.1). The expectations state that users and carers value their contact with social workers. They do not want social workers to cut the contact short through missed or late appointments, by ending appointments too soon, or failing to keep in contact. Meeting these expectations requires managing time efficiently, keeping a diary and planning realistically how much can be achieved in a day – with some allowance made for crises requiring speedy responses.

Box 2.2: Second Cluster of Expectations – Use of Relationship and Communication

Social workers must:

Be accountable to individuals, families, carers, groups, and communities for their practice.

Be good at starting, continuing, and closing relationships.

Respect confidentiality, and explain when there is a need to share information with others.

Involve individuals, families, carers, groups, and communities in all meetings that may affect them.

The cluster of expectations presented in Box 2.2 is concerned with the nature and quality of the *relationship* and the style of *communication* that the social worker establishes with users and carers. People who use services and carers want to know that the social worker serves *their* needs, not the needs of the social work organisation, and is accountable to them for their actions. Service users appreciate the use of good social work communication skills in beginning, maintaining, and ending relationships. They want their social worker to observe confidentiality and explain any limitations to confidentiality – an additional example of communication within a professional relationship. People who use services and their carers want social workers to involve them with open shared communication in meetings that might affect them. To fulfil these expectations, the social worker carries out their practice according to the professional value of respect for persons. The social worker needs to value the social work relationship, understand its potential as well as its boundaries, and develop the effectiveness of their communication skills.

Box 2.3: Third Cluster of Expectations – Use of Assessment Skills

Social workers must:

Assess needs properly, making sure that all options are explored before deciding on a plan.

Look for options when the services needed are not available.

Be creative involving individuals, families, carers, groups, and communities in setting goals and when developing a care plan.

Be honest about the limitations of choice and the options, when reviewing and changing plans.

Assess risk and support risk-taking when appropriate.

The expectations of *assessment skills* (Box 2.3) emphasise individual creative use of professional skills and values when assessing need. Users and carers want social workers to involve them in assessment and planning, to search for all possibilities with them, and ultimately to be frank and open about any resource shortfalls that might limit choices. Although recognising the need to assess risk, users and carers want social workers to give their support to risk-taking when (following a process of consultation) risk-taking is judged appropriate. A pro forma for assessment is a useful tool, but cannot substitute for listening carefully and picking up issues that people may struggle to express. Similarly, being creative about possibilities requires a strong values base and knowledge of what is possible. Risk-taking requires realistic assessment, honest communication, and a values base that accepts the need to take risk, particularly when promoting independence.

Social workers' duty to support and protect vulnerable people requires different kinds of decisions. The Benchmark Statement argues that social workers 'practise in ways that maximise safety and effectiveness in situations of uncertainty and incomplete information; help people to gain, regain or maintain control of their own affairs, insofar as this is compatible with their own or others' safety, well-being and rights' (QAA, 2000: §2.4). A potential polarisation of practice can occur, where taking a decision to prevent a likely risk might subvert the support desired by a person using services. The dilemma requires a careful judgement on the amount of risk-taking that is reasonable and feasible. On the one hand, social workers should promote full participation of service users, and on the other, social workers must manage risk. Managing risk can mean undertaking protective activities in opposition to some users' expressed wishes. The Benchmark Statement states that social workers must learn about 'the complex relationships between justice, care and control in social welfare and the practical and ethical implications of these, including roles as statutory agents and in upholding the law in respect of discrimination' (QAA, 2000: §3.1.3).

Box 2.4: Fourth Cluster of Expectations – Service Users' and Carers' Wishes for Services that Promote Independence and Recognise Their Own Expertise

Social workers must:

Work with individuals, families, carers, groups, and communities to develop and/or maintain independence.

Recognise the expertise of individuals, families, carers, groups, and communities about their own situation and have regard for their wishes.

The expectations of Box 2.4 state the preferences of service users and carers for services that take account of users and carers' *own expertise*, and develop and maintain *independence*. To meet these expectations, social workers must examine their practice values to ensure they remain motivated to promote independence and value the contributions of people who use services and carers.

Box 2.5: Fifth Cluster of Expectations – People who Use Services and Carers Want Services that Establish Contacts with a Range of Provision

Social workers must:

Help individuals, families, carers, groups, and communities to access benefits and services.

Link individuals, families, carers, groups, and communities to support groups and networks and support them to extend involvement with groups and networks.

The final expectations (Box 2.5) are concerned with social workers' ability to assist people who use services and carers to forge *links* with other services to access benefits, services, support groups, and networks. The expectations recognise that the social worker cannot provide every service that is needed, but will supply information about how to access a wider range of support. To meet these expectations, the social worker should be well informed about available benefits, services, and networks.

Themes for Developing Practice

In addition to the expectations, social workers can develop their own individual approach by drawing on selected conceptual themes that point the way to good practice:

- art of practice;
- use of self;
- importance of relationships.

Learning the Art of Practice

'It's sort of like instinct. It's understanding what needs to be said and done and then using yourself in exactly the right way at exactly the right times. I don't have words to explain it well, but it's that instinctive knowing of what to do because you're so focused and in touch with your client. It seems to go so effortlessly and beautifully when you're in that place,' Powell (2003: 457) quotes from an American colleague working in children's services, and claims that *social work as art* is difficult to achieve because the practitioner has to confront their use of values.

Social work both in Britain and the USA pursued science, logic, and positivistic frameworks for knowledge and practice, prompted by its search for professional recognition. Powell argues that social work began to separate 'head from heart, mind from spirit, practice from research, education from practice, knowing from understanding, and theory from the contingencies of real-world circumstances' (2003: 3). Siporin (1988: 178) drew attention to the art of the practitioner's 'creative use of style, the helping relationship, and metaphorical communication'. The art of practice may lie in seeing what may otherwise not be seen, recognising possibilities, and affirming the value of people who use services. Powell (2003: 459) suggests that art is 'recognising what is, what might be, and sharing that recognition so that [service user] and worker share a moment of [recognising] the work to be done'. Although social work draws on the social sciences for its knowledge base, and accepts the value of evidence-informed practice, practice is more of an art than a science. That is why social work students need opportunities to learn how to practice over a period of time in different situations, with different organisations, and with different groups and individuals.

Use of Self

The concept of the 'use of self' was popular when the one-to-one casework approach dominated social work practice, but now deserves revival because of its compatibility with contemporary social work roles. England (1986: 35), the leading British proponent of social work as art, links the art of social work with the use of self and argues that 'a pervasive use of self is the crucial centre point of social work'. The 'use of self' suggests that one of the social worker's main tools is an individualised personal style for communicating with others. Davies (1994: 181) argues for the use of self because social work is not simply a matter of what is done, but how it is done. Jordan (1979: 26) argued that 'to be effective the [social worker] must be a real person ... helping is not simply a skill or expertise or technique. Helping is a test of the helper as a person [involving] the disciplined use of the whole of the personality'.

Payne (1991: 60–3) reviewed some of the conceptualisations of 'use of self', and located this approach within a personal/interpersonal social work narrative. 'Use of self' is usually associated with goals of personal growth for people who use services. Its emphasis on the practitioner's creativity fits well with the expectation that social workers will be 'creative [in] involving individuals, families, carers, groups and communities in setting goals'. 'Use of self' is the means by which the social worker translates the different requirements of people who use services, carers, legal statutes, agency procedures, and competing methods and theories into a meaningful purposeful communication with service users and carers. Seden (2005: 72) argues that when social workers use 'the self', their practice reflects their 'interpersonal style rather than the theories or methods'. Seden (2005: 72–3) associates the concept of *use of self* with skills that convey understanding, such as attentive listening, reflecting back and summarising the content of the discussion. She distinguishes between personal qualities (e.g. the desire to help and encourage) and the use of skills that convey respect and understanding.

Payne (1991: 60) warns that the purposeful use of self could lead to social workers wielding covert power over people who use services, while Sainsbury (1970: 100–1) argued that the social worker should be aware of their 'own capacities and limitations' by appraising their use of skills and using supervision 'to avoid distortion ... and in selecting goals'. Howe (1987: 113) claims that the 'reference point for understanding of others is one's self' – being aware of one's own thoughts and feelings that either contribute to or interfere with being helpful to others. The importance of 'use of self' is implied in the expectation of people who use services and carers that social workers will 'be good at starting, continuing and closing relationships'.

Importance of Relationships

The Benchmark Statement asserts that:

> Social workers should engage with service users in ways characterised by openness, reciprocity, mutual accountability and explicit recognition of the powers of the social worker and the legal context of intervention. (QAA, 2000: §1.12)

These relationships differ from those that characterised social work when psycho-social models of casework (Hollis, 1972; Perlman, 1957) dominated practice. In psycho-social casework, 'relationship' between the social worker and the service user was accepted as an unequal power relationship, where the expert social worker helped service users to gain more insight into their problems.

Biestek (1961: 7–8) traced how the concept of *relationship* in social work practice emerged from attempts to identify the essence of a helping interaction in terms of personal qualities rather than precise skills, eventually replacing concepts of friendship, rapport, contact, sympathy, empathy, and transference. The fall from favour of psycho-social casework directed attention away from defining the nature of a professional relationship with people who use services and carers. As early as 1951, Hamilton (1951: 27) proposed that the professional relationship 'involves a mutual process of shared responsibilities, recognition of the other's rights, acceptance of difference'. This interpretation fits with power-sharing relationships in contemporary social work.

Relationship continues to be important within counselling and psychotherapy. Rogers (1961) developed a person-centred approach to psychotherapy and counselling that identified three core conditions that he considered necessary and sufficient for effective helping:

- empathy;
- unconditional positive regard;
- genuineness.

Carkhuff (1984) tried to discover whether these three conditions were sufficient for bringing about change. On the basis of his research he argued that psychotherapeutic interventions could bring about positive or negative change, depending on the skill of the counsellor. Therapy could bring about change 'for better or for worse' (1984: 21). He argued that professionals could become mechanistic and technical and therefore ineffective when they were too distant from those they were trying to help. This observation resonates with the contemporary perceptions of relationships in social work.

Howe (1987: 117) argues that good social work practice relies on intuition, use of self, the quality of relationship, gaining understanding of experience, searching for meaning, and communicating understanding, with an overall aim to help people who use services recognise their experiences and so gain understanding. This humanist approach to practice assumes that understanding will trigger change for the better. The emphasis on achieving understanding suggests that social workers who use this approach might ignore the practical purposes of social work – addressing shortfalls in resources. However, Davies (1994) argues that the use of self (in professional relationships) fits with a range of approaches to practice, and claims that social work should provide a wider range of resources but not abandon the use of self. Sainsbury's suggestion (1970) of the need for supervision provides a countervailing influence to the possible misuse of power in professional relationships.

Case Study 2.1 – Use of Relationships

Jodi is 16 years old with a history of violence and truanting from school. Her father left the family home many years ago, and Jodi witnessed domestic violence as a young child. Jodi is unemployed, drinks heavily, and left school with no qualifications. Her mother's lifestyle is erratic and Jodi's relationship with her mother is stormy. Two years ago Jodi became pregnant, but did not reveal who the father was. Social Services placed Jodi's baby, Michael, with foster carers because of concerns to protect the child. Jodi is now pregnant again and continues to drink heavily.

Halima Khan, a newly qualified social worker who was assigned to work with Jodi, felt some trepidation at meeting Jodi and doubted her ability to intervene effectively. There were several issues: the welfare of Michael, Jodi's 14-month-old child, the welfare of the expected child, and the welfare of Jodi, technically a child herself. Halima met Jodi and recognised her anger and feelings of being betrayed initially by her parents, and more recently by the men in her life. Jodi had low self-esteem – she had no qualifications or skills and had never been employed. Halima recognised Jodi's sense of hopelessness. However, Halima also recognised the need to work towards the welfare of all three of those involved. Halima had to find out whether Jodi wanted to continue with the pregnancy or not. She needed to find out whether Jodi would be willing to enter a programme to deal with her drinking, and what her goals were. Did Jodi want to work towards the return of Michael? If Jodi was not motivated towards this goal, or did not actively want Michael to return, then plans for permanency and adoption might be the best strategy for Michael's welfare. But had Jodi been encouraged to keep in contact with Michael? These were all sensitive issues that if presented quickly and impersonally to Jodi, however rational Halima's explanations might be, the likelihood would be that Jodi would become angry and refuse to listen. Halima took some time listening to Jodi in an attempt to recognise Jodi's feelings, before she began to explain the concerns and choices. Because Halima recognised the depth of Jodi's anger against social services, she arranged for Jodi to have contact with an informal mentor who was not linked to social services. Jodi was interested in this possibility and began meeting with the mentor. With the support of the mentor, Jodi began to look ahead to the future. She decided to continue with her pregnancy and seek appropriate help to stop abusing alcohol. She agreed reluctantly but with a great deal of thought that plans for Michael's adoption should proceed. She wanted to try to gain a qualification and find employment. The turning point was the initial respect given by Halima, and the positive relationship of trust formed with the mentor, which helped Jodi to develop more maturity. Only then was Halima able to link Jodi to appropriate services.

The example of Jodi (Case Study 2.1) reveals the power of social workers on the one hand, and on the other, the apparent hopelessness of the situations into which they are expected to intervene. There can be no miracles in situations like these, but instead of forgetting the humanity of the person who reluctantly and angrily uses services, the social worker who reaches out to acknowledge feelings and facilitates a trusting relationship is unlikely to cause harm and may be able to achieve some good. Forming a relationship was not the end goal, but provided the key to enabling change and constructive decision-making.

❓ Question for Reflection – Developing the art of practice

What kinds of support might help you develop the art of practice, as well as meet requirements and employers' expectations? It is likely that you would select from a range of strategies that include practice supervision, availability of a mentor, peer-group discussion, regular individual reflection on practice, and appropriate selection of continuing professional development activities.

Understanding the Concept of Competence

The concepts of social work as art, use of self, and relationship were almost swept away after 1989 by a new emphasis on competence – the demonstration of an acceptable standard of practice performance. To achieve the social work qualification, students must demonstrate that they can practise to required acceptable standards of competence. It is best to approach these competence requirements with an overall understanding of the combinations of knowledge, skills, and values that result in interactions called 'practice'. Practice learning opportunities take the student outside the classroom into the world of the caring services, the helping professions, and the needs of people who use services and carers.

Social work students need time to develop competences, particularly if they lack previous experience in social care or if they have been away from formal study for a considerable time. The degree sets higher standards for practice than predecessor awards. Although social work always welcomed older experienced candidates and more recently, candidates from diverse ethnic backgrounds, the profession did not try to attract younger applicants who may have had little or no previous social work experience. A previous age bar meant that the British social work qualification could not be awarded to anyone under the age of 22 years – thus discouraging school leavers from choosing social work as a career. Instead, potential social workers chose professions like teaching or nursing that welcomed school leavers. Now that the age bar has been removed, social work can attract younger students from school as well as mature students who may be sponsored by their employer to study part time. Mature students may have been away from formal education for some time, and feel 'de-skilled' by the educational setting. Both groups of learners will have particular challenges to overcome as they develop their competences. Competence suggests a minimum acceptable standard for professional practice at the point when students obtain their 'license to practice'. Benner (1984) captured the stages of learning leading to competence and the stages beyond competence in her adaptation of the Dreyfus model of skills acquisition (Box 2.6).

Box 2.6: Model of Skills Acquisition (adapted from Benner, 1984)

Expert
An expert practitioner has an intuitive grasp of situations based on deep tacit understanding, sees situations holistically rather than in terms of aspects, and has a vision of what is possible.

Proficient
A proficient practitioner uses guidelines for action based on attributes or aspects, and after some prior experience can recognise the global characteristics of situations. The proficient practitioner now sees action at least partially in terms of longer-term goals, sees what is most important in a situation, and can cope with the crowdedness of pressurised contexts where there are many separate factors vying for attention.

(Continued)

Box 2.6: *(Continued)*

Competent

The competent practitioner no longer relies solely on rules and guidelines; uses maxims for guidance, according to the variable meaning of a situation, uses conscious deliberate planning, and can perceive deviations from the normal pattern.

Advanced beginner

The advanced beginner's perception of situations is still limited. All attributes and aspects are treated separately and given equal importance. Decision-making is less laboured. Analytical approaches are used only in novel situations or when problems occur.

Novice

The novice is not able to use discretionary judgement. The novice adheres rigidly to taught rules or plans. The novice has little perception of how individual situations may differ.

When students begin the social work degree, they may be at the novice stage, the advanced beginner stage, or in certain aspects, a competent practitioner. Their actual situation is likely to represent a mix of these attributes. The Benner stage of *being competent* approximates the end stage of the social work qualification, but the stages of *proficiency* and *expertise* lie beyond the stage of competence, and need to be developed through post qualifying study and practice.

Practice Requirements for the Social Work Qualification

The social work qualification is generic, rather than specialist, enabling graduates to develop their careers in different directions rather than being restricted to working with only one user group or in one type of service organisation. The requirements for practice learning reflect the need for variety and breadth of learning. The DH (2002b), the SE (2003), the CCW (2004) and the NISCC (DHSSPS, 2003) have specified requirements for practice.

In England, student social workers undergo assessed preparation for direct practice to ensure their safety to undertake practice learning, including opportunities to develop greater understanding of the experience of people who use services, and to shadow an experienced social worker. This learning takes place at the beginning stages of the degree. Universities structure this and subsequent practice learning in different ways. By the end of the degree, student social workers in England will have undertaken at least 200 days of practice learning outside the university in at least two practice settings, will have gained experience of statutory social work involving legal interventions, and will have provided services to at least two service user groups. No credit is given for previous learning from practice.

In Scotland (SE SiSWE, 2003), social work students' practice learning must comprise 200 days, of which at least 160 must be spent in supervised direct practice (40 days may be recognised through previous experience and learning in practice). The Scottish requirements also include preparation for direct practice, and must include statutory social work tasks, involving legal interventions; work in at least two contrasting settings; providing services to at least two user groups; and taking account of and valuing diversity.

Northern Ireland requires staged practice learning of 240 days if the student is not able to gain credit from previous practice. The 240 days are the most structured of all the UK requirements, sharing the requirements for practice in at least two different settings with at least two user groups, but also requiring group care practice and work with two other professions. The student undertakes 25 days preparation for practice, 185 days in direct supervised practice, and 30 days in individual practice learning.

In Wales, social work students undertake a 20 day placement at level one, and then two practice learning opportunities of 80 and 100 days, of which at least one placement must be in a statutory setting, and they will need to work with two service user groups.

National Occupational Standards for Social Work Practice

The Benchmark Statement (QAA, 2000: §1.4) did not try to define professional competence because its writers, all social work academics, believed that this was a task best undertaken by a partnership of all the relevant stakeholders. In 2001 relevant stakeholders (comprising employers, people who use services, carers, practitioners, regulatory bodies, professional bodies, providers of practice learning, and social work academics) were convened to begin the task of identifying competence standards for practice. The competences were published as the *National Occupational Standards for Social Work* (Topss UK Partnership, 2002), key aspects of which were incorporated into the SE's *Standards in Social Work Education* (2003). The Standards identify six key roles of social work that provide the basis for assessment of students' practice. Twenty-one supporting units of competence are grouped under the key roles, a summary of which is presented (in Box 2.7).

Box 2.7: Key Roles

KEY ROLE 1 *Prepare for and Work with Individuals, Families, Carers, Groups, and Communities to Assess Their Needs and Circumstances*
Unit 1 Prepare for social work contact and involvement.
Unit 2 Work with individuals, families, carers, groups, and communities to help them make informed decisions.
Unit 3 Assess needs and options to recommend a course of action.

KEY ROLE 2 *Plan, Carry out, Review and Evaluate Social Work Practice, with Individuals, Families, Carers, Groups, and Communities and other Professionals*
Unit 4 Respond to crisis situations.
Unit 5 Interact with individuals, families, carers, groups, and communities to achieve change and development to improve life opportunities.

(Continued)

Box 2.7: *(Continued)*

Unit 6 Prepare, produce, implement and evaluate plans with individuals, families, carers, groups, communities, and professional colleagues.
Unit 7 Support the development of networks to meet assessed needs and planned outcome.
Unit 8 Work with groups to promote individual growth, development and independence.
Unit 9 Address behaviour which presents a risk to individuals, families, carers, groups, and communities.

KEY ROLE 3 *Support Individuals to Represent Their Needs, Views and Circumstances*
Unit 10 Advocate with, and on behalf of, individuals, families, carers, groups, and communities.
Unit 11 Prepare for, and participate in decision-making forums.

KEY ROLE 4 *Manage Risk to Individuals, Families, Carers, Groups, Communities, Self, and Colleagues*
Unit 12 Assess and manage risks to individuals, families, carers, groups, and communities.
Unit 13 Assess, minimise, and manage risk to self and colleagues.

KEY ROLE 5 *Manage and Be Accountable with Supervision and Support, for Your Own Social Work Practice within Your Organisation*
Unit 14 Manage and be accountable for your own work.
Unit 15 Contribute to the management of resources and services.
Unit 16 Manage, present and share records and reports.
Unit 17 Work within multi-disciplinary and multi-organisational teams, networks, and systems.

KEY ROLE 6 *Demonstrate Professional Competence in Social Work Practice*
Unit 18 Research, analyse, evaluate, and use current knowledge of best social work practice.
Unit 19 Work within agreed standards of social work practice and ensure own professional development.
Unit 20 Manage complex ethical issues, dilemmas, and conflicts.
Unit 21 Contribute to the promotion of best social work practice.

It is apparent that some key roles are more detailed than others, although all are of equal importance. Key roles one (prepare) and two (plan, carry out, review, evaluate) are the 'bread and butter' roles that social workers undertake in many different situations with different kinds of people, with key role two the most detailed and lengthy. Key role three (support) and Key role four (risk) portray a contemporary understanding of the social work role. Key roles five (manage and be accountable) and six (professional competence) point to the ongoing development of the social worker after gaining their professional qualification, and ensure that social work is a profession. The unit 18 requirement, (for key role six) *research, analyse, evaluate and use current knowledge of best social work practice*, and the unit 21 requirement (also for key role six) *contribute to the promotion of best social work practice* are the hallmarks of a professional practitioner.

A practice assessor/practice teacher assesses the student's activities during the required days in practice to ensure that by the end of the degree the student has attained the standards for beginning their professional practice. Assessment is based on evidence that includes students' own accounts of their activities, anonymised file notes, students' analyses of their interventions, practice teacher/assessor observations of students' practice, and contributions from people who use services. An assessor report is prepared following each practice learning opportunity, ensuring that practice assessment takes place throughout the degree. The feedback from each report gives students opportunities to develop their competence further.

The Benchmark Statement argues that practice should be assessed not as a list of: 'discrete practical tasks, but as an integration of skills and knowledge with relevant conceptual understanding' (QAA, 2000: §4.5).

It is best if the student can avoid a tendency to think about assessment, and practice itself, as a list of requirements. Professional practice should be developed from the requirements into individually crafted endeavours that typify the art of social work. The social work student with little previous work experiences in the caring services will be able to reflect on life experiences and then combine these reflections with insights from new learning and experiences. Experienced practitioners studying for the degree may have to re-think some of their assumptions, particularly in areas of tension between the professional role, agency procedures, and resource shortfalls. A potential pitfall may be their loyalty to their employers that may make it difficult to cast a critical eye over policy and practice. The example in Box 2.8 illustrates how organisational loyalty can prevent employees from recognising flaws in practice. This also illustrates the challenge of looking at self when it means an appraisal of actions and attitudes that may be open to criticism.

**Box 2.8: Denial and Rejection – Misplaced Reactions to
Criticisms of Policy and Practice**

A group of social work students (mostly experienced practitioners who were sponsored by their employers to attain the social work qualification) heard a foster parent present a lecture. The foster parent expressed criticisms of the way some social workers communicated with her and the foster children. She also criticised some of their decisions. After the lecture, when the foster parent had left the room, the students expressed anger at the foster parent's criticisms of social services. They rejected her criticisms, but also began to reject her. They cast doubt on the efficacy of her skills and knowledge as a foster parent. They could not accept that her rather mild-mannered criticism of their employers and their colleagues might be justified and that she, as a foster parent, had a right to express criticism.

Using a Staged Approach to Demonstrate Competence in the Six Key Social Work Roles

Demonstrating attainment of the six key social work roles calls for a developmental learning process that builds students' practice competences over time. Individual students need opportunities to practice and develop their skills, demonstrate their values, and apply their knowledge to practice. This takes time – and the National Occupation Standards (NOS) are very long and detailed. To make the Standards more approachable, each university programme has developed its own strategy (called a 'practice curriculum') for enabling students to demonstrate the requirements in different practice learning opportunities.

Learning to be competent in the six key roles and their supporting units is best tackled in a staged approach. Green and Statham (2004) provide a helpful template to organise cumulative learning in three stages, as presented in Box 2.9.

**Box 2.9: A Staged Approach to Attaining Safety,
Capability, and Readiness to Practice
(adapted from Green and Statham, 2004)**

Foundation Stage: Safety to Practice
(corresponds to the first year of undergraduate study; and the first year of study for graduates undertaking a postgraduate social work qualification)

At the Foundation Stage students should be working in support of a named person responsible for their work. Learning opportunities should enable students to learn and demonstrate their potential to become safe, reflective social work practitioners. Students will need opportunities to shadow an experienced social worker within the practice learning opportunity, at arms length, or as a separate practice learning opportunity. By the end of the Foundation Stage practice learning opportunity students should, under supervision, be able to carry out safely and reflect on the agreed activities.

Intermediate Stage: Capability to Practice
(corresponds to the second year of undergraduate study [and in Scotland, the third year as well]; and probably the last quarter of the first year and first quarter of the second year of study for graduates undertaking a postgraduate social work qualification)

At the Intermediate Stage, students will need to justify the appropriateness of their judgements and interpretations with their supervisor/practice assessor/practice teacher. Learning opportunities should enable students to learn and demonstrate their knowledge and skills of social work practice but will not require legal intervention and statutory risk assessment at this stage, although some students may undertake this level of activity. Students will need opportunities to undertake direct work with people using services to promote health and social wellbeing. By the end of the *Intermediate Stage practice learning opportunity* students should be capable of carrying out activities under supervision within a specific area of practice.

Final Stage: Readiness to Practice
(corresponds to the final year of undergraduate study, and the final three quarters of the second year of study for graduates undertaking a postgraduate social work qualification)

(Continued)

Box 2.9: *(Continued)*

At the Final Stage students should be able to take initiative, justify their judgements and actions and be responsible for their own workload under regular supervision. Learning opportunities should enable students to demonstrate that they are ready for practice. They will need opportunities for direct social work practice, including legal intervention and statutory risk assessment. By the end of the *Final Stage practice learning opportunity* students should be able to carry out activities competently and safely that demonstrate their readiness for competent practice.

Different Kinds of Practice Learning Opportunities

Social workers' practice will encompass different roles in multi-professional teams located in different kinds of organisations. Rather than learning to be a social worker only by undertaking practice in a team of social workers within a social services department (although this kind of experience remains important), the student social worker will experience a broad range of practice learning opportunities within statutory, private, and voluntary organisations whose primary purpose may not appear to be 'social work' but which play important roles in delivering co-ordinated services.

Some initial learning will focus on what it feels like to be a service user or carer. The changed culture of social work practice emphasises understanding the user and carer experience to help develop appropriate interventions. Organisations providing opportunities (Green and Statham, 2004) for social work students include:

- Voluntary sector organisations: Policies for neighbourhood renewal and regeneration (McGregor et al., 2003) have created strategic partnerships with voluntary sector organisations that promote community development as a strategy for addressing poverty and social exclusion. In this kind of practice learning opportunity, social work students learn to engage with a community's grass roots concerns.
- Supported housing organisations: Some challenging work with vulnerable children, young people and adults takes place in the supported housing field, determined by a policy of enabling service users to live as long as possible in the community with their own families and in their own homes. Practice learning opportunities provide students with understanding of the perspectives of tenants and their families, and the contributions of housing and care workers for maintaining tenants' independence. An important learning point is gaining awareness of partnerships with the other organisations necessary for delivering effective support.
- Private-sector organisations: Private-sector social care organisations constitute the majority of commissioned social care provision, and range from very small organisations to large corporations that provide residential homes, nursing homes, hostels, day care facilities, and home care services. Practice learning opportunities in private social care organisations illuminate the quality and standards of social care providers and the actual living arrangements that result from social work assessments of need.

- Educational organisations: Schools can provide practice learning opportunities for learning about the importance of educational attainment for all children, including children looked after by local authorities, and children from black and minority ethnic groups. Undertaking practice in schools helps student social workers understand how good social and educational skills increase life opportunities. Students also gain direct contact with children and young people in ways that are difficult to achieve in many other settings.
- Children and young people's services: Children and young people's services contribute opportunities for direct work with young children that increase understanding of child development, and parents' and local communities' perspectives about the services and support they need. Early years services that include day nurseries, playgroups, and nursery schools are important for promoting individual growth and development, and also for engaging with parents. Sure Start schemes tackle deprivation and exclusion by improving children's life chances and involving parents in planning and developing services. The schemes are being 'mainstreamed' – integrated in children's centres or into other broad organisational provision comprising multi-professional teams and a comprehensive range of services.

  Services to young people include youth and community work in different communities. The Connexions Personal Adviser service (in England only) provides advice and information for 13–19-year-olds on overcoming the barriers that prevent attainment in education, employment, or training. Connexions has particular targets to reduce teenage pregnancies, address the needs of care leavers, and intervene with substance misusers. Connexions Personal Advisers work in multi-professional teams that may comprise social workers as well as careers advisers, youth workers, and teachers.

  Social work students whose practice learning takes place in children's services must become aware of the protective regulatory aspect of social work practice that is intended to protect vulnerable individuals from harm. Although students are not meant to carry out responsibilities for this kind of regulatory practice, they will need to learn all they can about protective interventions because they will be expected to carry out the regulatory aspects of practice once they are qualified. (When working with adults, social workers have to be alert to the possibility of possible abuse and exploitation, for example of older frail people, although the law does not offer as much protection for adults.) Child protection is a form of practice where social work takes the lead role. Contemporary emphasis on service users' participation privileges the empowering nature of social work at the expense of paying attention to its protective function. The social work student must deal with the contradictions between empowerment and protective, regulatory functions.
- Health and social care organisations: Partnerships between health and social care have become essential for providing services for adults. Social worker attachments to primary health care practices and multi-professional health and social care teams help to promote a more coordinated service to vulnerable people living in the community. The primary health care GP practice supplies a range of services designed to maintain people in their own homes, such as podiatry, osteopathy, physiotherapy, counselling, welfare rights, and complementary medicine. Practice learning opportunities in these settings provide opportunities for partnership and joint working to address individual needs with shared perspectives.
- Service user led organisations: A student social worker might undertake a practice learning opportunity within a service user led organisation whose main purpose is to advocate for the rights of people who use services. The student will learn how power is exercised through the use of agency records, and will begin to understand that whatever is written down in agency records must be agreed with the individual service user, and that the focus of writing down information

must be from the service user's or carer's perspectives of what they want to achieve. They will begin to appreciate service users' difficulties (in comparison to professional staff) in accessing information (Turner and Evans, 2004); begin to understand risk-taking differently from statutory organisations, and perceive the causes of lack of service provision for people with mental health problems, learning disabilities, Alzheimer's disease, or carers. The experience of working in equal relationships with people using services, and handling disagreements and conflicts within this framework can provide a useful preparation for operating within policy frameworks.

- Themed practice learning opportunities: A different approach to practice learning involves undertaking thematic practice learning opportunities across organisational boundaries, with a focus on the experiences of people using services, rather than on service inputs or outputs. The student works with a diverse range of providers, developing skills in problem solving, negotiation, conflict resolution, and partnership by tracking the experiences of people who use services with the organisations with which they are most likely to come into contact. This approach is consistent with the contemporary emphasis on partnership with service users.

Guiding Principles for Practice: Three Examples

The requirements for practice are clear and detailed in stating what social workers should be able to do, but practitioners need to find some way of organising their approach to situations and problems. Occupational Standards and the Scottish Standards cannot determine precisely how an individual social worker actually undertakes their practice on a day-to-day basis. Practice comprises the activities the social worker undertakes in accordance with the Standards; how the social worker 'gets there' is a matter of professional skill and judgement.

Social workers should practice in an integrative way, rather than ticking boxes for achievement of separate tasks. The flaw of the National Occupational Standards is that the length and detail of the requirements for evidence to demonstrate the Standards and units can result in box ticking unless a more creative means of tackling the Standards is found. A *guiding principle* represents a constellation of ideas that are linked conceptually. The selective use of a guiding principle can help the social worker to see the 'wood' not just the 'trees' when thinking about how to approach their practice. Three examples of guiding principles include the: social model; group care practice; and the balancing dilemma of promoting both empowerment and emancipation on the one hand, and support and protection on the other.

'Social Model' as a Guiding Principle

The predominant model for contemporary practice is a *social model* rather than a *medical model* of intervention. The *medical model* is a stereotypical shorthand designation for an individual model of intervention (Oliver, 1996) that relied on the professional's expertise and power to diagnose and fix the 'problems' of people who use services. The individual model is not linked irrevocably to the medical and health professions, although traditionally doctors occupied positions of power and tended to practise an individual model that located sources of problems (illness) within the individual. Nursing in the UK promotes a social model of intervention within an appropriate focus of practice (most evidently within learning disabilities nursing and some areas of mental health nursing), although its position within an essentially hierarchical health service structure creates challenges for practising the social model.

The medical/individual model assumes that it can draw on an essentially stable body of expertise and social policies (Payne, 1991) but the world of social work is one of change, where new ideas challenge old assumptions. The disability movement (Oliver, 1989) champions the *social model of disability* which deals with structural factors that impede disabled people's full participation in society. Normalisation or social role valorisation (Wolfensberger, 1982, discussed in Chapter 5), a theoretical approach that promotes a valued life style for people who use services, is consonant with some elements of the *social model*. The essence of the social model is that it locates causal factors of problems (impairment) within society rather than within the individual; therefore the remedy for problems is for society to respond with appropriate strategies. The *social model* is appropriate for social work intervention, because it deals with power inequalities and forges a new kind of professionalism based on partnership, participation, and emancipation. However, Morris (1991) challenged its applicability to other forms of oppression (for example, gender inequality) where female service users may not be able to exercise choice in the same ways as mentally able male adults.

Group Care Practice: a Guiding Principle for Individualising Social Care

Chapter 1 discussed the modernisation process that challenges the assumption that social care is not a field of professional practice. Two major scandals in the 1990s that took place in residential children's services (the 'pin-down' experience in Staffordshire and the Frank Beck case) prompted efforts to improve the standards of social care practice. The Utting (1991) review of residential children's services in England resulted from the 'pindown' experience in Staffordshire in which children in care were subjected to extreme and demeaning methods of punishment. An Expert Group (CCETSW, 1992) recommended changes in residential children's homes' care training and practice.

The Expert Group re-supported the concept of *group care practice* that had been developed 11 years earlier as a domain for professional social work (Ainsworth and Fulcher, 1981; CCETSW, 1983). The Report recognised that the essential characteristic of group care is its complex networks of diverse relationships between staff and people who use services and between individuals and groups. The Report acknowledged its debt to an ecological perspective (Bronfenbrenner, 1979; Whittaker and Tracy, 1989) that values different environments within social care. Essentially, group care practice seeks to individualise practice in environments where institutionalisation and standardised treatment can too easily gain hold.

Group care practice (Ainsworth and Fulcher, 1981) first focused on residential care for children but then broadened its remit. From 1981, the term *group care* was understood broadly as encompassing all of social care – residential care, day care, and home-based care in a variety of settings and with a range of service user groups. Ainsworth and Fulcher (1981,

1985) established group care practice as a domain of practice, identifying a framework of eight areas of knowledge and skills (CCETSW, 1983):

- organisation of the group care environment;
- team functioning;
- activity programming;
- working with groups;
- on-the-spot counselling;
- nurturing care;
- developmental scheduling;
- formulation of individual care and treatment plans.

The CCETSW commissioned and published guidelines for group care practice with older people (Biggs, 1989; Kerr, 1985) to stimulate good practice and standards of care. The guidelines exposed the gaps between theory and practice, because in the pre-modernisation period of the 1980s and 1990s, the reality of life within many residential homes fell short of the standards demanded by the group care practice model (Stevenson, 1989). Group care practice represented a bold attempt to create a more theoretical and professional social care practice, but it remained a low priority for social work.

Also in 1992, the Warner Report (Warner, 1992) addressed the staffing of children's homes, triggered by a different scandal, in which Frank Beck, the head of a children's home in Leicestershire, was convicted of sexual abuse. Economic considerations about the cost of professional training, rather than theoretical considerations about good practice, may have prompted the Warner Report's recommendations against professionalising residential work with children as part of social work (Warner, 1992) and instead calling for better screening of applicants for posts in children's homes, and separate training for residential child care workers.

More rigorous quality assurance systems for social care were developed in the following years (discussed in Chapter 1). Social care has become professional in its own right, rather than seeking to become a branch of social work. In the UK as a whole, care councils and sector skills councils address the issue of standards in social care and in children's services. In England, a Children's Workforce Development Council works with children's services to develop standards and qualifications that will produce better outcomes for children. The ever-increasing outpouring of guidance on standards fits the paradigm identified by Booth (1985), in which the detrimental effects of institutionalisation (Townsend, 1962) that had been characteristic of social care since the days of the workhouse are attributable to the shortcomings of practice. The assumption is that bad practice is capable of improvement, rather than regarded as an inevitable aspect of the experience of social care.

The concept of *group care practice* with its eight knowledge and skill areas represents a humanistic approach that focuses on individual development rather than managing an institution. The group care practice model can help social care workers to recognise that the tasks and activities they perform can make a positive difference to the lives of people who use services. Group care practice deserves careful consideration as a guiding principle for professional social care practice.

The 'Balancing Dilemma' – a Guiding Principle

The Benchmark Statement asserts that: 'service users and carers comprise a wide and diverse set of individuals, groups and organisations who are involved in, or who benefit from the contribution of social work to the well-being of society, ... including some service users that are involuntary or unwilling recipients of social work services' (QAA, 2000: §1.12). This sentence hints at one of the most difficult aspects of practice: that some people who use services do not want to see a social worker or receive help, or may disagree with the approach taken. People who use services may desire empowerment and emancipation while the social worker is concerned to protect them from harm. Social work practice has to try to balance the dilemma of managing the tension between these two purposes, empowerment and protection, a difficult endeavour particularly when the user of services is angry or disagrees with the need for a particular course of action. There are no easy answers for resolving the balancing dilemma, which is a recurring feature of practice. Not to be aware of the balancing dilemma might mean that the social worker exercises power without self-awareness – and this could sabotage attempts to develop practice that aligns with social work values.

Some criticisms about the way professionals have exercised power are justified. To counter the oppressions resulting from decisions made without consultation or explanation, contemporary social work places a high value on working in partnership with people who use services and those who care for them. British social work promotes empowerment, participation, and emancipation. The growing influence of the consumer movement requires social workers to share power with people who use services (Holman and Bewley, 1999). Williams (1993) argued that health and social care professionals should work in partnership with people who use services to exchange knowledge. In this approach, the people using services would provide expert knowledge and reciprocal expertise. Social workers are expected to respect service users' and carers' diversity. Social workers are encouraged to focus on contributing to outcomes that people who use services want and that promote independence and autonomy, but social workers also must not neglect their duty to protect individuals from harm and abuse, requiring a regulatory investigative and monitoring role that can push the social worker into actions that some service users will want to reject.

The best way of preparing for situations where the social worker must confront the balancing dilemma between protection and regulation on the one hand and empowerment and emancipation on the other is to be honest in portraying the social work role and purpose to the person using services. The social worker must uphold ethical standards of protecting and safeguarding vulnerable individuals in disputed decisions. The person using services and the carer should be made aware of this social work duty from the start. Social workers should communicate clearly the principles that guide decisions to people who use services and those who care for them. The social worker who develops reflective practice and uses practice supervision constructively is better equipped to deal with the balancing dilemma.

? Question for Reflection – The Balancing Dilemma

How can you prepare to address the dilemma of balancing empowerment and emancipation with protection and regulation? You might consider learning more about the issues through practice learning, supervision, reading, discussion, and reflection.

▶▶ Conclusion

'Practice', an integral part of social work that must be organised around service users and carers' expectations of social work, is conceptualised as transferring from classroom to agency-based practice learning opportunities and back. Competence is a central concept of contemporary social work requirements which must be developed over time as part of a continuous learning process. Therefore students' practice learning should be carefully designed to move gradually through the stages of *safety to practice*, *fitness to practice* and *readiness to practice*. Practice learn-ing will develop beyond competence as social workers begin their professional practice after graduation. Practice learning should be recognised as life long learning that moves beyond competence to proficiency and then expertise, with social workers using guiding principles of the use of self, the importance of relationships, and the balancing dilemma rather than ticking boxes for shaping practice.

📖 Further Reading

Barnes, C. and Mercer, G. (2003) *Implementing the Social Model of Disability: Theory and Practice.* Leeds: The Disability Press University of Leeds.
This book provides an explanation by leading scholars in disability studies of the challenges of implementing the social model.

Boddy, J., Cameron, C. and Moss, P. (eds) (2005) *Care Work Present and Future.* London: Routledge.
This book discusses cross-European social care work that illuminates issues for social care, childcare work, and the social pedagogue model.

Seden, J. (2005) *Counselling Skills in Social Work Practice*, second edition. Maidenhead: Open University Press/McGraw Hill.
Seden's updated edition incorporates aspects of the concept of social work as art and use of self.

3 DIFFERENT CONTEXTS FOR PRACTICE

Social work is located within different social welfare contexts, with different traditions of social welfare influenced by legislation, historical development and social attitudes. (QAA, 2000: §2.2.1)

Introduction

An important step towards becoming a member of the social work profession is to begin to understand how and why social work practice has developed in particular ways in the UK and elsewhere – knowledge of social policy is essential for acquiring this understanding.

Chapter Structure

This chapter considers the complexity of practice within different welfare traditions, typified by balancing the dilemma between empowerment and emancipation on the one hand, and protection and regulation on the other. Two questions are posed about the distinctive 'art' of social work before tracing the inter-related development of social policy and social work. The chapter discusses concepts of citizenship and social exclusion, and resources for social policy that include human rights legislation, formal and informal social care, and sustainable environments. A particular feature is the discussion of social policy for social care (including social work), international social welfare, and the policy implications of the European social pedagogue model of social work.

Complexity of Practice and Different Welfare Traditions

The Benchmark Statement (QAA, 2000) draws attention to the complexity of social work practice. Social workers engage with a range of different people involved in social situations that rarely lend themselves to straightforward solutions. The apparent intractability of some situations may be the reason why people seek, or are allocated, social work help. Social policies that determine helping strategies are continuously changing. Social work practice draws on different expectations of social welfare that seemingly conflict with each other – the balancing dilemma of Chapter 2 where social workers are expected to empower and emancipate, but also regulate and protect vulnerable individuals. In Case Study 3.1, presented below, a social worker facilitates social change in an individual when she performs an advocacy role promoting direct payments.

Case Study 3.1 – Direct Payments

We return to the story told in Chapter 1 of Mrs Elsie Green, the 87-year-old widow whose Care Manager was Jane Clark, a social worker in an Adult Services Team. Jane managed to establish some continuity of staffing for the provision of social care support, following Mrs Green's expressed feelings of loss following the transfer of her care worker Denise Michael to other people who use services. After a period of time, Mrs Green's son John and her daughter-in-law Susan returned from Canada and bought a house about 10 miles away. John and Susan expressed concern over whether Mrs Green was receiving adequate support at home and hinted that she might be better off in residential care. They were worried about the possible risk of her falling.

Mrs Green subsequently asked to see Jane, and enquired tentatively about receiving direct payments or an individual care budget that she would manage herself. A neighbour had told her about their availability and so she wondered about giving them a try. Jane was initially taken aback. She had thought Mrs Green was too frail to manage the organisation of care funded by direct payments, and so had not mentioned their availability to Mrs Green. She thought that Mrs Green was about to request help to move to residential care.

However, Jane was aware that the Community Care (direct payments) Act 1999 and regulations governing direct payments had extended their availability to older people since 2003, and that the Department of Health in its Green Paper (2005) was urging her employers to improve the take-up of direct payments, which so far had been very slow. Jane recalled that her employers had appointed a direct payments manager and a system to ease the process and help the service user to get started with direct payments. She knew that the purpose of direct payments was to enable people who use services to buy in and manage their own support services, thus giving them more independence and control. Jane was aware of direct payments and individual budgets because her employer had provided a training day on the topic for all staff.

Jane decided to explore the idea of direct payments with Mrs Green, which meant determining eligibility and assessing any risks. Mrs Green was found to be eligible and motivated to receive direct payments. The risk assessment did not pose insuperable problems. A legal agreement covered the responsibilities of the user and of the council, explained the amount Mrs Green would get, and stated how funds would be monitored. A voluntary agency was able to assist Mrs Green with the employment and management aspects of direct payments. Jane found herself adopting an advocacy role, positively supporting the user's wishes, and allaying some of the fears expressed by her son John who remained very worried about his mother's care.

In a contrasting Case Study (3.2), Jane promotes adjustment and adaptation.

Case Study 3.2 – Providing Support During a Life Transition

In an alternative version of events, Mrs Elsie Green, the 87-year-old widow, contacted her Care Manager Jane Clark. When Jane and Mrs Green met together, Mrs Green said that she wanted to discuss going into residential care, because 'my son worries about me'. Jane discussed the range of choices including alternatives to residential care, the cost, and what residential living would be like. She gave Mrs Green a chance to express some of her doubts. It seemed that Mrs Green had made up her mind, saying that she felt too isolated and unsure of herself while living on her own. Jane assessed Mrs Green's suitability for residential care, and then arranged for Mrs Green and her family to visit a home that had a vacancy. Jane provided Mrs Green with the opportunity to change her mind. Jane was aware that this proposed move represented a significant transition for Mrs Green and that emotional support was required. Jane also liaised with John and Susan Green to explain the steps involved in the transition and how they could help. Jane liaised with the Registered Care Manager of the home and the social care staff to prepare them for Mrs Green's admission.

In the second scenario Jane plays a supportive role, but she presents a range of information to Mrs Green to enable her to make an informed choice. Jane's role draws on the principles of evidence-informed practice, where the facts, choices, advantages and disadvantages of a particular choice are presented to the service user to help make an appropriate choice. Promoting social change through advocacy and helping people with transitions are both aspects of practice that can be brought together in a series of interactions with the same service user. In the next Case Study (3.3), Jane adopts a combination of practice roles: advocate, supporter, and organiser.

Case Study 3.3 – Combining Different Kinds of Social Work Practice

Jane Clark acted as an advocate for Mrs Elsie Green when Mrs Green expressed her wish to receive direct payments. Jane assessed the risk and determined that the risk was acceptable and that Mrs Green had a right to direct payments and an individual budget if that was her wish. When setting up the arrangements, Jane became aware that Mrs Green needed support as well as advocacy to ensure that the arrangements worked well. Jane was sensitive to Mrs Green's understandable uncertainties, and tried to provide emotional support. Jane's statutory employers had contracted with a direct payments voluntary support service for people who use services that would provide the information, practical advice, financial information, and ongoing support that Mrs Green needed for managing her individual budget and direct payments. Jane involved them in providing support and building Mrs Green's confidence. Four months after taking up direct payments, Mrs Green expressed satisfaction with direct payments, saying that they were proving a great success that gave her more independence. She thanked Jane for her initial advocacy, her support, and for help in organising the arrangements.

Two Questions about Social Work Practice

The different practice situations in which social workers engage, and the flexibility of social work practice may cloud recognition of social work's distinctive contributions. The first question is: What is distinctive about social work practice when there are so many different roles and duties for social workers?

A second issue also clouds our understanding of social work: practice appears circumscribed by a range of statutory, regulatory, and policy requirements. Stringent audit procedures, evolving social policies, and a multitude of project-based initiatives make demands on social workers. For example, practice has to be consonant with employers' procedures and relevant legislation. The second question asks: Is there any opportunity in social work's crowded agenda for developing the art of social work practice? To help answer these two questions, the chapter considers the parallel development of social policy and social work.

Social Welfare Policy and Poverty

Manning and Shaw (2000) argue that social policy has always been concerned with the problem of poverty. Redistributing resources to alleviate poverty is a historic goal of social work practice, and explains why social work practice exhibits a range of concerns that cover the life course of vulnerable people from childhood, adolescence, and adulthood to old age, and the particular situations of people with physical disabilities, learning disabilities, mental health problems, and chronic degenerative health conditions – poverty is the common factor in social workers' involvement. Social work's historic *raison d'être* is the desire to promote social justice by addressing the causes of poverty.

Box 3.1: Definitions of Poverty

The relative nature of all definitions of poverty means that there can be no single agreed definition. Considering whether or not certain individuals are poor involves comparing their available resources with those of other individuals in society. Some people move into or out of poverty, and others remain trapped in chronic poverty. In 1984, the European Community elaborated the 1975 definition of persons living in poverty to 'persons, families and groups of persons whose resources (material, cultural and social) are so limited as to exclude them from the minimum acceptable way of life in the Member State in which they live' (Eurostat, 2000: 11).

In the UK, the Household Below Average Income (HBA) statistics, the Poverty and Social Exclusion Survey in Great Britain (PSE, 1999) and the Poverty and Social Exclusion Survey in Northern Ireland (PSENI) (Hillyard et al., 2003) provide indicators of poverty. The HBA statistics define the poverty line as 60% of median income. Poverty is defined by the PSE and PSENI as occurring when 'people lack a number of essential items or services because they cannot afford them and, in the PSENI, have a low household income' (Flaherty et al., 2004).

Social Policy Development

Social policy, the bedrock academic subject for social work practice, developed as an academic subject as part of the struggle to combat poverty; professional social work developed around the same time with similar goals. Like social work, social policy relates in a flexible manner to (and in some instances overlaps with) the study of sociology, economics, and politics; like social work, social policy's flexibility and versatility create difficulties in identifying its distinctive attributes. Alcock (2003a: 1) provides a useful overview of social policy's development. Social policy (as an academic subject) investigates the development and delivery of policy and the actions of policy makers. Social policy also refers to the body of strategic decision-making by planners and legislators that determines social support mechanisms for society as a whole, and in particular, for its vulnerable members. Manning and Shaw (2000: 1) argue that 'social policy is … the creature of social change generated elsewhere in society, and to which social policy is a response'.

Social policy became a focus of study towards the end of the 19th century just as social work began to win recognition, having as its primary interest the debate about poverty and how to replace the 1834 Poor Law. History reveals different explanations of poverty (Jones, 1997); it was once regarded as the fault of the individual or as an inevitable feature of a hierarchical society where social class predominated, rather than attributable to an unjust social system. For centuries, the Poor Law of 1601, religious bodies, and local charities constituted a rudimentary welfare system that administered relief to indigent people. Families were expected to provide care for their sick, old, or disabled members. Before the industrial revolution of the late 18th and early 19th centuries, Christian churches (prompted by their beliefs in charitable giving) and emergent local government systems at parish level administered a limited social welfare system for poor people, who included orphans, widows, people with disabilities, and frail older people unable to work whose families were not able to give them financial support. The industrial revolution changed British social structure with the introduction of mass factory production; the urban population began to rise, and work and home became separate, in contrast to the rural community of the farm and large estate where work and home merged together.

The Poor Law Amendment Act 1834 introduced a more stringent system of relief, where laziness was viewed to be the cause of destitution. The Poor Law remained the primary mechanism for welfare support, sending the poor to workhouses, which provided punitive experiences that segregated family members by gender and age. The social shame of entering the workhouse served as a negative incentive to make poor people avoid turning to public relief. At the same time, conditions for the general population were improving. Smales (1975) identified a second industrial revolution from 1850 to 1914 when improvements in communication and technology (invention of the railway, the steamship, the telegraph, and the telephone) brought about improved communication. Introduction of state funded education in 1870 increased literacy and opened opportunities for the growth of a popular press that provided the first example of mass communication to reach the newly literate working class. The right to vote was extended in 1884.

Accompanying the rise of capitalism and industrialisation was a growing interest in human rights. Social theorists like Rousseau (1998), Voltaire (1994), and Paine (1995) had provided philosophic ideas about human rights that triggered the American Revolution of 1776 and the French Revolution of 1789, resulting in independence for the American colonies and the overthrow of the French monarchy. Gradually the punitive spirit of the 1834 Poor Law reform lost support as the rise of trade unions in the late 19th century challenged the *laissez-faire* principle of the state, and Charles Dickens and other writers portrayed the effects of poverty in popular novels such as *Oliver Twist*.

Charity and philanthropy became powerful change agents. The Charity Organisation Society (COS), established in Britain in 1869, developed systematic casework to distinguish between the deserving and undeserving poor and determine who would be eligible for charitable help. During the Boer war at the end of the 19th century, the public was shocked by the poor physical health of army recruits attributed to widespread poverty, and following a public outcry, free school meals and health examinations were introduced.

In 1884 Beatrice and Sidney Webb established the Fabian Society in England, which encouraged critical evaluation of social issues, believing in the need for some kind of social protection to mitigate the perceived impoverishing effects of capitalism on much of the population. The Fabians argued for a more benevolent state intervention than the Poor Law. Their clamour for state intervention was fuelled by contemporary social survey research by Rowntree (1901) and Booth (1889–1903) into the causes of urban poverty. New ideas about the causes of poverty began to shift blame from the individual to the social and economic system. Gradually more members of the public recognised that a capitalist economic system without the mitigation of a welfare safety net could result in widespread unemployment that left individuals with few opportunities for alternative work, and left frail older people and those with severe disabilities who were not able to work in destitution. The urban poor could not turn to extended families for help, because everyone was affected by economic slumps.

In 1905 the Royal Commission's Review of the Poor Law resulted in a majority and minority view. Both views agreed that further reform of the Poor Law was needed, but disagreed about how to go about implementing the reform, the minority view arguing for more state intervention, the majority view for action through voluntary organisations. Signs of progress towards social justice were evident when the Lloyd George government provided old age pensions in 1908, reducing the likelihood of older people being forced to enter the workhouse because of poverty. During this period, suffragettes began to campaign for votes for women.

The COS School of Sociology became part of the London School of Economics in 1912, establishing a training base for social workers, and bringing together the two different views about how to tackle poverty. Two world wars in the 20th century triggered even more rapid social change: the First World War led to women finally receiving the right to vote, partly in recognition of the contribution women factory workers had made to the war effort. Gradually more state provision was introduced, but widespread unemployment during the economic slump of the 1930s left memories of means testing that humiliated the poor. The Second World War required sacrifices from the civilian population who were subjected to bombing and food shortages, but also brought employment and a broader consensus about how to tackle poverty.

The shared experience of war diminished the divisive influence of social class and created social cohesiveness that stimulated support for further welfare reforms. The Beveridge Report of 1942 introduced the plan that led to the introduction of the welfare state in 1948.

The period after 1948 initially achieved consensus about how to tackle social problems. Through the 1950s Conservatives supported welfare state reforms introduced previously by the Labour Party. Comprehensive state provision was intended to meet basic needs that Beveridge had characterised as the five giants. The giants were the outward representations of poverty, and by providing a comprehensive welfare system, it was hoped to defeat poverty itself (Box 3.2).

Box 3.2: The Welfare State of 1948

The welfare state provided:

- Free education up to 15 years (later 16) designed to defeat the giant of IGNORANCE.
- A free (at point of service) national health service to combat the giant of DISEASE.
- Full employment policies to overcome the giant of IDLENESS.
- Affordable public housing to banish the giant of SQUALOR.
- National insurance benefits to destroy the giant of WANT.

During this period of consensus, *social policy* was known as *social administration*. Alcock (2003a) argues that *social administration* taught social workers to act as providers of welfare. Social work training courses disseminated the views of social administration academics (Titmuss, 1950, 1976; Townsend, 1962) who studied poverty and other associated social problems to find evidence for more state intervention to resolve the issues by measuring the quantity of social need, rather than defining need or questioning whether the responses to identified needs were appropriate (Alcock, 2003a: 5).

By the mid-1970s the welfare state consensus began to collapse. Alcock identifies three challenges to the model of state intervention: the New Left, the New Right, and People's Movements. The New Left criticised the welfare state for not doing enough to address social problems and continuing to perpetuate a capitalist system that arguably exploited poor people. The Left proposed radical changes to the economic system, and many social workers joined the campaign for more extensive welfare systems and more generous benefits to combat poverty, which showed no signs of disappearing altogether.

In contrast, the New Right, exemplified by Thatcherite policies introduced from 1979, argued that state welfare was not compatible with promoting a successful market economy that would bring more prosperity and therefore reduce poverty, and that state welfare should be reduced or transferred to the private sector. In the 1970s and 1980s the Thatcher government introduced extensive privatisation of services and a quasi-market for purchasing care services in the private and independent sectors rather than relying on state-run services. During the 1980s, social care in the independent sector (provided by private or voluntary organisations) grew. The National Health Service and Community Care Act 1990, for example, encouraged a range of independent providers for residential care and day services. Some social workers disliked privatisation because they argued that standards of services would be compromised, and mourned what they perceived as the demise of the welfare state (Jones, 2002). Relatively few social workers, it would seem, supported privatisation, but because social workers were employed mainly in local government-run social services departments, it could be argued that social workers viewed privatisation as a threat to their own roles.

The third challenge to the welfare state came from groups characterised as People's Movements or New Social Movements (Oliver, 1999), which gained support from social workers. Feminists (Dale and Foster, 1986; Pascall, 1986) advocated reform of the welfare state to increase opportunities for women, perceiving a male bias in the payment of national insurance benefits (with the exception of family allowances that were paid to the mother) which had been constructed on the assumption that women would not be employed outside the home following marriage, and that men would be the family wage earners. Disabled people's organisations (for example, Shaping Our Lives; Hearing Voices) became powerful as disabled individuals grew tired of their invisibility within state institutions (Oliver and Barnes, 1998) and began to demand their rights as human beings to participate in society and make choices. The anti-racism movement recognised the pervasiveness of institutionalised racism and wanted to challenge this injustice. The welfare state of 1948 had said little about these members of society, and in the intervening years as society had become more diverse, the limitations of the welfare state vision were exposed.

Alcock (2003a: 9) argues that because of attacks from the New Left, the New Right, and New Social Movements, Britain has shifted from the *welfare state* to a *welfare mix* in which the state regulates and subsidises the partnerships of welfare providers. The long-term goals of contemporary social policy depend on networks and partnerships that need to remain in existence for a considerable length of time. The future danger is that policies will not be given an opportunity to prove themselves because of political pressures for changing direction. Britain could experience a policy shift away from the *welfare mix* although it is unlikely that social welfare policy will revert to the state run services of 1948.

Cultural Influences and Social Policy

The New Social Movements attacked the predominant culture within social work and social policy, and over time, were successful in changing dominant cultural beliefs to an increased acknowledgement of the diverse needs of particular groups within society. The shift in social policies towards women, minorities, and disabled people was triggered by changed cultural beliefs (Baldock, 1999). Social policy academics and sociologists played an important part in changing public attitudes, and influencing the future directions of social work and social care practice.

Box 3.3: The Literature of Dysfunction and Its Role in Bringing about Cultural Change

Leading academics published research in the 1960s that exposed the devastating conditions experienced by people living in long stay hospitals and residential homes – the literature of dysfunction. Their research and publications brought about a cultural shift in attitudes that resulted in changed policies towards residential social care and long stay hospital care, leading eventually to the introduction of care in the community legislation in 1990. Townsend (1962) revealed that years after the welfare state had been introduced, social workers were placing frail older people in geriatric wards of long stay hospitals, or in gender-segregated residential homes in former workhouse buildings. Goffman (1961) revealed that professionals placed people with mental health problems in locked wards of large mental hospitals. Morris (1969) revealed that professionals placed people with learning disabilities in long stay mental handicap hospitals. Goffman (1961) attacked long stay hospitals as constituting 'total institutions' and accordingly drew attention to surviving workhouse influences. The concept of *stigma* as a spoiled identity drew attention to prevalent attitudes that perpetuated discrimination (Goffman, 1963) and helped to change cultural perceptions of identity.

The literature of dysfunction (Box 3.3) changed public understanding and led to policy change. Social policy and social work argued that living in the community was more life enhancing than living in an institution. Closure of large institutions and a re-thinking of choices and life styles for previously institutionalised people soon followed.

New Pragmatism

The declining support for the 1948 welfare state can be explained by its failure to recognise the existence and rights of these excluded groups. Inequalities persisted among some groups – particularly women, and people who were institutionalised. Manning et al. (2003) explain the public's general perception that the traditional welfare state is under threat, partly because of the effects of globalised economies driving down labour costs and diminishing the resources required by the welfare state, and partly because of demographic changes resulting in an increased older population presenting challenges to health and social care provision. These perceptions of social changes led to the recent policy pragmatism of *The Third Way* (Giddens, 1998) that claims to adapt social democratic principles to contemporary social conditions.

Box 3.4: The Third Way (adapted from Giddens, 1998)

- Is concerned with exclusion at different levels of society.
- Emphasises both rights and obligations that promote social inclusion and social justice.
- Views globalisation positively rather than as the cause of inequalities.
- Believes in combining the culture of competitive markets with the public interest.
- Requires partnerships that develop relationships between communities and government, between public and private sectors, and between individuals and communities.
- Acknowledges the links between social and economic policies.
- Argues that spending on social policies should consider the consequences for the economy.
- Seeks to reform the labour market by developing active welfare e.g. getting people back to work through 'carrot and stick' motivation.

Giddens (1998) contributes the core values of *inclusion, community, opportunity, responsibility* and *accountability* to the Third Way, and proposes modernising social democracy to take account of a changing globalised world, placing emancipatory politics and social justice in the context of a new social contract of 'no rights without responsibilities'. Jordan (2000: 218) elaborated these ideas in the context of social work, concluding that the Third Way as promoted by the New Labour government was an opportunity for social work but potentially could be a cul-de-sac.

The Third Way's approach to tackling the five giants of the Beveridge Report (*inter alia*) is to set targets for reducing child poverty and raising educational standards, but not to address overall income inequality directly. Contemporary social policy seeks to influence investments and wealth creation as well as develop strategies for wealth distribution: its pragmatism is based on theoretical pluralism – what counts is what works. Some academics (Goldson, 2002; Jones, 2002) criticise the apparent abandonment of the aim to create social justice through direct income redistribution, perceiving an increasing amount of regulation and coercion in schemes designed to develop skills and improve employability.

Concepts for the *Welfare-mix* State

The next section explores some of the concepts that underpin the 'welfare-mix' state: *citizenship* and *social exclusion*.

Citizenship

Drake (2001: 119) identifies four prerequisites for *citizenship* that essentially echo themes of the Third Way (Box 3.5).

Box 3.5: Four Prerequisites for Citizenship (adapted from Drake, 2001)

- *Membership*: Citizens are *members* of the society in which they live, and are recognised as such by their ability to vote and live permanently in the country to which they belong.
- *Participation*: Citizens *participate* in society by contributing to their neighbourhoods, by involving themselves in community action, and by supporting regeneration of their community.
- *Entitlements*: Citizens are *entitled* to opportunities for realising their potential abilities and to supportive measures for preventing poverty.
- *Obligations*: Citizens have *obligations* to obey the law, be good neighbours, exercise prudent choices for managing their resources, pay taxes, serve on a jury, and if called, serve in the forces.

Attempts to clarify the concept of citizenship are particularly relevant as people from other cultures seek residence and eventually citizenship in the UK, and as the European Community (EC) extends its borders. 'Citizenship' appeals to the altruistic side of human nature that Titmuss (1962) explored in his analysis of the blood donor system as a gift relationship, arguing that the welfare state's provision of state support would enhance the generous side of human nature. Now, the emphasis on citizenship seeks to do much the same thing, but adds the proviso of *obligations* as well as *rights*.

For example, public organisations' citizen charters explain the standards of services they provide to their customers (e.g. the Student Charter explains students' rights to teaching, learning and assessment, and their obligations to attend class regularly and to undertake assessments). Charters demonstrate the concept of citizenship based on rights and responsibilities, but there are some implied risks in publicising the rights and obligations of citizenship. People who use services may not regard themselves as full citizens because of their history of exclusion: they may perceive a denial of their rights and consequently reject their duty to fulfil their citizen obligations.

Social exclusion

Contemporary British social policy tackles the problem of poverty holistically through the concept of social exclusion, and its opposite, social inclusion (defined in Chapter 1). In 1997 the government established the SEU as a policy body, now located in the Office of the Deputy Prime Minister. The SEU's Policy Action Team argued that traditional organisational structures for social work, social care, health, education, and criminal justice led to fragmentation. The subsequent policy thrust is to encourage 'joined up' solutions to 'joined up' problems, through programmes that focus on building skills for employment integral to social inclusion strategies – hence programmes such as Welfare to Work, the New Deal, and (in England) Connexions personal advisers for 13–19-year-olds. Regeneration of communities is a prominent goal of inclusion strategy.

Efforts to tackle poverty need continuous monitoring to check whether progress is being made. The New Policy Institute (Joseph Rowntree Foundation [JRF], 2004) monitors poverty and social inclusion, and its 2004 analysis established that the number of people in low-income households was falling. In contrast, the number of working age adults without dependent children who experience poverty has risen. Short-term work of less than six months is characteristic of jobs at the lower end of the labour market; the number of children and young adults with minimum levels of education qualifications has not improved although numbers did rise from the mid 1990s to around 2003.

? Question for Reflection

What contribution can social workers make to promoting social justice in the welfare mix of social inclusion projects and strategies?

You may want to consider social workers' roles in multi-professional teams that tackle social problems 'in the round' by bringing health, social care, education and the independent sectors together, and about social workers' roles in new projects that tackle the effects of poverty and exclusion, for example, Sure Start. Are there other opportunities for social workers? Craig (2002) argues that social workers can promote social justice in four different ways, by repositioning themselves with skills of community development to:

- accumulate and disseminate evidence about continuing injustices;
- facilitate and advocate for poor people on the margins of society to ensure that regeneration partnerships actually consult with the most vulnerable groups;
- promote the ideal of joined-up policies when gaps are discovered;
- address social services' deficiencies in providing for marginalised groups, including black and ethnic minorities.

Resources for Social Policy

Shaw (2000) argues that successful implementation of social policy depends on having sufficient resources of governmental funding. Social policy initiatives also require less tangible resources that include human rights legislation, sufficient availability of formal and informal social care, and in the long term, investing in sustainable environments that promote health and well-being. The next section reviews these resources.

Human rights legislation

When human rights are abused, individuals cannot participate fully in society and overcome their social exclusion. Professional social workers are expected to identify and challenge injustice that contravenes human rights, therefore they should be aware of international social policy on human rights. Social workers now have recourse to the Human Rights Act 1998 that took effect in the UK in October 2000. The Human Rights Act supports people's right to freedom from abuse, and their right to family life (Butler, 2004) and incorporates the European Convention on Human Rights into UK law, with implications that when service provision does not comply with human rights, a means of challenge is available in domestic law. McDonald (2001) argued that because the Act is rather conservatively framed, its interpretation and applicability would be developed over a period of time in response to individual and collective actions. Further discussion in Chapter 6 suggests how the Human Rights Act can be used by voluntary organisations to promote rights.

Availability of formal and informal social care

Demographic change and the changing roles and functions of families affect the availability of resources for achieving social inclusion. Demographic issues include the increasing number of older people who survive longer, and potentially may place more demands on pensions and social care support systems. Glenister (1997: 166) argues against a strict correlation between increasing age and frailty in old age, although the incidence of disability rises for people over 75 and therefore health care becomes more expensive for this group. The ageing of the population (Table 3.1) suggests that social care and social work will need to devote more resources to supporting older people who are living longer.

Table 3.1   Population of the United Kingdom (millions)

	1991	2001	2011 (projected)	Percentage change	
				1991–2001	2001–2010
Total population	57.4	58.8	60.5	2	3
Aged under 16	11.7	11.9	11.1	1	–7
Working age	35.2	36.2	37.5	3	4
Pensionable age[1]	10.6	10.8	12.0	3	11
85 and over	0.9	1.1	1.3	29	19

[1]Between 2010 and 2020 the state pension age (now 65 for men and 60 for women) will be increased to 65 for both sexes.

Sources: Office for National Statistics; Government Actuary's Department; General Register Office for Scotland; Northern Ireland Statistics and Research Agency.

Caution is necessary when considering gloomy predictions of a crisis for health and social care provision triggered by increasing demands from older people. Brooks et al. (2002) suggest that proximity to death, rather than greater longevity, is a key factor for explaining the extra demand on services, and it is not proven that all older people will need continuously increasing levels of care. If health and social care policies continue to develop effective prevention and rehabilitation programmes, older people will survive with better health, needing relatively little support until they are very close to death, and fewer older people will require ongoing intensive health and social care support.

The number of people of working age who participate in the labour force has reduced (particularly for men) because of the decline of traditional industries like steel and coal; in contrast, the number of women in the workforce has risen (Vickerstaff, 1999). These demographic trends raise issues about the supply of both formal and informal carers to meet increased demands for care posed by longevity (Shaw, 2000: 27). The rising numbers of women entering higher education and the workforce diminishes the potential supply of informal care from women family members, because wives and mothers are more likely to be employed outside the home. The rise in divorce and single parenthood also places more demands on informal carers. Social policy resources require interconnected strategies to address these issues – providing good quality child care, introducing flexible working patterns, and more easily accessible rehabilitative care. The outcomes of social work and social care practice usually rely on the availability of health, education, and social care (including child care) resources to provide day-to-day support for users of services. Professional caring roles, such as social work, teaching, and nursing, are experiencing staffing difficulties, as women who have traditionally entered these professions gain wider possibilities for career development. Social care employers need to develop human resources strategies that include workforce development programmes that will both recruit and retain social work and social care staff.

Sustainable environments

Concerns about resources extend to the wider social policy issue of sustainable environments. The World Commission on the Environment (Bruntland, 1987: 43) defines sustainability as 'Development, which meets the needs of the present without compromising the ability of future generations to meet their own needs'.

The industrial revolution brought prosperity and increased longevity, but a reduced quality of the environment for many people, particular those living in cities. Pollution and contamination caused by the use of destructive industrial materials without protection for workers and people living in the surrounding areas resulted in increased industrial diseases such as asbestosis and silicosis with long-term negative health effects. Concerns about the environment have led to bans on smoking in public places because of the potential carcinogenous effect of active and passive smoking. The increase in childhood asthma and the pollution of the atmosphere with traffic fumes and noise are now social policy concerns (Jacobs, 1996).

Recognition that social and environmental variables are key factors for determining health and life opportunities is gaining ground, so that future social policy is likely to be concerned with public health issues of managing the ecology of the environment. The Public Health White Paper (DH, 2004a) promotes principles that will assist the public to make informed choices about their health, including tackling health inequalities, health in childhood, and health at work through health improvement programmes. Information and practical support from the government will try to motivate people to make healthier life choices on diet and exercise. Social workers located in multi-professional teams will therefore begin to recognise environmental factors as issues to be considered when seeking ways to improve the quality of life for particular individuals. Although health workers may take the lead in promoting awareness of the causal effects of environment, social workers will need to consider the importance of health improvement and sustaining the environment.

Resource Planning for Social Policy

The levels of resources required to sustain the contemporary *welfare-mix* model may be threatened by the prevalence of individualism in society. The notion of the *common good* is present within Etzioni's (1997) communitarianism that influenced the Third Way brand of social policy. For example, anti-smoking campaigns have an opportunity to succeed only when smoking is recognised as affecting the common good. In contrast to the post-war years when the public accepted high levels of taxation in return for the welfare state, voters are unlikely to support policies that evidently require high taxation. This suggests that resources should be targeted at vulnerable individuals who need them most, but the notion of targeting tends to offend those whose ideal is the 1948 welfare state supplying universal free services. A current dilemma is what to do about retirement policy. Public opinion may not accept the need to rethink retirement policy and yet not accept higher levels of taxation – a conundrum for social policy (Box 3.6).

Box 3.6: Retirement Policy – a Contemporary Social Policy Issue

The rising numbers of older people who live for a very long time on pensions pose a resourcing issue for governments. Walker (1991) argued that the dependency of older people is socially constructed: compulsory retirement policy linked to inadequate state retirement pensions and occupational pensions' insufficient coverage of the population create social dependency in older people whose incomes are not large enough. The level of the state pension could be raised but that would create a large tax burden on the population. There is a case for introducing flexible retirement policies that would permit older people to stay in work beyond the current mandatory retirement age of 65, but keep pensionable ages at 65. Alternatively, pensionable age could be raised to 67 or to 70 in recognition of the increased longevity of older people since the introduction of the state pension.

The Risk Society

Social workers work with the concept of managing risk when they assess risk in situations involving vulnerable people (discussed in Chapter 2). Risk assessment also operates at the policy level. Dingwall (1999) explores the concept of the *risk society* in contemporary life by drawing on the contributions of Giddens (1990, 1991, 1994) and Beck (1992). He portrays changes in traditional capitalism as the starting point of the risk society, with society's resulting transformation to *late modernity* (a continuation of modern society into more radical globalised structures) or *post-modernism* (a way of viewing society not as an organised systematic structure but as different constructions of reality where individual self-reflexivity becomes important). The core theme of Beck's risk society is that modernity failed to deliver its promised freedoms, and instead created new enslavements. For every advance in wealth production that benefits society, there is an increase in accompanying risks. Societal risks can be global as well as personal, but these risks ultimately affect individuals.

For example, the destruction of South American rain forests and the possible plundering of Alaska's natural environment for oil would realise short-term benefits, but also create longer-term risks of climatic change that might endanger the food supply and lead to flooding of cities. The problem of risk management becomes a social policy issue that requires sufficient expert predictive knowledge of risk and belief in the effectiveness of scientific solutions. Responsibility for managing risk of the more long-term variety is not straightforward, because its management is linked to political priorities. Changes in political priorities mean that responsibility for managing risk can be avoided.

Social Policy for Social Care and Social Work

Social care and social work are the focus of current social policy change that seeks to modernise services and raise standards (discussed previously in Chapter 1). Roche and Rankin's (2004) policy seminars for the Institute of Public Policy Research reviewed some major policy trends for social care (including social work) and examined the impact of modernisation on the social care workforce. Their critique is made less clear by an interchangeable use of *social work* and *social care*, thus obscuring the issues that are particular to professional social work. In the discussion that follows, social work is identified separately where relevant, but *social care* indicates both social work and social care unless otherwise noted. The key issues are the *identity, image, organisational structure, recruitment and retention* of the social care workforce, *qualitative changes* in practice, *integration* of care services, and developing a *career pathway* within social care.

Identity

Modernisation (DH, 1998) introduced the social policy goal of creating a highly skilled and knowledgeable social care workforce, but unfortunately the social care workforce is invisible and anonymous because few statistics were kept about numbers and types of workers. In response, Skills for Care (2005), its predecessor body Topss England (2003) and the SE (2004) set up workforce intelligence projects to gather more accurate information on the workforce. In Scotland, the labour demand has increased faster than supply. Social care employment has been growing faster than the average, with male employment doubling and qualification levels and the number of staff with full time contracts increasing.

In England, an estimated 922,000 people were employed in social care in 2003, with most working in services for older people (Skills for Care, 2005). If the early years workforce and social care employees of the health service are added, the number is 1.6 million employees: 50% of these work part time; 80+% are female, and 76,100 are social workers. The social care workforce is ageing. As discussed previously, most social care jobs are part time and filled mainly by women, but men predominate in management level jobs. In 2000, attention was drawn to the fact that 80% of the social care workforce had no qualifications for their work (Topss England, 2003). Since then, targets for attainment of vocational qualifications have been introduced, linked to inspection criteria of social care establishments. However, it is unlikely that all these targets will be met by the end of 2005, leaving the sector with considerable problems to resolve.

The CCW, as part of its strategic plan, is reviewing its workforce intelligence data systems that are available to ensure the best information is available. The NISCC is in discussion with the Department of Health Social Services and Public Safety (DHSSPS) (Northern Ireland) about workforce intelligence, and will be influenced by its membership of the UK Alliance for the Sector Skills Council for Care.

Image

Social care has an image problem that hinders raising its standards. Social care's identity is amorphous (Roche and Rankin, 2004: 5) – comparatively few members of the public know about social care or understand what social care workers or social workers do. Social care workers and social workers are employed in the NHS and in local authority social services departments, and also work for private organisations, charities and temporary care agencies; some are self-employed in independent practice. Social care employers are nationally, regionally, and locally based, and they range from very large to very small establishments that provide care services to a widely diverse range of people who use services.

Organisational structure

To raise standards, the *organisational structure* of social care services has been reformed. Children's organisations in Wales campaigned for a children's commissioner for more than 10 years to speak up for children and young people's rights and help protect them. In 2000 the Waterhouse Report *Lost in Care* (which had enquired into child abuse in children's homes in north Wales) recommended a Children's Commissioner, and this led to the Children's Commissioner for Wales Act 2001. Scotland established a commissioner for children and young people under the Commissioner for Children and Young People (Scotland Act) 2003, to promote awareness of the views and interests of children. In Northern Ireland, the Commissioner for Children and Young People (Northern Ireland) Order 2003 established a similar role. More recently, a major review of services for children and young people resulted in the Green Paper *Every Child Matters* (Department for Education and Skills [DfES], 2003) that appointed a Minister for Children and moved responsibility for services to children and young people in England from the DH to the DfES. The Children Act 2004 establishes a Children's Commissioner for England, later than the other countries of the UK.

The Children Act requires public services to cooperate to promote the well-being of children and young people, and requires local authorities with responsibilities for education and social services to appoint a Director for Children's Services and a Lead Member for Children. It also seeks to establish a database called the Children's Index that will enable professional workers to track children and to ensure all children and young people in an area receive their entitlement to services. The reform of children's services in England is intended to give them a clearer identity and enable them to work together in a more co-ordinated manner.

In April 2004 the Parliamentary Under Secretary of State for Community announced a new vision for adult social care. The Green Paper *Independence, Well-being and Choice* (DH, 2005) puts adult social care into a wider context of public health, universal services, community leadership, and healthy sustainable communities. Integrated working will be embedded across the care system; professional social workers and social care workers will still be needed, but in different roles that offer appropriate empowering support.

Different models of social care services will place greater emphasis on direct payments and individual budgets, risk-taking, self-assessment, and other ways to promote independent living and extend choice and control to people who use services. A growing perception that professional activity to protect individuals has emphasised reducing risks so that the capacity for independent living has been stifled will result in more emphasis on self-assessment of needs instead of professional assessment. People who use services might be made responsible for realistically assessing the resources required to deliver the outcomes of their self-assessment. The Green Paper will explore whether the single assessment process (SAP), the care programme approach (CPA) and person-centred planning (PCP) could be developed into an assessment framework for use with all people who have complex needs.

? Question for Reflection

The introduction of direct payments, individual budgets and self-assessments for adult social care will change service users' entitlements and service provision. What will be the likely responses of older people? Consider also the likely reactions of people with mental health problems, learning disabilities, and physical disabilities. What are the likely challenges for social workers?

You should consider the extent to which it is possible to identify a response that is typical of a group as a whole, and whether it is more accurate to think about a range of individual responses.

Recruitment and retention

While optimism is expressed about building a new professionalism and promoting social work values, questions arise about whether enough is being done to resolve the long-standing problem of *recruitment and retention* that the Social Services Inspectorate (SSI) (2003) viewed as the biggest threat to raising standards in social care. Social care is one of the fastest growing sectors of the public sector workforce (DH, 1998). Competition with other sectors to recruit employees makes creating a skilled workforce harder. Successful attainment of higher standards therefore depends on resolving the issue of a largely unqualified work force that is too small in numbers. Roche and Rankin (2004: 17) suggest that any reduction of the social care workforce will sabotage the goal of a health oriented NHS rather than a disease oriented service.

The problem of creating a skilled workforce is exacerbated by limited arrangements for 'return to work' courses for experienced social workers who have taken a career break. A recurring dilemma is the need to find a balance between generic and specific roles. Social workers report that they have too much paperwork, feel undervalued, and are underpaid. To address these issues, employers are urged to make more investment in their workforce and become *learning organisations* that commission training and education to create the necessary knowledge and skills for the future. Developments in the children's workforce mirror these trends but the outcomes of this long-range policy will take time to emerge.

Qualitative changes in practice

Qualitative changes in service delivery will affect social care's traditional culture which provides *care* but also *control*. Members of the public want more flexible social care services delivered in different ways. People who use services express the desire for services that help them lead integrated lives. Changing contexts of practice in statutory, voluntary, private and temporary employment agencies, and in independent practice require new relationships with people who use services and carers, with the social care workforce becoming a 'powerful force to … promote the model of the state as an enabling force' (Roche and Rankin, 2004: 20). Consultation with people who use services in the design of service provision represents a step towards empowerment, with direct payments and individual budgets becoming a major part of the new practice and policy. The CSCI (2004) reported that 73% of people surveyed welcomed the idea of direct payments but only 9600 people received direct payments in 2004. Some people who had not previously used routinised services took up direct payments (Stainton, 2002). Many local authorities are reluctant to promote direct payments; professional reluctance and a general lack of awareness of their availability hinder progress in expanding their take up (Roche and Rankin, 2004: 21).

Social work pioneered public service reform with the introduction of 'personalisation, choice, user empowerment, and user involvement aspirations' (Roche and Rankin, 2004: 1). One of the most successful achievements of professional social work is the colonialisation of its values to the wider social care workforce. The social care workforce now shares social work values of promoting social inclusion and better life opportunities for people who use services. All social workers need to be able to exhibit empathy and demonstrate interventionist and entrepreneurial skills, as well as the ability to reframe a problem (Rankin and Regan, 2004a, 2004b; Smale et al., 1993). It could be argued that these professional skills should permeate more of the social care workforce instead of remaining the preserve of professional social work. Some social workers have expressed concern that the perspective of social work may be lost as familiar organisational structures (social services departments) fragment, but it could also be argued that social work's perspective may become more influential in shaping practice.

Integrated organisational structures

Increasingly, social care will manage a complex 'integrated care landscape' (Roche and Rankin, 2004: 13) enabling its workers to navigate the continuous changes taking place in service provision. Social care services will be integrated across a range of services, including health, housing, social services, and small and large private and voluntary organisations. The two major integrations are between health and social care for adult services, and between education and social care for children and young people's services. The Health Act 1999 established the legal framework for health and social care partnerships followed by Care Trusts. Similar arrangements will create Children's Trusts or 'trust-like' partnerships that bring together local education, social care/social work, some health services, Sure Start schemes, and in England, Connexions and possibly Yots into an integrated commissioning strategy for service provision. Other partners that might be involved include the police, housing and leisure, and voluntary organisations. Currently, social care workers are employed within, and managed by, health service organisations, housing organisations, and social services, as well as private and voluntary bodies. New configurations of employment within multi-professional teams will add to social care's complex landscape. Service integration has implications for training the workforce, developing defined career paths, managing social care, and maintaining autonomy of practice (Roche and Rankin, 2004: 13).

A future challenge is to make new partnerships and collaborations work effectively. Peck et al. (2001: 18) argues that partnerships may falter if there is insufficient consideration of cultural changes in practice. All social care employers need to take an active role in promoting the importance of knowledge in the workplace, but to do this effectively they may need to increase their investment in information technology networks.

Building a career framework: the Skills Escalator

Social care needs to develop a career framework, and should consider the applicability to social care of the National Health Service Modernisation Agency's (2004) proposed career framework for health. The framework's centrepiece is a generic analysis of job roles in health care that categorises roles on a hierarchical scale. Workers' exercise of decision-making becomes more autonomous and responsible the further up the scale they are placed. The Changing Workforce Programme (2004) across the UK, which is part of the NHS Modernisation Agency, examined the need for new roles and for working in different ways. In England a Skills Escalator provides a template for further developing new roles for members of a range of existing professions (Box 3.7).

Box 3.7: Skills Escalator (adapted from NHS Modernisation Agency, 2004)	
Level 9	More senior staff with responsibility for 'clinical caseload decision-making and responsibility'.
Level 8	Consultant practitioners.
Level 7	Advanced practitioners.
Level 6	Senior practitioners.
Level 5	Practitioners.
Level 4	Assistant/associate practitioners.
Level 3	Senior care assistants/technicians.
Level 2	Support workers.
Level 1	Domestic workers or 'cadets'.

The hierarchy begins with generic entry-level jobs and moves gradually up to practitioner level and beyond. The most senior staff with ultimate practice accountability are placed at the top of the escalator. Under the Skills Escalator principle, some nurses' skills will be developed through additional training and qualifications to become prescribing nurses who will be able to carry out some of the responsibilities formerly reserved for medical practitioners. Mental health social workers could become mental health consultants on the social aspects of policy and law, or on implementation of the social model.

The social care sector has not embraced the Skills Escalator concept probably because the diversity of its employers and workforce seems to preclude reaching agreement on strategy. Roche and Rankin (2004) suggest that workforce strategies are needed for social care, but a Skills Escalator that could align pay and skills development would not work at national level. Rejecting the concept, however, limits the vision of social care. Ideas within the Skills Escalator could help develop new roles for social workers that would be underpinned by continuing professional development and commissioned post-qualifying awards. At present there are no comprehensive clear strategies for linking post-qualification social work education, training, and research with senior and advanced social work roles – an area of workforce development that social care employers need to consider.

International Social Policy

The Benchmark Statement contains implicit references to international concerns, suggesting (QAA, 2000: §1.9) that the student social worker 'takes account of European and international contexts of social work'. The UK is part of the EC, and therefore social policies in the UK are influenced by what is decided in Brussels. The UK Action Plan on Social Inclusion 2003–2006 (Department for Work and Pensions, 2003) is an example of the influence of international social policy: the plan was constructed in alignment with a common outline agreed by member states and the European Commission, and is designed to contribute to the European Union's goal of eradicating poverty in Europe.

Social workers are more likely to become aware of global issues when they work in countries other than their own (Box 3.8). Charities and voluntary service organisations provide opportunities for social workers to spend a year or more working in Africa, Asia, or South America.

Box 3.8: Awareness of International Practice

Laird (2002), a British social worker who worked for four years in Ghana, argued that she was more directly exposed to the influence of globalisation than when she worked in the UK. Laird found that in Ghana, action to improve children's basic survival took preference over action for detecting child abuse. She concluded that 'best practice' differed from one country to another because of the country's particular socio-economic contexts. British social workers should not assume the superiority of western (British) social work models. The key question to ask is: 'what are the priorities in terms of social problems for this particular society at this particular time, and to what extent might the solutions to these problems be facilitated or obstructed by the social, political and economic structures already in place?' (Laird, 2002: 19).

To gain some understanding of international social policy, the social worker has to avoid Eurosceptic thinking – judging policies and practice according to British culture and assumptions. The section explores the social policy issues of globalisation, migration, subsidiarity, European models of social work practice and the social pedagogue.

Globalisation

Yeates (2001) argues that globalisation (explained as the global flow of capital, people, and information) is a contested term in academic and political debate, particularly about whether globalisation is 'good' or 'bad'. No matter which side one takes in the debate, people generally accept that globalisation brings about changes in the world's socio-economic structures. Yeates (2001: 2) identifies a reciprocal relationship between globalisation and social policy, in which political agency, social conflict, and struggle remain important influences. Global social governance includes human rights legislation; non-governmental organisations (NGOs) exert influence at international levels; and state regulation of health and safety, competition, and environmental concerns are examples of movements that counter the effects of globalisation. Single-issue groups opposing globalisation engage in social dialogue, protest, and direct political action against global corporations.

Migration

Migration is a global issue with major implications for social policy and social work activity. Globalisation encourages global movement – and it is difficult to control the flow of people. Castles and Miller (1998: xiii) argue that international migration is a constant and continuing historical fact, prompted by famine, war, economic push–pull factors, urbanisation, and ethnic and religious discrimination. In recent years, refugees moved within and from Rwanda, Burma, Zaire, Tanzania, Afghanistan, the Middle East, and countries of the former Soviet Union and the former Yugoslavia. In almost every situation, migration to countries with more developed economic structures leads to permanent settlement and creation of ethnic minority populations. In Western Europe, migration policy has focused on protecting national borders, securing trans-border agreements on regulating illegal entries, and speeding up and regulating the process for asylum. Castles and Miller (1998: 285) argued a case for planned and controlled entry of migrants.

A fortress mentality, economic fears, and racist thinking prompt some British people to view migration as a threat to a seemingly overcrowded island rather than as a potential asset. Migration leads to issues of political participation, cultural identities, and national citizenship. The Third Way emphasises citizenship and exhorts citizens to participate in local communities. Despite the possibility of protection by human rights legislation, as yet there is no universal protection of the rights of refugees. Some social workers argue that denial of asylum seekers' personhood arises from the policies of the National Asylum Support Service (NASS) (2005), established in 1999 as a specialist provision service within the Immigration and Nationality Directorate of the Home Office. NASS administers the provisions of the Immigration and Asylum Act that removed asylum seekers from mainstream welfare provision, and is responsible for basic support mechanisms for destitute asylum seekers. Asylum seekers must show that they are destitute, have no other means of support, or are likely to become destitute in 14 days.

NASS funds six voluntary sector agencies across the UK (including the Scottish Refugee Council and the Refugee Council in different regional locations in England and Wales). The six agencies function as a partnership to provide some emergency support and advice to asylum seekers through 'one-stop shops'.

Box 3.9: Breach of Human Rights

From January 2004, under Section 55 of the Act, access to support was limited to those who can prove they made application for asylum 'as soon as reasonably practical' after entering Britain. The Refugee Council states that in May 2004 a Court of Appeal test case found a breach of human rights in the implementation of Section 55 of the Asylum policy. From June 2004 the implementation policy was changed so that support is denied only if staff find that applicants do have an alternative means of support.

British social workers find themselves expected to intervene with economic migrants, refugees, asylum seekers, and new immigrants to the UK.

?   Question for Reflection

How can social workers develop appropriate strategies for working with refugees and asylum seekers?

Here are some suggestions:

- Developing successful social work strategies to address globalisation and migration depends on social workers forming alliances with other professionals and with people who use services.
- Knowledge of social policy leads to informed views of migration.
- In the short term, social workers should be alert to situations when individual families of asylum seekers and migrants seemingly are excluded from full human rights entitlement.
- Social workers can use appropriate advocacy skills to promote human rights perspectives for migrants.
- Social workers can also support efforts to increase migrants' access to information through the Internet. Migrants, because of their poverty, may be excluded from full access to knowledge available through computer information technology.

ICAR, the Information Centre about Asylum and Refugees in the UK based in King's College London (ICAR 2005 http//www.icar.org), is an independent centre funded by charitable trusts that aims to raise the level of public debate and promote better understanding by collecting, recording, compiling, and disseminating up-to-date, comprehensive and academically credible information about UK refugees and asylum seekers. ICAR provides navigation guides on issues of current concern.

Subsidiarity

The post-war welfare state in Britain was founded on a social welfare vision of universal services, but after 50 years, the stigma of receiving help from 'the welfare' remains. Crisis intervention rather than preventive services occurs too frequently. Service delivery patterns perpetuate social exclusion. The policy emphasis on 'joined up' services as a way of dealing with social exclusion has led to service coalitions and collaborative working. Adult services are merging with health; and children's services are merging with education. Social work practice in the UK is beginning to adopt certain aspects of international social welfare models, which both resemble and differ from those used by British social workers.

One feature of European social work that is notably different from how social work developed in the UK is the principle of *subsidiarity*, which delivers services through smaller independent agencies, some private, some voluntary, and some church related, rather than through large state agencies (Cannan et al., 1992: 31–5). This principle is seen as protecting the individual from the power of the state. The *subsidiarity* principle is meant to ensure that decisions are taken as closely as possible to the citizen's local community. *Subsidiarity* is being adopted within the UK through an emphasis on partnerships at local and regional levels to deliver services, and the increased use of independent sector service provider agencies.

European models of social work practice

A significant importation of a European model of practice is the emphasis on promoting education and individual development rather than traditional social welfare. As well as social welfare as the driving force for social policy, educational strategies have become important tools for reducing social exclusion and bringing about change. Significant causes of social exclusion are attributed to low educational attainment, subsequent skills shortages, and unemployment. The Labour government, under Tony Blair, has promoted expanded participation in education and training through linking benefits to training, increasing funding for further education, widening access to higher education, modern apprenticeships, and vocational qualifications. Policies were introduced to raise literacy and numeracy levels within schools and colleges. Organisations are expected to become *learning organisations*, with *life long learning* now a popular slogan.

The social pedagogue

The fall of communism in the former Soviet Union and countries of Eastern Europe triggered the introduction in these countries of professional social work and also social pedagogy (Higham, 2001), a European model of social work practised (*inter alia*) in Germany, Denmark, and The

Netherlands. In 1991 Russia introduced both professional social work, portrayed as *applied sociology*, and social pedagogy, portrayed as a *pedagogical science*. Social pedagogy differs from social work, because the social pedagogue exerts an educational influence on the service user. Box 3.10 describes how the Russian Orthodox Church promotes and uses the social pedagogue role as a means of social intervention. In reading this account, it is important to appreciate the value placed on spirituality, which differs from the values of secular social work. An analogous role in the UK might be a church youth worker, but there is no adequate direct parallel.

Box 3.10: Social Pedagogy in Russia (adapted from Sklayarova, 2004)

Sklayarova argues that industrialisation in the second half of the nineteenth century prompted the Russian people to move to urban centres, thus threatening the perpetuation of traditional values. This prompted the rise of social pedagogy to 'accomplish tasks that were beyond the traditional educational system' including re-educating individuals who 'did not fit in the social system or who violated its norms … to help them readjust themselves to the new conditions'. As with social work, there were two traditions of social pedagogy: the emancipatory view that social pedagogues should work to address causes and effects of anti-social behaviour; and the ameliorative view that social pedagogues were like 'ambulance paramedics' giving material and psychological aid to individuals to help them live successfully in society. A matter of concern is whether the primary focus of intervention is with children or adults, or both.

Traditionally 'social education' was the responsibility of the Orthodox Church and the family, therefore the Russian Orthodox Church trains and employs social pedagogues. The curriculum emphasises an anthropological view of human openness to change, seeking to assess and address external factors, working with individuals of all ages and social conditions while reaching out to the inner person to get them to turn to 'the spiritual richness of Orthodoxy and to introduce [them] to the liturgical life of the Church'. It is argued that 'both unsuccessful and successful people, families and other groups need pedagogical influence'.

This model of social pedagogy seems to emphasise helping individuals to 'adjust', but social pedagogy could in principle empower and emancipate. Cannan et al. (1992) argue that social pedagogy shares some aspects of Freire's pedagogy of the oppressed (1972, discussed in Chapter 5), a popular education movement from South America that seeks to liberate individuals from their oppressions.

The British practitioner of social pedagogy was introduced almost by stealth within services such as Sure Start programmes for parents and children under five, and in England, Connexions personal advisers for young people aged 13–19. Participants in the Roche and Rankin seminars expressed the view that the identity crisis of social work is heightened by the establishment of services that practise a different kind of social work under a different name – e.g. Sure Start and Connexions services. Kornbeck (2000) argued that describing the social pedagogue role is easier than defining the role, a view that echoes Lorenz' efforts to explain social pedagogy (Lorenz, 1991, 2003).

Europe has developed two distinct traditions of professional social work: social casework that emphasised psychoanalytic ideas (imported from the USA and prevalent in the UK, Ireland, Portugal, Italy, Greece and the Scandinavian countries); and social pedagogy (prevalent in Belgium, Denmark, France, Germany, The Netherlands, and also in Eastern European countries). Social pedagogy's particular approach was developed in Germany in the later part of the 19th century. During this period, reactions to industrialisation led to the founding of new philosophical movements that accord with some of the ideals of social pedagogy. These philosophical movements emphasised human potential as a spiritual aspect of human existence but within a secular conceptual framework rather than an overtly religious belief system. Three philosophies, theosophy, anthroposophy, and ethical culture (Cross, 1958) contributed ideas that are consonant (arguably) with the ideas of social pedagogy. The Rudolf Steiner movement (Box 3.11) is an example of a social philosophy applied to education and development, resulting in a particular model of a therapeutic community.

Box 3.11: Steiner Communities

Rudolf Steiner (1861–1925) developed anthroposophy (Steiner, 1925) as a philosophical movement that promotes spiritual awareness and identity. His followers spread beyond his native Germany to the USA, the UK, and many other countries. He inspired the founding of Waldorf schools for children, Camphill Communities for adults with learning disabilities, and eurhythmy, a form of physical movement. Today the schools and communities are established on a worldwide basis. Social services organisations have placed children in Steiner schools, and middle-class parents have supported Steiner education. Adults with learning disabilities are placed within Camphill communities, which are self-contained 'village communities' set apart from local communities.

Some criticisms may be made of village communities for institutionalising people with learning disabilities in groups that are peripheral to the rest of society, but the communities generally continue to receive public support. A study commissioned by the DH in 1998 studied the costs and quality of village communities and dispersed housing, and concluded that, when village communities were established by organisations with little experience of this model for the purpose of re-provisioning accommodation following mental health hospital closures, the quality was poor. However, the study also concluded that village communities were economical and could offer effective choices to some people with learning disabilities (Emerson et al., 1999).

Social pedagogy belongs to a developmental model that plays a part in the *welfare-mix* pattern of services. Lorenz (2003) considers social pedagogy to be part of a wider framework of *socio-educational care work*. Pedagogy questions how a society reproduces itself culturally, socially, and intellectually. The key role of social pedagogy is to promote individual well-being through informal educational strategies that empower people with the knowledge and skills to manage their lives. Lorenz (2003) argues that social pedagogy can pose questions about the individual identities of people who use services, and pushes beyond traditional self-definitions to explore wider possibilities for individual identity. Cannan et al. (1992) suggest that social pedagogues renew society by developing individual potential through preventive, developmental, and educative forms of intervention with children and communities outside the formal classroom. The *animateur* in France practises in a similar way. Crimmens (2001) discussed efforts to develop a British social pedagogy through new approaches to practice, including residential children's services. Arguably, Connexions personal adviser teams, early years workers, learning mentors, education welfare officers, Sure Start workers, and youth and community workers practise aspects of the social pedagogue model.

Cameron (2004) argues that social pedagogy is concerned with the relationship of the individual to society. Based on research on social pedagogy practice in Denmark and Germany, she claims that social pedagogy could provide a suitable practice strategy for children's residential services. The Thomas Coram Research Unit's research programme on care work in Europe (Boddy et al., 2005) engaged in work with partners in Denmark, Hungary, The Netherlands, Spain, and Sweden to explore care work with children, young people, young adults with disabilities and older people. The study revealed differences, but also commonalities in demands for:

- qualities and skills for reflecting;
- making contextualised judgements;
- communicating and listening;
- networking and teamworking;
- supporting development, autonomy, inclusion, and citizenship;
- working with diversity and change;
- adopting a holistic approach; and
- combining theory and practice.

The study concludes that there may be a case for developing a generic care worker like the Danish pedagogue who is educated to work with people from birth through to the adult years.

The shift in responsibility for children and young people's services in England from the DH to the DfES, the appointment of a Children's Minister in 2003, and the appointment of Children's Commissioners in all four countries of the UK signalled the growing importance of an implicit social pedagogue model of social work for some of the new services. The social welfare model was not deemed sufficient in itself to offer help aimed at reducing social exclusion, because of the perceived stigmatising features of social welfare in the UK. The British tradition of casework based on statutory intervention came to be perceived negatively. Social pedagogy, which Europe views as part of a broad range of roles that encompass social work, offers an alternative model by combining community development and broad educational strategies in multi-professional partnerships and non-stigmatising access to services.

The emphasis on education is underpinned by a belief in each individual's capacity to learn and develop. This belief prompted the decision to introduce the Connexions Service in England, a programme whose goal is to emphasise the attainment of skills and qualifications, and personal advisers, who are employed by the Connexions Service to tackle social exclusion by seeking to prevent young people aged 13–19 from dropping out of education, employment, and training. The personal adviser role differs from current British social work models and does not duplicate the roles of education welfare officers, careers advisers, youth and community workers, and members of Yots. They are not teachers, although they promote education and training – their consonance with the social pedagogue model is evident (Higham, 2001; and Box 3.12).

Box 3.12: An English Model of Social Pedagogy

Connexions provides a universal, comprehensive, non-stigmatising approach in England to guiding and supporting the transition of all young people to adulthood and working life (DfEE, 2000: ch. 6). The Connexions service aims to end the perceived fragmentation of young people's services (2000: 3). Initial targets comprised general educational goals of reducing truancy, preventing school exclusions, increasing attainment of educational qualifications, improving participation in employment, and specific targets of better outcomes for care leavers and reductions in illegal drug use, youth offending, and teenage pregnancies. The personal adviser pursues the goals of enhancing human development, life long learning, and working towards developing a person's inherent potential. Similar to Sure Start, this programme will face the challenge of continuity and survival within the new mix of children's services.

The Connexions partnerships, founded out of Careers Guidance companies and the Careers Services in England, will undergo change. Similar to Sure Start, they face the issue of aligning with new policies for integrated children's services. The professional organisation for careers guidance officers (who comprise the majority of personal advisers) has expressed a desire to return to the role of careers adviser serving all young people, rather than the targeted Connexions service that has come to resemble social work (The Guidance Council, 2004).

In the late modern era of fragmenting systems that Alcock calls the *welfare mix* rather than the *welfare state*, social pedagogy may provide a new model of practice within social work. Despite considerable diversity of roles and functions, international and European associations of social work education acknowledge common aims and ideals. They have agreed a definition of social work that was adopted in the UK. An international definition of social work is a starting point. Social work's international networks should result in more broadly based opportunities for practice in the 21st century.

Returning to the Two Questions about Social Work Practice

Evident from the discussion is the current dynamic turbulence of social policy and its effects on social work practice. Social work's broad practice base can be viewed as a strength that facilitates appropriate responses to new social problems, or alternatively social work's wide range of approaches to practice can be perceived as a weakness that prevents social workers from acquiring a recognised body of knowledge and skills. After this discourse on the development of social policy and its key themes for practice, consider again the two questions posed at the beginning of the chapter. The first question was: What is distinctive about social work practice when there are so many different roles and duties for social workers?

New service delivery requirements want 'joined up' integrated services that tackle social exclusion. Social workers' practice has the potential to develop whole systems thinking about situations and people, rather than being limited to perceiving just a part of a situation. Social work education is generic and therefore provides a good basis for understanding the totality of the issues confronting people who use services. Insights from social policy, social work theory, psychology, sociology, and human growth and development provide a knowledge base for practice.

Social workers sometimes find it hard to identify the skills they possess compared with the task oriented skills of other professions. For example, unlike nurses, social workers do not give injections. To feel inadequate about this misses the point about social work's potential to work holistically with situations and with individuals. When considering the desire to create multi-professional partnerships, a positive attribute may be found in the amorphous nature of social care and social work (Roche and Rankin, 2004). Cozens (2004) argues that social care and social work's diversity gives them the ability to wrap around other services and be flexible. Social workers' distinctive strengths are found in their ability to be interactive and work collaboratively with other disciplines and professions (Higham, 2005).

The second question asked was: Is there any opportunity in social work's crowded agenda for developing the art of social work practice? The preceding discussion of social policy revealed the dynamic changing nature of social work and social care shaped by changes in social policy. The transformation of the *welfare state* into the *welfare mix* challenges professional social workers to form new relationships with people who use services and their carers that require working in partnership and listening to their wishes. Co-working with social care workers and other professionals in multi-professional teams should not be difficult for social workers. The changes are meant to deliver the better quality services that people who use services and carers want, posing a challenge for social work because there are no blueprints for the new kinds of practice that are needed. Social workers' creativity in helping to construct new ways of working will be valued.

Manifesto for Social Work and Social Justice

Jones' (2003) manifesto for social work and social justice is a response to contemporary social policy changes that argues that British social work has lost direction because of its domination by managerialism, service fragmentation, financial restrictions, increased bureaucracy, and use of private sector organisations. The manifesto echoes social workers' views in the findings of the Roche and Rankin report. Jones attacks budget-driven social work, and claims that social workers feel frustrated and angry. The manifesto takes an anti-capitalist, anti-war, and anti-globalism stance, and suggests that democracy, participation and justice are anti-capitalist values. Asserting the need for a new social policy direction, the manifesto sees 'resources of hope' in forming partnerships with the new user movements. Jones advocates a genuinely anti-oppressive social work. Aspects of the manifesto are consonant with current social policy for social care, for example, user participation, and the concept of citizenship, but the manifesto implies that the art of social work is incompatible with the higher levels of accountability required in public services.

▶▶ Conclusion

The loss of social work as 'art' is not necessarily inevitable. Much depends on social workers asserting a strong collective professional voice that examines work roles and accountability in relation to quality of outcomes. Is British social work mature enough to assume a professional role? Ladyman (2004) criticised some of the responses to the consultation on adult social care for their preoccupation with process rather than with a vision of change, and the initial reluctance of some social workers to enrol on the Social Care Register. At the London-based GSCC Annual Meeting Conference in November 2004 some English social workers asked the GSCC to tell them the specific competences they had to meet for their continuing professional development, rather than assume responsibility for making their own choices. Notwithstanding the more structured continuing professional development requirements in the other countries of the UK, social workers should not always ask to be told what is best for them. Social work practice needs to gain confidence in its own ideas and begin to express its professional voice, thus influencing the direction of social policy.

📖 Further Reading

Alcock, P. (2003) *Social Policy in Britain*, second edition. Basingstoke: Palgrave.
This book provides an overview of social policy including the concept of the 'welfare mix' provision of services.

Ferguson, I., Lavalette, M. and Whitmore, E. (eds) (2004) *Globalisation, Global Justice and Social Work*. London: Routledge.
The book discusses the theories of Gramsci and Freire, and presents case studies of the global effects of welfare policies in different countries, including Senegal, France, Argentina, and Mexico.

Jordan, B. with Jordan, C. (2000) *Social Work and the Third Way: Tough Love as Social Policy*. London: Sage.
This is an eloquent analysis of the Third Way's policies and their influence on the roles and purposes of social work.

4 SOCIAL WORK ROLES

There are competing views in society at large on the nature of social work and on its place and purpose. Social work practice and education inevitably reflect these differing perspectives on the role of social work in relation to social justice, social care and social order.

Social work … evolves, adapts and changes in response to the social, political and economic challenges and demands of contemporary social welfare policy, practice and legislation. (QAA, 2000: §§ 2.2.2, 2.2.3)

Introduction

Social work's distinctive quality is its holistic practice working with a range of situations and people, an ideal attribute for developing the multi-professional partnerships that are now seen as essential to better service provision. The amorphous nature of social care (and social work) noted by Roche and Rankin (2004) constitutes a strength in undertaking new roles in partnership with people who use services and their carers. Professional social workers have to combine multiple roles that balance empowerment and emancipation with protection and support. Balancing this dilemma is a challenge that is not easily resolved; sometimes there may be no single choice of role that seems best. A further issue is how to balance generic roles with practice specialisms. Social workers' roles will change as people who use services and carers exercise more choice and take up self-assessments of need and direct payments, with needs assessments becoming shared exercises in which the social worker adopts an enabling supportive role.

Chapter Structure

This chapter argues that social workers must practice multiple roles in order to deal with complex situations, and suggests that *use of self* can help them avoid an unwitting misuse of power by developing more self-awareness. The chapter surveys a range of roles for specialisms in individual, group, and community-based fields of practice, and introduces the concept of maxims for practice. The dilemma of balancing regulation and protection with emancipation and empowerment is reiterated, before concluding with a discussion of complex needs and a possible new social work role of *service navigator*.

Multiple Social Work Roles

The concept of *role* is an important tool in the development of an understanding of the complexity of social work practice. The social worker selects, combines, and carries out a number of roles as part of their interaction with individuals, groups, and communities. Whittaker and Tracy (1989: 101) argued that the professional social worker operates within the framework of complementary roles that constitute 'multiple pathways to helping', calling for a dual focus on face-to-face assistance and indirect activities, for example environmental change, thus echoing the Barclay Report (1982) recommendations.

Social work roles are characteristic patterns of behaviours that are influenced by professional values and requirements. Linton (1936) portrayed *role* as the qualities and behaviours that denote a particular social position. When a person carries out a role, they apply rights and duties to selected patterns of behaviour, and demonstrate aspects of status. Status is defined by norms that indicate how an individual is expected to act. Norms help to construct social roles that regulate behaviour. Mead (1934) portrayed *role* as the social interactions that link society, personality, and communication; an inter-actionist interpretation that recognises the sometimes ill-defined nature of roles and allows room for role negotiation. Merton (1957) developed the idea of the *role set* to denote more than one social relationship and one behaviour pattern. *Role-playing* is sometimes portrayed as playing games, implying manipulation or insincerity, but multiple roles are an essential feature of human relationships and are integral to complex social work practice.

Box 4.1: Examples of Multiple Roles

A *male adult* may play multiple roles of:

- son;
- husband or partner;
- father;
- householder;
- employee.

A *female adult* may play multiple roles of:

- daughter;
- wife or partner;
- mother;
- householder;
- employee.

(Continued)

Box 4.1: *(Continued)*

A *young person* may play multiple roles of:

- son or daughter;
- grandchild;
- sibling;
- pupil;
- member of a peer group.

The role examples in Box 4.1 imply a set of shared expectations of social relationships, status, behaviour, and conduct. However, not all women and men may have a partner or spouse; some may not be a parent and some may be without work. An indicative list of roles could extend beyond those noted, yet the assumption that women may simultaneously play roles of wife, mother, and employee would not have been acceptable when the welfare state was established in 1948 because women were expected to give up their roles as paid employees when they married and assume full time unpaid caring roles as wives and mothers.

Parsons (1951) argued that a values consensus is necessary to maintain social order in society. Roles constitute the means by which a values consensus is translated into action so that role definition is rooted in the expectations of society. An unthinkingly rigid application of previously defined roles may restrict opportunities for developing new kinds of roles. The role of wife or husband is defined differently depending on culture, tradition, and choice. The roles of men, women, and children can conflict at times because of the multiple expectations that each person has to meet. For example, a young person may find the role of friend may conflict with parents' expectations of the son or daughter role, and the changing roles of women and men can result in dissonant expectations and lead to role conflict.

Professional roles that social workers adopt include a versatile and flexible range:

- planner;
- assessor;
- evaluator;
- counsellor;
- supporter;
- advocate;
- manager.

Compton and Galaway (1984: 428) defined 'interventive roles' in social work as the behaviours by which users and workers expect helping functions to be jointly carried out. They warn that these roles do not represent functional specialisms. Social workers demonstrate their professionalism by combining roles appropriately within service user situations and professional environments. Social workers need more than 'one string to their bow'. They have to combine roles for effective practice.

Case Study 4.1 – Susan: 'One string to her bow'

Susan, who was a newly qualified social worker, returned to the intake team she had left a few years previously when she obtained sponsorship for the qualifying social work programme at a nearby university. Susan had gained many years of social care experience before undertaking the social work qualification. On her return she felt frustrated at what she perceived as insufficient resources. Susan held high expectations that the welfare state should meet identified needs. She did not place much value on undertaking psycho-social casework with people who asked for help.

One day during the team meeting, the team leader tried to allocate a new referral concerning a poor family with debts, housing problems, and whose children were truanting from school. Susan became annoyed at being asked to take the new case. She repeated over and over: 'There are no resources!' She said that her intervention would be useless unless she could supply the family with ample provision of benefits and services. She attributed the family's problems to their poverty. She thought that she, the social worker, had no adequate means of alleviating poverty, so what was the point of her intervention?

In the example given in Case Study 4.1, Susan is a 'one-string-to-the-bow' social worker. She analyses the family's problem as poverty – an analysis that does not a consider the complexities of every situation. Susan was persuaded to visit the family. This is what she discovered and what she did, thus adding more strings to her bow (Case Study 4.2).

Case Study 4.2 – Susan's Multiple Roles for Multiple Problems

Susan visited Mrs Rose who was a single parent with three children, aged 14, 13, and five. Mrs Rose had several debts, looked depressed, and was very worried about the oldest boy, Michael, who was truanting from school and associating with a single man who showered him with expensive gifts. Mrs Rose worried that the man was a paedophile. She told Susan that things had got on top of her after her husband died six months ago as the result of a road traffic accident. Susan realised that there were multiple problems in the family. First, she listened to Mrs Rose express her feelings of loss and anger. Then with Mrs Rose's help and agreement, the two of them drew up a plan of action to address the debts, Mrs Rose's feelings of loss, and Michael's situation. Susan did some of this work herself, but also made referrals to other agencies for appropriate support, and Mrs Rose participated fully in expressing her needs, forming and carrying out the plan. The help supplied was a combination of advocacy to other agencies, counselling, support, and child protection, as well as addressing the financial situation. By the end of the intervention, Mrs Rose began to recover from her depression and assumed more leadership of the family's relationships and finances. Susan realised then that her social work practice with Mrs Rose involved playing multiple roles to address the multiple problems.

Susan was able to practise effectively with Mrs Rose because she played a number of roles. Initially she took some control (a principle of crisis intervention, O'Hagan, 1986, 1991; Roberts, 2004) because Mrs Rose was in a crisis state. Then she gradually handed control back to Mrs Rose and sought to enable Mrs Rose to address her own problems. Susan played the role of advocate for the family with the housing department and the school and obtained resources for the family. The starting point was Susan's focus on demonstrating respect to the individual members of the Rose family, recognising that they, like other people who use services, wanted to identify for themselves their own desired outcomes of social work intervention (Brunel University and NISW, 1999). Respect established the professional relationship and led to the family's gradual unfolding of their issues. From that point, Susan and the family were able to work together to address the multiple issues that required multiple helping roles within a variety of helping strategies that were deployed both consecutively and simultaneously. This case study example illustrates three characteristic features of social work roles:

- First, a focus on valuing human beings, through which the social worker acts as a *guardian of values*.
- Second, a focus on promoting individual and collective well-being and people's strengths, through which the social worker acts as a *promoter/advocate*.
- Third, a focus on protecting vulnerable individuals from harm, through which the social worker acts as a *protector*.

These three areas of focus can lead to role conflict. Susan found that her multiple helping strategies and multiple roles were not always perfectly tuned with each other (Case Study 4.3).

☐ Case Study 4.3 – Susan's Role Conflict

Susan discovered that Michael Rose, the 14-year-old, welcomed her involvement with the family only as long as the focus remained on help for his mother. Michael had felt overburdened with responsibility for his mother and the younger children. He missed his father. He wanted Susan to put things right for the family. However, he became very angry when Susan asked about his truancy from school and his association with a suspected paedophile. He denied Susan's right to interfere, and said that Susan didn't understand and was just a busybody. Mrs Rose also objected to Susan's child protection role because it made her feel uncomfortable. Susan worried that the positive supportive relationships she had formed with the family were being threatened by her child protection role; she feared that the family might reject her and all the other kinds of help because of this role conflict. The family in turn feared that Susan would remove the children from home. Fortunately, the relationship with the family was strong enough to survive this crisis. Susan exercised tact whilst being assertive. She was able to empower Mrs Rose to deal with Michael's truancy and the relationship. Michael became better able to face school once he had expressed his own feelings.

The Social Worker's Use of Self

Social workers invest a great deal of themselves in their multiple roles. Their *use of self* is essential to successful practice. Chapter 2 argued that the *use of self* is intended to develop understanding of others and that being self-aware leads to the effective use of self. Williams (1996: 62–3) argues for wider acceptance of the role of the fragmented nature of the self and the Freudian concept of the unconscious as tools for understanding human behaviour. The contributions of Freud's (1986) psychoanalytic theory to social work practice have been disputed since the eclipse of psycho-social casework, but social workers can gain some useful insights from considering how the unconscious internal mechanisms of defence against anxiety (Freud, 1936) can block self-awareness and impede a purposeful rational use of self. Not all of the mechanisms are relevant to social work practice, and some people argue that Freud's ideas are not proven (Masson, 1984, 1993).

According to Freudian theory, the ego (or conscious part of the mind) tries to defend itself from anxiety caused by urges from the id (the unconscious part of the mind). The ego also has to deal with anxiety threats from the super ego that functions like an over zealous conscience. The defence mechanisms (Box 4.2) defend the ego – our conscious self – against excessive anxiety but they succeed only when the ego is unaware of them. Freud suggests that awareness of how we use the mechanisms can help us confront reality and understand ourselves.

Box 4.2: Defence mechanisms (adapted from Freud, 1936)

Transference is the act of unconsciously transferring emotional reactions and behaviours from previous relationships into current relationships.

Counter-transference occurs when the person who receives an initial transference responds with transference of his or her own.

Denial is refusing or being unable to admit a threatening situation, which occurs when an individual loses control of a situation and is in crisis.

Dissociation, which can sometimes result from traumatic experiences, involves behaviour that disassociates itself from the immediate moment by forgetting a painful moment and thus distorting reality.

Regression involves reverting to previous behaviours and feelings that are now inappropriate.

Repression is the act of pushing unacceptable thoughts and urges into the unconscious to be revealed only by slips of the tongue or in dreams.

Suppression involves pushing unpleasant thoughts or impulses away, but not vanquishing them entirely into the realm of the unconscious.

The defence mechanisms may impede objective evaluation of situations and distort understanding. Social workers engaged in helping relationships should be able to recognise the mechanism of *transference* that occurs within professional helping relationships as well as in everyday relationships, and also should be aware of potential *counter-transference* that can sabotage efforts to bring about change, where the worker and the user of service may be caught in an emotional dynamic based on previous relationships rather than on current situations. For example, a person who uses services may transfer the characteristics of the relationship they previously had with a parent onto the current relationship with the social worker, and the social worker in turn may counter-transfer the kind of relationship he or she had with their own child. Then they begin to respond unconsciously as if a child to a parent, and vice versa, rather than as adults.

Good practice supervision builds self-awareness and helps to neutralise any tendency towards counter-transference. Social workers' use of defence mechanisms should not be employed to construct covert oppressive explanations for service users' behaviour, but used as potential tools for understanding the use of self. Interpretations of behaviour should be mutually shared and agreed as potential guides to understanding, but not as 'facts'. The same provisos apply to use of *transactional analysis* (TA), which Berne (1964) developed from Freud's theory as a way of understanding how unconscious motivations can distort the use of self (Box 4.3).

Box 4.3: Transactional Analysis (adapted from Berne, 1964)

TA analyses interpersonal interactions or transactions between people according to the inter-relationships of three ego states: the Parent, the Adult, and the Child.

The *Parent* represents an inner voice of authority acquired through childhood experiences.
The *Child* represents our emotions and reactions to the world around us.
The *Adult* represents the thoughtful reflective self that makes rational decisions.

TA suggests that individuals play unconscious roles of Parent, Adult, or Child to initiate or respond to communication (or transactions) with others; Adult-to-Adult communication is considered the most desirable kind of transaction.

The Use of Power

Social care organisations exercise power in ways that can either promote or undermine well-being. Social workers embody their employing organisation's power relationships through performance of their roles. This power dynamic operates within social care relationships, and is particularly evident within residential social care (Box 4.4).

Box 4.4: The Power Dynamic in Residential Care

A research project in a home for older people sought to gather residents' views about the quality of their care. The interviewer found that many residents declined to participate, and those who did take part in the project praised the home in over-enthusiastic tones. She felt that she was not able to gather a truly representative valid picture of residents' opinions. On reflection, she realised that the residents were fearful of what might happen to them if they voiced negative views. They perceived themselves as dependent on the staff and feared that criticising the staff who controlled their lives could result in some form of punishment. The interviewer realised that she would have to provide some safeguards to confidentiality before she could hope to gain the residents' participation.

Weber (1958) provides a classic analysis of power, distinguishing between:

- *charismatic authority* stemming from the qualities of leadership;
- *traditional leadership* based on custom and belief; and
- *rational legal authority* based on law and impersonal rules.

Lukes (1974) considered the influence of power on decision-making and avoidance of decision-making, while Hugman (1991: 33) argued that decision-making becomes most difficult when different constituencies display open or latent conflict and little ownership of an established agenda. Mills (1959) analysed the operations of an American military-governmental-industrial complex as a 'power elite'.

The neo-Marxist Gramsci (1971) argued that dominant blocks within society perpetuate power over others; the hegemony of the ruling classes controls political and civic society. The idea of hegemony corresponds with the *control* aspect of social work practice, where the social worker plays a dominant regulatory role in their relationship with the person who uses services. Hegemony helps to explain how social work functions as a powerful state intervention. Nevertheless, Gramsci recognised that the state always has to make some concessions to people who are subject to the hegemony of the ruling class. Exchange and reciprocity theory (Dowd, 1975; Homans, 1974) argued that power and status should be balanced between giver and receiver, but the balance is disrupted when people who use services have to adopt exclusively recipient roles and are excluded from *giving* roles.

Foucault (1971, 1979, 1980) analysed the social control mechanisms of the asylum, the body, and power. His concept of the *disciplinary society* also helps to explain the regulatory control element within social work. He (1980: 19) argues that human lives are shaped by *normalising truths* that exercise power over individual lives. Power (Foucault, 1980: 98) is something that circulates or functions in a chain: professionals exert power over people who use services, applied in different proportions according to identities of class, gender, user power, and position in a hierarchy. Radtke and Stam (1994: 74) claimed that feminism rejects a one-dimensional, single-sourced concept of power, preferring instead a view that theorises diverse sources of power in which different voices set different agendas. Parton (1996: 12) noted that changes in practice (the quasi-market in adult social care, increased legislation and reduction of direct social work practice) shift the nature of power relationships between people who use services and social workers by limiting the discretionary use of professional power. People who use services are regarded now as consumers who require accountability from social workers (Clarke, 2003; Cornwall and Gaventa, 2001). The consumer movement challenges traditional power imbalances in social care, and consequently power relationships that were weighted in favour of social workers have altered because of these ideas that challenge familiar assumptions about power relationships.

Fields of Practice

The next part of the chapter discusses roles located within the three main fields of practice: casework, group work, and community work, categories taken from American social work and Younghusband's (1951, 1978, 1981) account of British social work. *Individual helping roles* are the first point of discussion.

Individual Helping Roles and Casework

Social workers practise individually with individuals and families, undertaking *casework* and carrying *caseloads*. The social worker who adopts an individual helping role as a caseworker is usually said to be practising in the *field* – working from a *fieldwork* office and offering help to people living in their own homes within neighbourhoods and communities rather than to people in residential establishments. The *caseworker* role remains important within social work despite the theoretical eclipse of psycho-social casework. Richmond's (1917) casework model, previously discussed, was not based on psychoanalytic theory and although avoiding the objections to psycho-social casework, it triggered discomfort because of its association with giving help only to the 'deserving poor'. These objections should not prevent social workers from selecting appropriate knowledge and skills from traditional casework.

Whittaker and Tracy (1989: 102) discuss the *therapist-counsellor* as an individual helping role which uses face-to-face work for supporting people through life transitions, helping service users reach decisions, gain insight, modify behaviour, and regain confidence. The therapist-counsellor listens, helps people articulate their feelings and wishes, and the social worker adopting this role is advised to be aware of human growth and development theories and diversity issues that influence identity.

A social worker using an individual approach will use enabling strategies, draw on information networks, and when appropriate refer the person who uses services to other agencies for help – therefore the social worker/caseworker must be knowledgeable about a range of services, must work in partnership with people who use services and their carers, and be skilled in dealing with a range of matters, including unemployment and poverty.

The *caseworker* can adopt the role of *advocate* or *role mediator* (Compton and Galloway, 1984). The *role mediator* resolves disputes between people who use services and service providers by seeking a common ground of agreement on procedures for ongoing communication, and negotiating a process about when to agree and when not to agree. Being able to use good communication skills contributes to the success of efforts to resolve disputes.

The NHS and Community Care Act 1990 introduced the *care manager* role for adult services (Lymbery, 1998). A care manager undertakes a needs assessment of adults seeking community care support or residential care, and then organises a *package of care* to meet the needs, drawing on the contributions of social care staff from the independent and voluntary sectors. Community care introduced a mass welfare system for adult care, particularly older people. Because of the larger numbers of older people seeking services, the care manager role became dominated by standardised procedures that were organised to address the mass market of those seeking care. The role differs from the personalised approaches that some social workers remember, but reaches more people in need of care and offers a wider range of choices than the previous historic reliance on residential care.

The contemporary British statutory model of care management is not the only care management model; wider availability of direct payments and personal budgets in the UK may lead to different care manager roles that will be commissioned directly by the person who uses services. An example, given in Box 4.5, is the specialised role of geriatric care manager (GCM).

Box 4.5: A Different Care Manager Role (adapted from Association of Professional Geriatric Care Managers [APGCM], 2004)

The geriatric care manager (GCM) is a consumer-oriented role in the USA that is commissioned individually by the person who uses services. The GCM helps older people and their families with care arrangements, conducts care planning assessments, arranges and monitors home services, reviews financial, legal and medical issues, and makes appropriate referrals to avoid future problems and conserve assets. The GCM role extends to helping the older person move to a care home, providing advocacy services, counselling and support, as well as 'consumer education', crisis intervention; and liaising with families living a distance from the parent to make sure of the older person's well-being, and alerting families if there are problems.

In the field of brain injury services in the UK, independent care managers work directly with people who use services and carers (Box 4.6).

Box 4.6: Independent Care Manager for Brain Injury

Brain injury is part of a wider group of *acquired brain injury* that also includes non-traumatic brain injury such as stroke. About three quarters of brain injured people who use services are men between 16 and 25 years of age. Road traffic accidents (RTAs) cause over 50% of head

(Continued)

Box 4.6: *(Continued)*

injuries. Falls, sports, and recreational injuries; domestic and industrial accidents; and assaults cause a further 33% (DH, 1994). Some brain-injured people receive compensation funds for their injury and loss of earnings that enable the service user, working through their solicitor, to contract with an independent care manager. The user and carer employ the care manager who assists them to assess their support needs and organises their support – a consumer model that results in ongoing supportive relationships (Washington, 2004).

Working with groups

Group work is a major field of social work, sometimes known as *social group work* to distinguish it from group work that is used within psychology, counselling, or education. The *group worker* role has been overshadowed in British social work by the predominance of one-to-one work, perhaps for reasons connected to the suitability of casework for assessing need and establishing eligibility criteria.

As part of their practice, social workers establish and lead groups (Preston-Shoot, 2006) but group work also is undertaken by other professionals or by social care workers. An effective intervention strategy for therapeutic purposes, for support, and for developing non-oppressive participation (Mullender and Ward, 1991), group work can help provide a very suitable support network for people tackling addictions, or depression. Some groups function as learning groups; others are therapy groups (Yalom, 1985). Issues of power, communication, and use of self permeate the functioning of groups, and these dynamics have to be recognised and managed skillfully to ensure effective interventions.

Another kind of group work is *group care practice* (Ainsworth and Fulcher, 1981, 1985) undertaken in residential homes or day centres (discussed in Chapter 2). Group care involves 'hands-on' caring work for the *group care worker* – the kinds of tasks that social work has always felt uneasy about but which nursing acknowledges as part of its core function. The Benchmark Statement includes provision of direct care as part of intervention and evaluation skills, but links direct care with dependency and also carefully avoids referring to residential homes: 'manage the complex dynamics of dependency and, in some settings, provide direct care and personal support in every day living situations' (QAA, 2000: §3.2.2.4). Registered care manager is the designated title of the qualified head of a residential home that is registered with the CSCI. About 37% of registered managers in local authority care homes (including children's) in 2003 held a professional social work qualification (Skills for Care, 2005).

Working with Communities – Building Social Capital

Younghusband (1959) defined community work as helping people in a community to identify needs, to consider effective ways of meeting needs, and achieve this within available resources. The Benchmark Statement includes building and sustaining 'purposeful relationships with people and organisations in community-based, and interprofessional contexts including group care' in its requirements for intervention and evaluation (QAA, 2000: §3.2.2.4), and also requires knowledge of: 'a range of community-based settings … at individual, group and community levels' (2000: §3.1.4). The Benchmark Statement views working with communities as a social work role, although for the last 50 years community work and youth work have been regarded as separate occupations in the UK with their own youth and community qualification. Community work is not a registerable profession like social work.

Smith (2004) provides a useful overview of the history and characteristics of community work, which initially was part of adult education. In 1968 the Calouste Gulbenkian Foundation published a report on the future of British community work, arguing that community work should be part of the practice of other professionals, including teachers, social workers, and health professionals, but also stating that community work could be a full time role (1968: 149). Community work received its greatest boost during the period 1969–1976 when the Home Office funded several Community Development Programmes, which were action-research projects meant to gather information and foster innovation and co-ordination in tackling poverty. Thomas (1983: 106–9) identified five approaches to community work:

- *Community action* that promotes collective action to challenge inequality.
- *Community development* to promote self help and problem-solving capacities.
- *Social planning* to assess and plan strategies for meeting community needs.
- *Community organisation* to promote shared initiatives.
- *Service extension* to extend services by increasing their accessibility.

Contemporary approaches to community work are linked to social integration and regeneration projects that build social capital, with the result that modern community work practice resonates with the goals of social work. The concept of *social capital*, which aims to develop people's strengths, fits with the National Occupational Standards Key Role 2–Plan, carry out, review and evaluate social work practice with individuals, families, carers, groups, and communities, and other professionals; unit 5–Interact with individuals, families, carers, groups and communities to achieve change and development to improve life opportunities; and unit 8–Work with groups to promote individual growth, development, and independence.

Social capital is the supply of active connections among people, with shared values and behaviours enabling cooperative action (Cohen and Prusak, 2001: 4). Another way of looking at social capital is to view it as the glue that holds together society's institutions, relationships, and expectations (World Bank, 1999). Putnam (1993, 1995, 2000, 2002) argues that society's supply of social capital – its connections with each other – has diminished because of changes in employment patterns, family structures, demography, and women's roles. Examples of social capital include informal neighbourhood relationships, faith communities, self-help groups, credit unions, and community safety schemes. Social capital has two dimensions:

- *Bonding capital* that builds reciprocity and solidarity but is exclusive, inward looking and may reinforce closed homogeneous groups, and can be oppressive if acceptance of diversity is not actively promoted.
- *Bridging capital* excels at information sharing and forming new networks, is inclusive, is outward looking and capable of bridging social divides (Putnam, 2000: 22).

    Putnam, an economist, extended the argument for social capital beyond economic benefit, arguing that joining and being involved in organised groups promotes individual well-being.

The National Strategy for Neighbourhood Renewal and Health Action Zones took up the idea of social capital (Health Development Agency [HDA], 2005). The HDA's Social Capital for Health Research Programme (Morgan and Swann, 2004) claimed that social capital affects health independently of other socio-economic indicators. Cropper and Ong (2002) suggest that more attention should be paid to supporting social networks and community participation as a way of promoting the strengths of individuals. These arguments support a strategic shift in emphasis towards a form of community work – *community practice* which is a new way of defining community work (Butcher et al., 1993).

Community practice requires a mixture of roles and approaches. A worker undertaking community practice may establish a group, work on a one-to-one basis, or offer training to volunteer groups. Community practice involves workers in identifying and consulting with *natural helpers* (Whittaker and Tracy, 1989: 120–1) who are volunteers and community leaders. Workers should avoid the pitfalls of: imposing different value systems on communities, assuming a hierarchical role, and possibly destroying or altering natural situations of helping by trying to professionalise them.

Old and New Maxims for Practice

To guide their practice, social workers frequently draw on maxims that function as shorthand expressions for particular approaches to practice. The next part of the chapter examines some familiar maxims for their continuing relevance to social work roles, and then discusses a new maxim for practice.

Advise, Assist, and Befriend

'Advise, assist, and befriend' is a maxim that describes a formerly dominant social work role in the justice field. The predecessor to the role of probation officers (who are no longer trained as social workers in England and Wales) was the police court missionary whose role was to advise, assist, and befriend offenders. The maxim characterised the traditional expectations of probation officers in the UK and other countries. As recently as 1993, the Probation Service Act 1993 (c. 47, 14) stated that the duty of probation officers was:

(a) to supervise the probationers and other persons placed under their supervision and to advise, assist, and befriend them; (b) with a view to assisting the court in determining the most suitable method of dealing with a person's case, to inquire (in accordance with any directions of the court) into, and make reports on, his circumstances or home surroundings; (c) to advise, assist and befriend, in such cases and in such manner as may be prescribed, persons who have been released from custody; and (d) to perform such other duties as may be prescribed.

The current probation aims of 'enforcement, rehabilitation and public protection' differ from previous aims, but 'rehabilitation' that assists offenders to lead productive lives corresponds to some extent with 'advise and assist'. 'Public protection' addresses the risk of further offending, and corresponds with social work's accepted aim of risk management. 'Enforcement' is a world away from 'befriend'.

'Advise, assist, and befriend' conveyed a general understanding of the historic role of the child care officer, the title given to social workers in Children's Departments from 1948–1971. The phrase 'advise, assist, and befriend' is still current, although less used than formerly. The Children (Leaving Care) Act 2000 extended the responsibilities of the Children Act 1989 so that children leaving care at the age of 16 would continue to be the responsibility of the local authority. Local authorities have the responsibility to 'advise, assist, and befriend' looked-after children and promote their welfare after they leave care until they are 21, or 24 if in higher education (Tregenna-Piggott and Daly, 2001).

The Corporate Parent

The former Children's Departments located within local authorities acted as 'corporate parents' for children in local authority care. Holman (1998) reviewed the achievements of the Children's Departments, claiming that they had improved the standards of care for many children, reunited children with their birth parents, and closed inappropriate children's institutions in favour of foster care provision. Most importantly, they provided a personalised touch to social work practice. Holman described how Children's Officers, the chief executives of the Departments, visited children' homes and carried caseloads.

The professional experience of the author as a social worker/child care officer in a Children's Department affirms the validity of reports about the corporate parent role. The child care officer was expected to form a personal relationship with the child, and required to undertake direct work with the child by ensuring that she saw the child on their own and sought the child's views at every visit. It was the custom for child care officers to report in person to a monthly local government councillors' sub-committee with a detailed oral report of activities on behalf of each child in foster care. The corporate parent role helped to make the Children's Departments effective. When they became part of larger social services departments in 1971, the personal touch was lost because of the larger size of the new departments and the more complex agendas for meeting needs across the entire life course. Another interpretation of the role of *corporate parent* is for organisations to take responsibility for combining fragmented resources for services into an integrated budget.

Holman argues that Children's Departments did not have enough qualified field work staff or residential staff (still a problem in contemporary social care, but one that the modernisation agenda is trying to address), and failed to provide for care leavers and children from ethnic minorities. Contemporary practice is more sensitive to issues of ethnicity and diversity, and the personal touch is more likely to be found in small community-based projects. As plans for children's trusts and children's centres seek to renew the specialist focus on children, a demand for the personal touch of child-centred practice is evident.

Care and Control

'Care and control' is a maxim that depicts the chief conundrum of social work: that social workers have to exercise both caring and controlling roles. Social workers want social work practice to be about *care* – that is offering support, concern, and championing the development and empowerment of the person who uses services, rather than exercising *control* through professional gate-keeping, rationing resources, and making quasi-moral judgements about eligibility for services. Social work practice has performed both of these roles and will continue to perform them, but will always feel uneasy about the control aspect of practice. Care and control poses a continuing dilemma for contemporary practice.

Social Care Planning and Counselling

The Barclay Report (1982) identified two roles of professional social workers: a *counselling* role (encompassing the characteristics of casework) and a *social care planning* role (comprising the service brokerage and resource finding roles of social workers). The Barclay Report also criticised social services departments for letting social work with old people fall to the bottom of the pile, which Barclay called rationing by age.

The Maintenance Mechanic

This approach to social work practice implies that the practitioner adopts a role as a *maintenance mechanic* rather than practising as a change agent or advocate. The maintenance mechanic role was a relatively modest aspiration, and its apparent acceptance of the status quo disappointed many social workers when Davies (1994) introduced the maxim. Davies did not intend to portray social work practice solely as a reductionist activity, but he did argue that social workers maintained the stability of society by acting as a buffer for vulnerable people against society's demands. However, no social worker would wish to have their work described as mechanical.

A New Maxim: Critical Thinkers and Fixers

The maxim *critical thinkers and fixers* expresses the tension between the requirement to acquire knowledge and skills that question the context and nature of practice (the *critical thinker* role), and the requirement to perform competently a range of skills (the *fixer* role). Braye and Preston-Shoot's (2004) systematic research review for SCIE of relevant knowledge for teaching, learning, and assessment of law in social work education identifies the same tension in social work education as in legal education. Twining (1967) compared the example of the law technician who is a *plumber* with the example of Pericles who practised law with knowledge, awareness, and integrity. Twining argued that providing only specialist knowledge and technical skills (plumbing) was not enough. Future practitioners (whether practising law or social work) need a breadth of education to help them acquire a critical capacity and a wide perspective of social contexts that develop their thought and judgement. At times this will result in criticising policies and practices, rather than conforming to the regulations. The critical thinker who is also a skilled practitioner will know how and when to raise issues effectively so that they can influence quality and standards of service provision.

Braye and Preston-Shoot (2004) sought the views of a wide range of stakeholders (including people who use services, carers, and practitioners) for their review. The consultation groups suggested that social workers should be *fixers* who also think critically about their actions – *plumbers plus*. People who use services stated that they expected to be involved in determining the issues that need fixing, and how the issues are fixed. Braye and Preston-Shoot conclude that social workers need to be both competent technicians but also *well-rounded professionals* who have sufficient knowledge and judgement to question their working context. Instead of developing two kinds of workers – *critical thinkers* and *fixers* (Preston-Shoot, 2004) – the future may require both kinds of roles within the same social worker. Preston-Shoot (2000) argues for practitioners who are:

- confident enough to challenge when appropriate;
- credible when presenting an explanation of their decisions; and
- aware of the need to make their practice accessible, to assess how policies affect people's lives, and to navigate through issues of ethics, rights, and needs.

? Question for Reflection

Can you think of a situation where you had to solve a problem by being a fixer? A critical thinker? Both of these roles? What might be the challenge of combining both roles in social work practice?

You may want to consider some of the pitfalls of each role – a fixer may rush into action to solve problems without thinking through the consequences of actions, and the critical thinker may find it difficult to move from thinking into action. Stepping back from busy activities to think through the issues may be less acceptable within the predominant practice culture than continuing with busy activities.

The New Professionalism of Social Work and Social Work Roles

As discussed in Chapter 1, a *new professionalism* of social work is based on:

- Promoting the social model of intervention in partnership with people who use services and carers.
- Working with other professional roles and with support workers.
- Intervening to protect vulnerable people when appropriate.
- Promoting human growth and developing individual capability.

Designated role clusters support each aspect of the new professionalism.

Roles that Promote the Social Model of Intervention in Partnership with People Who Use Services and Carers

A significant change in social workers' roles is the emphasis on partnership with people who use services and carers. The demand for partnership is embedded in the Standards, Requirements, and Benchmark Statement for the social work qualification.

Advocate

The National Occupational Standards Key Role 3–Support individuals to represent their needs, views, and circumstances, includes unit 10–Advocate with, and on behalf of, individuals, families, carers, groups and communities, and unit 11–Prepare for, and participate in decision making forums, both of which promote the idea of the social worker as an advocate.

Social workers who work in partnership with people who use services and carers will adopt the role of *advocate*. Issues that may require an advocacy role include service refusal, discrimination, denial of rights, and the user's inability or unwillingness to act on their own. Compton and Galaway described an advocate as a partisan representative who presents and argues users' cases. Whittaker and Tracy (1989: 104) portray the advocate as intervening on behalf of people who use services to help them obtain appropriate advice, benefits and services, and emphasises the importance of determining whether the advocacy issue falls within the law, what other attempts at helping have been tried, and whether the person who uses services agrees to an advocacy approach.

Advocacy requires confident, articulate, factual communication (Whittaker and Tracy, 1989: 105). To be an advocate should not involve doing more than is necessary, or needlessly alienating others. An effective advocate should be ready to concede on some points in return for winning success on the most important issues. Practising as an advocate involves:

- planting 'seeds of awareness' of future actions;
- avoiding 'burning bridges' through confrontations that preclude possible compromises;
- accepting that a particular strategy may not succeed;

- consistently following up action;
- being tenacious; and
- empowering people who use services.

The strategy of empowering people who use services is likely to encourage them to become their own advocates, with social workers adopting supportive roles. The example in Case Study 4.4 illustrates how an advocacy organisation can achieve changed policy.

⬚ Case Study 4.4 – Organisational Advocacy

Action on Elder Abuse, an organisation of concerned professionals, including social workers, which promotes greater awareness of the need for protection of older adults, drew attention to the Department of Health's focus since 1996 on protection of vulnerable adults (including those with mental incapacity) rather than on abuse and neglect of older people (Kingston et al., 1997). Action on Elder Abuse contributed to changing policy on worker registration. After a long period of advocacy by Action on Elder Abuse, a House of Commons Select Committee on Health Report on Elder Abuse called for registering home care assistants on the Social Care Register (HCSC) (2004), because they visit older people in the privacy of the domestic home and their practice is not easily open to scrutiny. The General Social Care Council in England announced in November 2004 that home workers will be recommended as one of the next groups (following social workers) to be invited to join the Social Care Register.

Enabler

This is a somewhat more modest role than that of advocate. Compton and Galloway (1984: 430–1) describe the enabler as undertaking intervention designed to help users identify their own coping strengths and resources to tackle issues themselves. The role encourages users to express and work for their own goals.

Roles that Promote Working with Other Professional Roles and Support Workers

Multi-professional working

Multi-professional working (also known as interprofessional practice and sometimes inter-disciplinary practice) is a significant new role for social workers. The Benchmark Statement (QAA, 2000: §1.10) refers to interprofessional practice:

Contemporary social work commonly takes place in an inter-agency context, and social workers habitually work collaboratively with others towards inter-disciplinary and cross-professional objectives. Honours degree programmes should, therefore, be designed to help equip students with accurate knowledge about the respective responsibilities of social welfare agencies and acquire skills in effective collaborative practice between these.

Knowledge about the nature of social work practice (2000: §3.1.4) will include: '... the factors and processes that facilitate effective inter-disciplinary, inter-professional and inter-agency collaboration and partnership.'

Multi-professional practice means that rather than working across agency boundaries, social workers are employed in multi-professional teams comprising professionals from health, housing, community, work, justice, education, and other professions. They could find that they work in a *skill-mix* team, where their colleagues will include social care workers, health care assistants, and educational assistants, an approach to multi-professional practice that has to transcend practice models associated with particular professions. Practice traditions within education, health, social work, social housing, and community development cannot succeed if they compete with each other – they have to develop commonality and complementary roles through shared staff development activities.

The number of multi-professional organisations across the range of service provision is increasing. Across the UK, mental health teams comprise *inter alia* professionals from social work and health care. Learning disability teams similarly comprise a range of health and social care/social work professionals. Teams in primary health care trusts are multi-professional and practice with older people, people with a disability or with mental health issues. Children's trusts or quasi-trust organisations will comprise multi-professional teams of early years workers, learning mentors, education welfare officers, nurses, and social workers. The Sure Start projects for children under five and their parents are organised on a multi-professional basis, with health visitors, outreach workers, social workers, and early years workers sharing their perceptions and skills. Examples in England include the Yots of the YJB, in which social workers, probation officers, teachers, housing officers, and police work together in one team; and Connexions personal advisers teams that comprise, *inter alia*, careers guidance officers, youth workers, social workers, teachers, and educational welfare officers.

Roles that Intervene to Protect Vulnerable People

Social workers have to choose appropriately from a range of roles when they carry out social work practice. The intervention phase of the social work process is captured in the National Occupational Standards Key Role 2:

Plan, carry out, review and evaluate social work practice with individuals, families, carers, groups and communities, and other professionals.

A great deal of social work intervention focuses on protecting vulnerable people, who may be young children at risk of abuse, and at the other end of the life course, old people whose frailty puts them at risk. Social work intervention in child abuse has played a forensic role, seeking to protect children from risk, but the protection of older people from abuse has not been so actively pursued (as Action on Elder Abuse has long argued). It comes as no surprise that a main focus of social work with children and families is to protect them from harm, typified by Key Role 4–Manage risk to individuals, families, carers, groups, communities, self, and colleagues.

Individual failures of protection – for example, the deaths of vulnerable children including Maria Colwell (Department of Health and Social Security [DHSS], 1974), Jasmine Beckford (London Borough of Brent, 1985), Kimberley Carlisle (Greenwich London Borough, 1987), and Victoria Climbié (Laming, 2003) – led to enquiries about what went wrong. Blame was often attributed to social workers' apparent failure to protect children adequately. A DH report (2002c) summarised the serious cases of child abuse deaths, and concluded that some of the key messages confirmed research findings about the incidence of mental health problems and domestic violence in the families. They found that the children's circumstances varied, with the abuse sometimes unanticipated. Sometimes tragedy occurred in families where the needs were considered low level, whereas in other cases abuse might have been anticipated from previous knowledge of family incidents. Some families were previously known and others were not known to the caring services. The research report suggested that the lesson to be learned was the need to institute better processes for managing risk rather than being able to identify which children are vulnerable.

Child protection work remains a high priority for social work intervention, but the regulatory control elements of this necessary kind of social work do not sit well with the current desire for empowerment and emancipatory social work. Although its purpose may be to protect vulnerable people, the power aspect of regulatory surveillance can dominate the role unless the social worker exerts a vigilant self-scrutiny of actions and uses supervision to safeguard against distortion of the role. Units 4–9 of Key Role 2 divide into roles that typify the balancing dilemma of practice. For example, unit 4–Respond to crisis situations and unit 9–Address behaviour which presents a risk to individuals, families, carers, groups and communities, suggest roles that manage crisis and assess risk. These roles place power in the hands of social workers.

Roles that Promote Human Growth and Develop Individual Capability

Other units of Key Role 2 suggest more empowering roles for social workers: unit 5–Interact with individuals, families, carers, groups and communities to achieve change and development to improve life opportunities; unit 7–Support the development of networks to meet assessed needs and planned outcome; and unit 8–Work with groups to promote individual growth, development and independence. Whittaker and Tracy (1989: 116–17) suggest a cluster of social work roles that promote human growth.

Social skills trainer, educator, teacher, network facilitator, mutual aid/self-help facilitator

The social worker as a *social skills trainer* who seeks to develop communication and other skills with people who use services can be an empowering role if the social worker does not ignore people's environmental needs and concerns. The *social skills trainer* role is almost indistinguishable from the role of *educator* or *teacher* (Compton and Galloway, 1984: 431) who provides new information and skills, models communication, and checks on the acquisition of skills.

In this role cluster, the social worker offers advice, information, and teaches skills. The approach helps the person using services to develop assertiveness and independent living skills. The learning and teaching approach is less stigmatising than other approaches, promotes empowerment, and is consonant with developing social capital, previously discussed. The social worker needs to be aware of how people learn, how they can acquire skills, and the advantages and drawbacks of role-play techniques. Giving positive but realistic feedback is essential for this approach.

Two additional roles in this cluster include *network facilitator*, where with user agreement, the social worker works with the service user's neighbours, friends, and relatives to develop a network of support. This approach may appear unreliable because the social worker has little control over the network. A shared assessment by the social worker and service user about whether this approach is realistic is a first step. Although the approach draws on users' own strengths and networks and is therefore empowering, some users may be isolated and unable to draw on sufficiently large or supportive networks. The other role is *mutual aid/self-help facilitator* where the social worker supports and enables the service users' initiatives.

The Dilemma of Balancing Empowerment and Protection

The essence of professionalism lies in exercising judgement in selecting and combining appropriate social work roles for a particular situation. The social worker's multiple roles will clash. The Benchmark Statement (QAA, 2000: §2.1) concurs: As an applied academic subject, social work is characterised by a distinctive focus on practice in complex social situations to promote and protect individual and collective well being. 'Promoting well being' could mean providing direct care and support by managing the complex dynamics of dependency and in some settings providing direct care and personal support in every day living situations (2000: 3.2.2.4). Alternatively, promoting well-being could mean that the social worker acts as a change agent: 'honours degree graduates in social work should be … enabled to analyse, adapt to, manage, and eventually to lead the processes of change' (2000: §2.2.4).

Balancing the dilemma may be less problematic in practice than at first glance. A social worker's initial assessment with the person who uses services may recommend that an initial intervention to provide support should be followed by a second shared assessment that would seek to shift the intervention role towards change. An initial assessment to protect from harm might be followed by an agreed need to provide support. The interchange of roles becomes more challenging when working with a family, a group, or a community in a volatile situation, when events occur at a fast pace. Balancing the dilemma between empowerment and protection/regulation will require tact and skill when social workers begin to act as mentors for the service user's self-assessment of needs.

Social Work Specialisms

The generic social work degree prepares social workers to practise in a variety of roles. During their practice learning, students begin to recognise particular kinds of expertise. Social work has developed specialist roles to deliver particular kinds of expertise that require specialist skills and knowledge in selected areas of practice. The 'big six' intervention categories of social work practice in the UK are:

- Children and young people.
- Crime and justice.
- Older people.
- People with learning disabilities.
- People with mental health problems.
- People with physical disabilities.

Social work with homeless people, people with HIV/Aids, migrants and asylum seekers, and people who misuse substances (including drugs, alcohol, and tobacco) are also specialisms but are less prevalent than the 'big six'. In the USA, social work with substance misuse forms a larger part of social work practice in comparison with the UK. In England and Wales, probation officers who work with offenders have their own training that is separate from social work, but in the other countries of the UK, the probation role is part of mainstream social work education and practice.

Social workers apply their core generic knowledge of human growth and development, health and disability, social policy, law, and social work theory to the contexts and requirements of their specialist roles. Good communication skills help to develop the art of social work in each specialist role. An example of specialised sub-divisions within a specialist role is found in work with children and young people. Social workers who work with children and young people may become specialists in:

- adoption and fostering;
- child protection;
- looked after children's care and development;
- prevention of risk;
- post-adoption support;
- residential children's services.

Some specialisms for working with children and young people have developed outside the remit of British social work, while in some European countries, analogous roles are considered part of social work. These roles that might be considered part of a broad interpretation of 'social work' include:

- careers guidance officers;
- Connexions personal advisers in England;

- early years workers;
- education welfare officers;
- outreach workers;
- probation officers in England and Wales;
- youth workers.

The potential for miscommunication and separate strategies among this variety of roles explains the drive for integrated services in which professionals are required to communicate with each other and practise together for the benefit of service users and carers.

New Social Care Roles

Dissatisfaction with the 'silo' mentality felt to be characteristic of individual government departments and individual caring services, combined with the desire to improve standards through modernisation, has led to development of integrated health and social care services for adults, and integrated education and children's services. Not content with that, the government is interested in developing new social care roles to fill perceived gaps in existing roles. The DH commissioned Topss England to develop new social care roles and pilot them over a three-year period 2003–2006 (Waddilove, 2004) to fill gaps in service delivery and assist with service integration (Box 4.7). Some of these roles may substitute for social workers but it seems more likely that workers carrying out the new roles will become skilled social care colleagues in multi-professional teams. The creation of new roles is particularly apt when considering how to address multiple complex needs.

Box 4.7: New Social Care Roles – Three Pilot Projects

Hybrid roles that bring together two or more already familiar roles and combine health and social care but also housing and education.

Ordinary life roles that blur formal and informal care, for example *community enablers* and *neighbourhood carers*.

Genuinely new roles that emerge as a result of challenges to traditional care by people who use services, and these may involve users as partners, educators, and providers.

Addressing Complex Needs

Recognising the complexity of needs requires integrated consideration of social inclusion issues, comprising, *inter alia*, mental health, poverty, and disability, without denying other inclusion/exclusion issues. Rankin and Regan's (2004a, 2004b) research on complex needs was conducted with people who use services in partnership with the voluntary organisation Turning Point. The findings provide a new understanding of the interrelationships between different kinds of needs, and a redefinition of the meaning of *complex needs* as a framework for better understanding interrelated needs that span specialised services in health and social care. Rankin and Regan argue that when services assess depth of needs for the purposes of eligibility, they fail to take enough account of breadth of needs. A person may experience mental health problems, poverty, substance misuse, and homelessness, but these needs might not meet eligibility criteria when considered individually. However, in terms of breadth of needs, they would be considered *complex needs*.

Social workers need to select multiple roles to intervene effectively in complex situations, using their own judgement to determine how to combine different roles in particular situations. The issue of complex needs has led to an impetus for overcoming the silos of separate organisations and separate professionalisms by creating multi-professional teams instead of relying on separate social services departments, health services, and education services. But it is not enough to put different professionals together in a team.

A question arises: which organisational arrangements can address complex needs most effectively? Acknowledgement that needs are never singular but multiple and interrelated is not a new discovery for social work. Hadley et al. (1987), who contributed to the Barclay Report on the roles of social workers in 1981, argued a case for the role of *community social worker* who would provide an integrated approach to needs assessment and re-invoke the spirit of community social work as envisioned by Seebohm in 1968. Social services departments did not adopt this role to any great extent probably because the post-Seebohm introduction of generic social services departments in 1970 overwhelmed many social workers from the previous specialist departments (children, social care, and public health), when suddenly the public required them to meet every kind of social need within a large new local authority department. Opportunities for post-qualification training to prepare social workers for an increased set of practice expectations were not widely available. Social workers preferred specialist roles because their scope and duties appeared to be clear, and best of all, manageable.

Arguably, a focus on specialisms offered a greater depth of expertise to people who use services, but specialist practice has a tendency to retreat into silos that ultimately do not benefit people who use services. Specialisms helped social workers to feel capable rather than de-skilled because it is harder to apply a sufficient breadth of knowledge and professional skills to generic practice, and have the level of confidence required. Generic and specialist roles can be combined at the point of contact with people who use services, and more work needs to be done on how this can be achieved.

Rankin and Regan (2004a, 2004b) draw attention to the current failure of some health and social care organisations to meet complex needs defined not by depth or magnitude but according to their breadth across a range of social issues (Case Study 4.5). An individual who experiences a breadth of needs may not be eligible for help according to the individual criteria of separate agencies, and so may fall through the safety net of service provision.

🗋 Case Study 4.5 – Defining Complex Needs According to the Breadth of Needs (adapted from Rankin and Regan, 2004a, 2004b)

Mary is a single unemployed adult in her early 30s with a recurrent substance misuse problem that includes use of prescription drugs and alcohol and previous experiences of self-harm. She recently became pregnant but had a miscarriage. She lives on her own but is being threatened with eviction for non-payment of rent and had a previous court appearance and conviction for shoplifting. Her family lives a distance away and she is estranged from them. She reports that she is isolated, has no friends, and lacks confidence. Where can Mary receive help and support? Which agency will address the range of her needs? Mary presents a breadth of needs that taken individually might not be enough to get her past the eligibility criteria for each need, but taken together the issues that trouble Mary constitute a breadth of needs that fit the definition of complex needs.

Rankin and Regan recommend a holistic understanding of needs. This approach to meeting complex needs comprises a single point of entry, creative whole system services, and user empowerment to ensure that service users own the decisions made. *Connected care centres* and a *reformed commissioning service* could provide more precisely targeted approaches to meeting complex needs. Connected care centres for adult services could be modelled on aspects of Sure Start's integrated approach (Box 4.8).

Box 4.8: Example of a Coordinated Programme Delivered at Local Level – Sure Start (adapted from Glass, 1999; Sure Start, 2004)

The Sure Start Programme offers a comprehensive service to children under five and their parents, delivered in local centres, inspired by the successful Headstart programme in the USA, and gaining governmental support following a Comprehensive Spending Review in 1997. The Review concluded that the earliest years in life, while most important for child development, were susceptible to environmental influences; multiple disadvantage for young children was growing, increasing the possibility of later social deprivation; and service provision for young children and families was uncoordinated and of variable quality across the country. The Review recommended that a comprehensive community-based programme of early intervention and family support built on existing services could have positive effects on child and family development, and could also break the cycle of social exclusion, thus providing long-term financial advantages to government spending. Effective early interventions would involve parents as well as children; avoid labelling 'problem families'; target numerous factors, not just education, or health; be long term; culturally appropriate; and consult with and involve parents and communities. Sure Start, which began in 1999, has won widespread acceptance as a government programme that aims to increase the availability of child care for all children, improve their

(Continued)

> **Box 4.8:** *(Continued)*
>
> health and emotional development, and support parents as parents and in their aspirations towards employment. England, Scotland, Wales, and Northern Ireland have responsibility for their own Sure Start programmes. The 10-year strategy *Choice for parents, the best start for children* (December, 2004) drew on Sure Start's example in seeking to develop comprehensive services for young children and families, including increasing the available child care places in nurseries and nursery schools, and developing children's centres that incorporate the Sure Start approach. The challenge is to maintain the involvement of parents and maintain the levels of support.

Rankin and Regan recognise that connected care centres already exist in some local areas as examples of social care's creativity. For example, the SEU (2004a) recommended that the NIMHE (2005) pilots new forms of social support such as connected care centres in deprived neighbourhoods. The principles of connected care centres aim to establish many services on one site, including health services, social services and social care provision, police, the justice system, housing and employment, with a single point of entry that provides managed transitions, a mechanism for bridging social inclusion strategies (often located in special initiatives like regeneration projects) and social care provision based in local authorities and private and voluntary organisations. The connected care centres would close the 'gap between the community-based approach and the individualised social care approach' (Rankin and Regan, 2000b: 6) and would include self-referrals from people who use services.

Rankin and Regan (2000b: 7) call for a reformed commissioning process for assessment, planning, contracting, and monitoring service provision, claiming that these functions are 'rarely fulfilled'. The targeted approach would begin with a local audit of community characteristics and needs, proceed to commissioning, and thus could be adapted to local conditions and local needs. The commissioning process needs to involve all stakeholders (including people who use services and carers) and work across budgets and funding streams.

The Service Navigator: a Professional Role for Social Workers?

Rankin and Regan (2004a, 2004b) propose the role of *service navigator* as part of a strategy to address complex needs. Although relatively unknown and underdeveloped in Britain, the role of *care navigator* is used in the USA. Franklin County Children Services (2002) in Columbus, Ohio employs a *kinship care navigator* to help carers of children who need support and resources; Montgomery General Hospital (2004) in Maryland employs a *cancer care navigator* to provide emotional support, information, and point the way to services. In the UK, the Children's Health Task Group Recommendations (DH, 2003) proposed a *care navigator/key worker/advocate* for parents and children.

The service navigator would:

- offer knowledge of the full range of services, including knowledge about benefits and employment law;
- work with people who use services to 'develop a sustained pathway of care'. (Rankin and Regan, 2000b: 6)

Every individual person who uses services would have a 'lead professional to case-manage their care, ensuring a coherent package of services to meet individual needs' (2000b: 6–7.) The service navigator would have to:

- understand the life situations and different cultures of people with complex needs;
- at times adopt an advocacy role.

Professional social workers are ideally suited to undertake the role of service navigator. Many of the requisite skills and areas of knowledge are part of social work, although Rankin and Regan do not designate the role for social workers and suggest that the service navigator role could be developed through inter-professional training and development of shared assessment frameworks. Social workers could undertake this training on an in-service basis that could be aligned to the social work post qualifying system (GSCC, 2005). A possible hindrance to developing the role might be an over expectation of the expertise required by the navigator. Effective information technology resources for accessing the knowledge base of services could prevent this potential threat; being able to use information systems as tools for practice would enable the navigator to focus on building relationships with people who use services and supporting their participation in provider partnerships.

The proposed role of service navigator deserves careful consideration because of its inclusion in the adult social care Green Paper (DH, 2005). The role fits with the importance of possessing knowledge, the key to capability within a consumer society. A navigator is not the same role as a care manager or a broker of services because the service navigator acts as an ongoing guide and pilot through the complexities of service provision. By trying to finding the best possible fit of services, the service navigator makes sure that the shoals that could cause a figurative shipwreck of provision are avoided. Most important of all, navigation requires staying with the person, forming a relationship, and working together using the social model of intervention.

Similar Roles

The role of navigator draws on previously defined social work roles such as Whittaker and Tracy's (1989: 117–20) *network system consultant* who uses natural social and personal networks to encourage reciprocity, friendship, and social support in users' social environments (similar to the concept of social capital). Whittaker and Tracy suggest that a network consultant can be effective in addressing loneliness, stress, and life changes.

The role of *broker of services and resources* (Whittaker and Tracy, 1989: 108–12) has a close but not identical correspondence with the navigator. The social worker who adopts the role of broker links the person who uses services to resources and opportunities by jointly assessing needs, locating resources that match needs, and then monitoring progress. Here the social worker must possess extensive knowledge of a range of services. Whittaker and Tracy comment that the broker role is more in demand when services become complex. The major skill of the broker is in expediting services (1989: 109), a three-part process of getting others' cooperation, performing tasks, and following up. The social worker has to be consistent in approach, organised, prepared, and should listen carefully, then make appropriate referrals. Whittaker warns against making inappropriate referrals where users will encounter failure, arguing that the broker role, although viewed as less 'professional' than that of counselling, requires as much skill and knowledge. Compton and Galloway (1984: 429) portray the broker role as connecting users, resources, and services. The navigator role also resembles aspects of the Connexions personal adviser role that provides information and advice to 13–19-year-olds in England and Wales – a role patterned on the social pedagogue (discussed in Chapter 3).

Communicator Role

The chapter concludes with a reminder of the most basic, and arguably one of the most important social work roles: being a good communicator. The social worker must be able to communicate clearly and effectively with people who use services, carers, and other professionals. The Benchmark Statement places importance on how social workers communicate:

> In providing services, social workers should engage with people who use services in ways that are characterised by openness, reciprocity, mutual accountability and explicit recognition of the powers of the social worker and the legal context of intervention. (QAA, 2000: §1.12)

Social workers' interventions and evaluations should: 'build and sustain purposeful relationships with people and organisations' (2000: §3.2.2.4).

Evidence-informed practice requires social workers to share more information than formerly with people who use services and with colleagues in multi-professional teams. Partnership working and information sharing across professional disciplines and agencies are important for future practice. Information giving has become a helping mechanism that can be empowering, depending on how sensitively information is communicated and whether appropriate safeguards for confidentiality introduced by the Data Protection Act 1998 and Freedom of Information Act 2000 are in place.

?   **Questions for Reflection**

Which roles do you think are most appropriate for contemporary practice? Do any of the roles described seem less well suited for social work practice? Give reasons for your choice.

You may want to consider the different purposes of social work in relation to each role, and the degree of power and authority implied by each role.

▶▶ **Conclusion**

Social work's amorphous nature is a strength that will enable it to develop further its range of roles. Being open to developing new roles is important for social work. Hughes (2002: 36) argued that social work is at a crossroads because of social work's identification with large social services departments, which now have become 'increasingly disconnected from the preventive agenda'. He asks why social work has not been more evident 'in the fight to overcome social exclusion and regenerate local communities ... Over time, social work has become narrower, and community and group work have been placed elsewhere', citing Yots (in England and Wales), Connexions personal advisers (in England), and Sure Start across the UK as examples of integrated wrap-around non-stigmatising services, from which social services departments have been marginalised, and hints at the development of a new role of 'social educator' – that is the social pedagogue (discussed in Chapter 3). Social workers can play a part in the new developments, he implies, once they are freed from working almost exclusively in large social services departments.

As people who use services and carers exercise more choice through self-assessment of need and use of personal or individual budgets, they pose a significant challenge to social workers' professional role of assessing need, which will become a shared exercise, with the social worker adopting an enabling supportive role instead of assuming an overtly powerful lead role. The National Occupational Standards Key Role 1–Prepare for and work with individuals, families, carers, groups, and communities to assess their needs and circumstances, unit 3–Assess needs and options to recommend a course of action places the responsibility of assessing need on the social worker, although unit 2–Work with individuals, families, carers groups and communities to help them make informed decisions, does share power. If self-assessment of need becomes the norm, social workers will be expected to place greater emphasis on facilitative skills for supporting service users' choices.

Sharing power is difficult for the professional because this inevitably means surrendering some of their previous power. Self-awareness gained through insights afforded by defence mechanisms and transactional analysis can help to prevent an inappropriate use of power. Maxims for practice, the three fields of practice, specialist roles, and different role clusters illuminate social work's potential to 'wrap around' new situations and embrace potential new roles (as identified by Andrew Cozens (2004), the then president of the Association of Directors of Social Services). Social work's versatility should enable practitioners to select and combine multiple roles that balance regulation and protection with emancipation and empowerment.

Professional social work must consider how it will adapt to new ways of working and new roles. Proposals for integrated services that address complex needs, together with the proposed role of service navigator, illustrate the drive for change that is transforming the caring services. Will professional social work be part of that change? Social workers in Britain now belong to an officially recognised profession that requires them to change the way they practise; they should not feel threatened by the possible demise of large social services/social work departments. The social work degree emphasises multi-professional working, integrated services, and partnerships with people who use services – good preparation for future practice. New combinations of roles will develop for social workers as a result of these changes, but the social work profession must seize the opportunities for change.

📖 **Further Reading**

Bateman, Neil (1995) *Advocacy Skills. A Handbook for Human Service Professionals.* Aldershot: Arena Ashgate/Gower.
This book provides an overview of an important social work role.

Social Work Services Policy Division (SWSPD) (2005) *21st Century Social Work Review.* Edinburgh: SWSPD Scottish Executive. www.21csocialwork.org.uk.
This significant review, in progress at the time of publication, seeks, inter alia, to explore social work roles.

Whittaker, J.K. and Tracy, E.M. (1989) *Social Treatment. An Introduction to Interpersonal Helping in Social Work Practice,* second edition. New York: Aldine de Gruyter.
This is a classic text, written for American social workers, the value of which lies in its detailed explanation of social work roles.

5 VALUES FOR PRACTICE

Social work is a moral activity that requires practitioners to make and implement difficult decisions about human situations that involve the potential for benefit or harm … at their core, social work values involve showing respect for persons, honouring the diverse and distinctive organisations and communities that make up contemporary society and combating processes that lead to discrimination, marginalisation and social exclusion. (QAA, 2000: § 2.4)

Introduction

Social work values contribute significantly to contemporary understanding of practice, and influence other vocations and professions. The care councils in all four countries of the UK insist that values are embedded in all relevant National Occupational Standards in health and social care, including those for social work, and in the councils' requirements for social work. Roche and Rankin (2004b: 4, discussed in Chapter 3) attribute values-based aspirations of 'personalisation, choice, user empowerment, and user involvement aspirations' to social care, including social work. Most social workers identify their social work values as one of the most distinctive features of the profession. Acknowledging shared aspects of values rather than claiming their exclusive ownership provides a way for social workers to establish multi-professional partnerships. The social worker is a *guardian of values*. This does not constitute a claim of exclusivity in relation to values, but guarding their integrity and making a consistent attempt to keep values at the forefront of practice.

Unfortunately, social workers' ownership of their values may imply an unintended arrogance. Social work has adopted values from outside social work; an example being the social model that originated in disability studies which now has become for social workers and to other professionals a rallying cry for change. An unwitting assumption of moral superiority in owning values can offend other professionals, people who use services, and their carers. Social work has made its values explicit and requires social workers to own the values in the care councils' codes of practice, but the nursing profession has its own code of conduct (Nursing and Midwifery Council [NMC], 2002) which differs from that of social work in some respects but demonstrates considerable consonance in requiring respect for persons, confidentiality, trustworthiness, and minimisation of risk. Social workers should analyse and compare different professional codes of ethics. They would find that similarities outweigh the differences.

'Ethics' is described by the Oxford English Dictionary as comprising a 'science of morals' and by Webster's New Collegiate Dictionary as 'moral principles, quality, and practice'. Social work values that are contained in codes of ethics can trace their origins to philosophical and theological systems of thought that sought to explain human existence and behaviour by producing explanations of human morality and definitions of 'good' or 'bad' intentions and actions. Every society and every human being lives according to a set of values, but most people's values are implicit and submerged within their particular culture.

The *categorical imperative* principle of Kant (1996), an 18th-century German philosopher, influenced the social work value of *respect for persons,* which also owes its origins to the Christian golden rule of *do unto others as you would have them do unto you* (Matthew 7:12) – expressing a reciprocity of respect and obligations to fellow humans which is found in most world religions and secular moral codes. Christian theology viewed human nature as flawed by original sin, but Kant believed that human nature was essentially good and thus could use reason to make 'correct' moral choices. He argues that human beings are moral agents who are rational and free (to make choices), and therefore able to judge whether any action is moral by asking if the action is consistent with the *categorical imperative*: judging an action to be moral by universalising it – imagining what society would be like if everyone lied, stole, committed murder, etc. The categorical imperative involves treating all humans, self and others, as ends in themselves rather than as a means of one's own happiness. Kant believed that freedom was a fundamental truth of the universe and that true morality involved a struggle to choose between right and wrong. A sense of duty should guide human action – therefore humans should try to discover what these duties are by careful rational analysis of the facts of each situation to become aware of what their duty is.

All social workers will make difficult ethical choices in their practice, and therefore should use a rational process to analyse the facts, including the precepts of ethical codes and their own particular values system, to guide their decisions. Part of their learning is to understand the origins of social work values and ethics and their possible conflicts with each other so that decisions are well considered (Shardlow, 2002). Values dilemmas continue to pose issues that are not easily resolved. Codes of practice for employers and workers specify levels of conduct expected to promote high standards and protect the public, but do not advise the social worker what to do in a specific situation involving personal and professional values. Social workers have to make sense of dilemmas by drawing on their understanding of personal and professional values and ethics as applied to particular situations. The ethical danger is that social workers will rely on codes of ethics or codes of practice rather than think through the issues. The codes can supply a false sense of security about values for practice; they are not meant to substitute for individual consideration of the issues.

Chapter Structure

This chapter traces how social work values have broadened over time from a preoccupation with individual values to awareness of emancipatory values, identifying different applications of values to new approaches to practice, and exploring casework principles, concepts of values clarification, moral competence, self-awareness, quality of life for people living in social care environments, concepts of group care practice, and social role valorisation.

The chapter considers how structural values, including empowerment, emancipation, and the pedagogy of the oppressed, tackle oppression and discrimination, and concludes by arguing that social work imported values from other disciplines, adopted these values and championed them as social work values, and now these values that have become aligned with social work are being exported to the wider world of social care. The responsibility for applying values to practice remains with the individual social worker, but employers must provide access to professional practice supervision.

What Kind of Values?

The Benchmark Statement establishes the relationship between social work practice and values. The BASW (2003) Code of Ethics which resembles the USA's NASW values (discussed in Chapter 1) but omits one NASW value – the importance of human relationships – suggests that social work is committed to five basic values:

- Human dignity and worth.
- Social justice.
- Service to humanity.
- Integrity.
- Competence.

The Benchmark Statement requires social work programmes 'to involve the study, application of and reflection upon ethical principles' (QAA, 2000: §2.4). Social workers should 'recognise and work with the powerful links between intra-personal and inter-personal factors and the wider social, legal, economic, political and cultural context of people's lives' (2000: §2.4). Social work values have been expressed at different times in a variety of ways. At their core they involve:

- Showing respect for persons.
- Intervening appropriately to protect vulnerable individuals.
- Promoting their quality of life.
- Honouring the diverse and distinctive organisations and communities that make up contemporary society.
- Combating processes that lead to discrimination, marginalisation, and social exclusion.
- Empowering and emancipating individuals, groups, and communities.

The scope of social work values expanded as social workers became more aware of the impact of social inequality and injustice on individual lives and extended their awareness beyond individual well-being to concern for the quality of life of people in residential care; diverse community groups; people experiencing injustice; protecting vulnerable individuals; and empowering and emancipating people who use services. The sequence of the discussion expresses this widening concern influenced by research-informed knowledge from the social sciences. Another way of expressing the range of values is to cluster them into four values concepts (Box 5.1).

Box 5.1: Values Concepts

Values Concept 1: Belief in the worth of the individual that prompts the practitioner to listen with respect and respond appropriately to the needs and wishes of people who use services and their carers.

Values Concept 2: Belief in change and development throughout human life, prompting the practitioner to understand the present within a context of change, and draw on knowledge of past influences.

Values Concept 3: Belief in the reciprocal influence of the environment on the individual, and the individual on the environment, prompting the practitioner to acknowledge the complex, multi-layered nature of social interactions and contexts, particularly when called on to protect vulnerable individuals.

Values Concept 4: Belief in empowerment and emancipation, prompting the practitioner to work in partnership with people who use services and their carers to build their strengths, abilities, and promote their independence.

Values for Working with Individuals

Felix Biestek was an American Jesuit priest who taught social work. His seven casework principles (1961) focused on the relationship between the social worker and the individual. Biestek's interpretation of professional values corresponds with values concept 1 'belief in the worth of the individual', and also with values concept 2 'belief in change and development', dividing the relationship conceptually into three directions: first, the need(s) of the person using services; second, the response of the social worker; and third, awareness of persons using services and the social worker (Box 5.2). Overarching these directions are the seven principles (Box 5.3) that function as elements of the relationship as a whole.

**Box 5.2: Conceptualising the Casework Relationship
(adapted from Biestek, 1961: 17)**

First direction: The need of the [person using services]

To be treated as an individual; to express feelings; and get sympathetic response to problems; to be recognised as a person of worth; not to be judged; and to make [their] own choices and decisions; to keep secrets about self.

Second direction: The response of the [social worker]

(Continued)

Box 5.2: *(Continued)*

The [social worker] is sensitive to, understands, and appropriately responds to these needs.

Third direction: Awareness

The [person using services] is somehow aware of the [social worker's] sensitivity, understanding, and response.

**Box 5.3: The Seven Principles in Relationship
(adapted from Biestek, 1961: 17)**

1. Individualisation
2. Purposeful expression of feelings
3. Controlled emotional involvement
4. Acceptance
5. Non-judgemental attitude
6. Self-determination
7. Confidentiality

Casework Principle 1

Individualisation is 'the recognition and understanding of each [person's] unique qualities … Individualisation is based upon the right of human beings to be individuals and to be treated not just as *a* human being but as *this* human being with [his or her] personal differences' (Biestek, 1961: 25). The prerequisites for individualisation, and suggestions for putting them into practice can be represented schematically, see Box 5.4.

**Box 5.4: Casework Principle 1 – Individualisation
(adapted from Biestek, 1961)**

Prerequisites for individualisation	*Practical means of individualising*
Freedom from bias and prejudice	Thoughtfulness in details
Knowledge of human behaviour	Privacy in interviews
Ability to listen and observe	Care in keeping appointments
Ability to move at the [person's] pace	Preparation for interviews
Ability to enter into the feelings of people	Engaging the [person]
Ability to keep perspective	Flexibility

Casework Principle 2

Purposeful expression of feelings is 'the recognition of the … need to express feelings freely, especially negative feelings. The [social worker] listens purposefully, neither discouraging nor condemning the expression of these feelings, sometimes even actively stimulating and encouraging them when they are therapeutically useful …' (Biestek, 1961: 35). The main focus should be on the service user's request for help, which may be practical in nature. The feelings that need purposeful expression will vary in intensity according to individual circumstances, and are a necessary but subsidiary focus of the intervention. Expression of feelings should serve a valid purpose (Box 5.5).

Box 5.5: Casework Principle 2 – Possible Purposes for the Expression of Feelings (adapted from Biestek, 1961: 37–8)

1. Relieve tensions and pressures and thus be able to see problems more clearly.
2. Reveal the nature of the problem for assessment purposes and learn about the person presenting the problem.
3. Provide psychological support.
4. Deal with negative feelings which may constitute part of the problem.
5. Deepen the interactive relationship between the social worker and the person using services in order to deal more effectively with psychological problems.

Biestek acknowledges the limitations of encouraging expression of feelings: feelings must be expressed purposefully and be directed towards the end goal of resolving the issues that led the person to seek help, and expression of feelings might need to be limited in some situations (Box 5.6). The role of the social worker is to prepare, create a relaxed atmosphere, listen well, encourage expression, be sensitive to pace, and most important of all, avoid unrealistic reassurance.

Box 5.6: When the Expression of Feelings Might Need to Be Limited (adapted from Biestek, 1961: 38–40)

1. Expression of feelings is focused on issues that fall outside the agency remit.
2. Expressing deep feelings too soon in the relationship leads to awkwardness and hostility.

(Continued)

Box 5.6: *(Continued)*

3. Encouraging too much expression of feelings results in overdependence on the social worker.
4. Expression of feelings is used solely as an attention-seeking device or as a test of acceptance.

Casework Principle 3

Controlled emotional involvement is 'the [social worker's] sensitivity to the [person's] feelings, and understanding of their meaning, and a purposeful, appropriate response to the [person's] feelings' (Biestek, 1961: 45). The social worker who notes and comprehends the significance of non-verbal communication (as well as verbal communication) demonstrates sensitivity. Developing understanding is a continuous process where the social worker draws on knowledge of human behaviour, their self-reflection, and their use of supervision to develop skill in interpreting the significance of what is said and observed (1961: 55). Sensitivity and understanding are useful insofar as they guide the social worker's responses to feelings, which Biestek argues are the most difficult aspect of the professional relationship to manage. The social worker's responses can be non-verbal as well as verbal, and should be carefully and selectively chosen.

Casework Principle 4

Acceptance is 'a principle of action wherein the [social worker] perceives and deals with the [person] as [he or she] really is, including … strengths and weakness, congenial and uncongenial qualities, positive and negative feelings, constructive and destructive attitudes and behaviour, maintaining all the while a sense of the [person's] innate dignity and personal worth. Acceptance does not mean approval of deviant attitudes or behaviour. The purpose of acceptance is … to aid the [worker] in understanding the [person] as [he or she] really is, and to help the [person] look at [him or herself] as [he or she] really is, and thus to deal with problems and [him or herself] in a more realistic way' (Biestek, 1961: 72). Two aspects of this definition are problematic: the assumption of agreement about how one determines 'deviant attitudes and behaviour' instead of acknowledging a disputed definition; and a similar assumption of an undisputed understanding of 'a more realistic way' of dealing with problems. Other aspects of the definition are helpful. The social worker's responses should first focus on the needs of the person using services, and second, recognise the potential for the person's self-help and growth in responsibility. (The second response is consonant with contemporary practice values.) The third response is to reflect back both thoughts and feeling elements (1961: 78–9). The fourth response is to shape the proposed action in consonance with organisational function. Biestek identifies obstacles to acceptance that arise from an excessive desire to help, lack of self-awareness, or unresolved prejudicial attitudes (Box 5.7).

Box 5.7: Possible Obstacles to Acceptance
(adapted from Biestek, 1961: 81–7)

1. Not enough knowledge of human behaviour patterns.
2. Lack of acceptance of a feature of the person's life that mirrors an unresolved situation in the worker's life.
3. Attributing one's own feelings to the feelings of the person seeking help.
4. Biases and prejudice based on differences in gender, race, ethnicity, religion, age, and other aspects of diversity.
5. Unwarranted and unnecessary assurances to the persons seeking help.
6. Confusing approval with acceptance.
7. Losing respect for the person seeking help.
8. Overidentifying with the situations of the person seeking help.

Casework Principle 5

Non-judgemental attitude is 'based on the conviction that the [helping] function excludes assigning guilt or innocence, or degree of … responsibility for causation of the problems or needs, but does include making evaluative judgments about the attitudes, standards, or reactions of the [person]; the attitude, which involves both thought and feeling elements, is transmitted to the [person seeking help]' (Biestek, 1961: 90). Biestek criticises the historic tendency of social workers to judge people's worthiness to receive help, but urges the social worker to maintain values and standards. This principle is difficult to put into practice in today's diverse society where different theories, ideas, and standards compete for acceptance as part of values and ethics. Biestek's advice is rooted in the certainty of a different place and time and is anchored in his religious faith. The useful learning for social workers is to become aware of the unintended bias that may be present in their judgements, attitudes, and personal value systems.

Casework Principle 6

Self-determination is 'the practical recognition of the right and need of [people using services] to freedom in making their own choices and decisions … [Social workers] have a corresponding duty to respect that right, recognise that need, stimulate and help to activate that potential for self-direction by helping the [person] to see and use the available and appropriate resources of the community and of his own personality. The … right to self-determination … is limited by the … capacity for positive and constructive decision making, by the framework of civil and moral law, and by the function of the agency' (Biestek, 1961: 103). Biestek identifies actions of the social worker that can either help or impede self-determination (1961: 105–9, see Box 5.8).

Box 5.8: Self-determination – Activities of the Social Worker (adapted from Biestek, 1961)	
Social worker activities that support self-determination	**Social worker activities that impede self-determination**
1. Helping the person gain a clear perspective on the problem/need.	1. Assuming responsibility and leaving the user of services in a subordinate role.
2. Informing the person about relevant resources.	2. Scrutinising every detail of people's lives even when their requests for help are modest ones.
3. Using strategies that stimulate the person's own resources.	3. Manipulating situations and people both directly or indirectly.
4. Creating an environment that enables the person to work out their problems themselves.	4. Persuading others in a controlling manner.

The supportive social worker activities are compatible with empowerment activities. Biestek (1961: 109–19) identifies limitations to self-determination that arise from the user's own capacity for making decisions; from civil and moral law, and from agency functions. Contemporary practice may feel uneasy about ascribing decisions to moral law; Biestek advises the social worker not to impose their own moral law on issues such as divorce or abortion, but to listen carefully to the moral law that forms part of the service user's beliefs. He avoids discussion of moral law in situations where self-determination may put an individual service user at risk of substantial harm and where the social worker has a duty to intervene.

Casework Principle 7

Confidentiality is 'the preservation of secret information concerning the [user of services] which is disclosed in the professional relationship. Confidentiality is based upon a basic right of the [user]; it is an ethical obligation of the [social worker] and is necessary for effective … service. The [user's] right … is not absolute … the [user's] secret is often shared with other professional persons within the agency and in other agencies; the obligation then binds all equally' (Biestek, 1961: 121). The availability of information on the Internet and through computerised records makes confidentiality a threatened principle. Shared confidentiality with legal safeguards is more typical of today's practice. Social workers are not individual therapists, but work within agencies where the requirement to protect vulnerable individuals can conflict with the confidences of service users. The social worker should ensure that the person using services is informed of the limitations to confidentiality.

in front of his peers. Blurting out a strong view just as you are leaving the room is a way of avoiding further discussion. It may be that the social work students did not have enough opportunity to explore their values and gradually learn to practise social work values through an honest exploration of their doubts, rather than having to express conformity. Alternatively, it could be argued that allegiance to social work values should be a criterion for selection to the degree.

Values Clarification

Values clarification (Simon et al., 1978) is an approach to moral and civic education that helps people identify their personal values. Techniques of values clarification were used in the 1960s and 1970s to build awareness of moral and cultural diversity at a time of civil unrest and conflict. Values clarification is practised today in schools and in some areas of professional education. The Royal College of Nursing (RCN) (2005) in the UK uses values clarification in its practice development training advice. The RCN argues that values clarification can be useful for developing a shared vision amongst a group of practitioners that helps to bring about cultural change. Values clarification could help multi-professional teams to establish a shared understanding of different team roles, and to determine strategic directions for future practice.

Values clarification does not try to teach values or ethics. Its purpose is to involve learners in participatory exercises that make them more aware of their own ideas, beliefs and values, so that they are better equipped to make well-informed moral choices (Simon et al., 1978). Values clarification should lead to congruence between what practitioners say and what they do. Its obvious flaw is an assumption that individuals already own a set of values that, once clarified, can be applied to practice. Some religious and community leaders (Kilpatrick, 1993) attack its moral neutrality, arguing that values clarification is an unworthy substitute for teaching moral choices, and that it is unacceptable to regard all responses to values issues as having equal merit. Kilpatrick advocates a return to *character education* that promotes character traits to build moral competence.

Values clarification requires listening to other people, and also learning about yourself through seeking feedback from others. You could imagine how a colleague perceives you, and how you might respond to practice issues. When undertaking a values clarification exercise with others, it is important to own your beliefs by preceding your statements with 'I' and avoiding jargon. Disagreements that emerge when providing feedback to each other can be acknowledged, but the area of focus should be on shared views.

Box 5.10: A Values Clarification Exercise (adapted from RCN, 2005)

To be completed individually and then shared in a small group of colleagues:

I believe that the purpose of social work is_____
I believe that what helps social work achieve its purpose is_____
I believe that what hinders social work from achieving its purpose are_____

An example of a values clarification exercise is given in Box 5.10. Responses to the final question in this exercise may be difficult to share if the originator of the response fears rejection and criticism for expressing negative views. A practitioner committed to values clarification should aim to create confidence amongst colleagues and others about expressing and listening to a variety of views.

Moral Competence

It can be argued that British social work has failed to think about techniques for building moral competence (Box 5.11) because it has been distracted by the requirement to demonstrate practice competence.

Box 5.11: Moral Competence

Moral competence is being able to:

- Identify one's own values and ethics and the basis for these.
- Avoid the pitfalls of imposing personal moral values unthinkingly on others.
- Translate values into practice that demonstrates commitment to social work values and the Code of Practice.

Bauman's (1993) discussion of late modernity argues that reliance on the rules and principles of traditional moral authority has collapsed. The rise of moral relativism makes a system of universal ethics impossible. He notes that the postmodern era is concerned with moral issues, but rejects rigid rules and precepts. Our sense of morals lacks an ethical code. Bauman argues that our humanity depends on members of society having a moral sense and being morally competent. However, the approach to moral issues is now uncontrolled and incoherent.

Practice cannot be sustained without a well-defined set of values. The generality of the values requirements leaves the social worker having to make choices when confronted with different cultural values and different individual values that conflict with a community's values and social work's values. Social work values promote tolerance, acceptance, and diversity, but on what basis can the social worker determine his or her decisions? Values clarification can help social workers think through their own starting points on values and ethics and explore their feelings as they develop moral competence. Values are not just about beliefs, they are also concerned with translating beliefs into actions. Values and actions should complement each other.

Self-awareness

Values clarification, together with the insights from the defence mechanisms and transactional analysis (discussed in Chapter 4), can assist in developing self-awareness, an important trait in achieving moral competence and working effectively with others. Self-awareness involves self-knowledge of personal prejudices and feelings, the realisation that a diverse society contains different communities of individuals with different prejudices and feelings, and that no community has an absolute right to moral superiority. Values clarification argues that by identifying personal prejudices and rigidly held but poorly argued beliefs, the individual will adopt better informed, more reasonable values that are more tolerant of other people's differences.

Joseph Luft and Harry Ingham (Luft, 1970) devised the Johari Window (an amalgam of their first names) at the University of California in 1955 as a device for building self-awareness (Box 5.12). The Window suggests that the self has four aspects that can conflict with each other: the *open self, hidden self, blind self,* and *unknown self.* Self-awareness grows when we recognise the way the different aspects of self interrelate to work together or conflict with each other. Multi-professional teams could use this device to develop trust and shared goals.

Box 5.12: Johari Window (adapted from Luft and Ingham, 1955)	
OPEN SELF *Known to self and others:* Communicates ideas, feelings, thoughts	BLIND SELF *Not known to self but known to others:* Actions and behaviour not recognised by self but evident to others
HIDDEN SELF *Known to self and not known to others:* Hides ideas, feelings, thoughts	UNKNOWN SELF *Not known to self and not known to others:* The unconscious self

Values that Promote the Quality of Life

Values concepts 2 and 3 are concerned with quality of life issues in residential care, a major concern of social work and social care from the late 1960s, prompted by the literature of dysfunction's revelations about institutional life (Goffman, 1961; Morris, 1969; Townsend, 1962). Social work values for working with individuals, particularly individualisation and confidentiality, began to permeate residential care, but the caring services defended the continuing existence of residential homes by advocating good care practice to address the problems. For example, Atherton (1989; based on Maslow, 1987) suggested that the care practices of residential life could be understood within a hierarchy of concerns ranging from meeting physical needs to encouraging individual therapeutic growth, and this understanding could help practitioners mitigate the effects of institutionalisation.

Brearley (1990) believed it possible to create 'good' institutions out of 'bad' ones: the negative effects of institutionalisation were attributable to regimes and interactions within care rather than to institutionalisation itself (Booth, 1985). Unlike the literature of dysfunction, the good care practice approach did not conclude that residential homes should be replaced – the care 'enterprise' (Estes, 1979) and 'industry' (Challis, 1990) used good care practice as a justification for retaining residential homes rather than developing community-based alternatives.

Problems in Finding Out What Residents Want

Booth's (1985) study of dependency in residential environments revealed the persistence of power and control (Townsend, 1986) in residential homes. Booth considered the complexity of trying to measure institutional environments and find out what residents wanted, drawing attention to potential sources of bias in staff's responses, and arguing that staff members may confuse what they would like to do with what they actually do in practice, while the residents' responses may not reflect their true feelings and opinions because of the power imbalance between them and the staff.

Sinclair and Payne (1990) echoed the same issues, attributing the well-documented problems of eliciting the opinions of residents to the reluctance of some residents whose care was subsidised by the state to complain about services they had not paid for. Some residents do not complain because their thresholds of satisfaction are lower than the rest of the population, and they fear retribution by staff. Part of the philosophy of good care practice is to enable users of services to become more powerful in expressing their wishes and preferences. Consumer views are important for discovering the nature of needs, but direct approaches to residents or service users may not succeed. The power imbalance is particularly acute when consumers with a disability are dependent on the provision of physical care, and living in an institution increases the power imbalance.

Taxonomy Approaches to the Quality of Life

Throughout the 1970s and 1980s, taxonomy approaches defined key characteristics that were considered essential for quality of life in residential care. Goldberg and Connolly (1982) adapted some individual values as well as taking account of the complexity of organisational relationships and environmental contexts. They identified nine features of a residential environment with potential to influence life in a home in a positive manner:

- Individualisation and autonomy for residents.
- Opportunities for privacy.
- Opportunities for social stimulation.
- Communication and interaction with the outside world.
- Social interaction between staff and residents (in addition to instrumental communication).
- Maximum delegation of decision-making to care staff and to residents.
- Good communication channels between staff.
- A minimum degree of specialisation of roles and tasks among staff.
- Flexibility of management practices.

Goldberg and Connolly foreshadowed the recommendations of the later research of Willcocks et al. (1987) who identified the need for privacy, individual control, choice, and social stimulation. The Avebury Working Party produced *Home Life* (Centre for Policy on Ageing [CPA], 1984) as a guide for inspection practice and for managers and homeowners in the independent sector. Ainsworth and Fulcher's (1981, 1985; discussed in Chapter 2) group care practice with its eight areas of knowledge and skills provided a template for developing good practice, first in residential care, then in all of social care. The Wagner Committee (1988) undertook an independent review of residential care, recommending practice standards for all user groups and extension of registration and inspection to local authority-run homes. Wagner's main recommendation was to make the decision to enter residential care a positive choice by introducing the Wagner principles (Box 5.13).

Box 5.13: Adapted from the Wagner Principles (1988)

Residential care should:

- Enable people who move into residential establishments to do so by *positive choice.*
- Be a *positive* experience ensuring a better quality of life than the resident could enjoy in any other setting.
- Meet the *special needs of people from ethnic minority communities.*
- Enable residents to *retain their rights as citizens.*
- Provide access to *community support services.*
- Promote contact with *local community, relatives and friends.*
- Value the contributions of *residential staff* as a major resource.

The NHS and Community Care Act 1990, implemented from 1993, was intended to reduce the need for residential care by providing community-based alternatives. Henwood (1992) and Sinclair (1990) argued that it was unlikely that residential care could be replaced entirely by community care, and the ensuing years have proved the accuracy of their prediction. Changes in style and design and the move towards professionalisation of care practices reflect a genuine concern about values and standards and improving the quality of the residential experience, but the question remains: what, if anything, can prevent or negate the stigmatising effects of institutionalisation?

Values within Community-based Social Care

Concern about quality of life was not limited to residential care provision. Wolfensberger's (1982, 1992) *normalisation* principles, later re-titled *social role valorisation,* provided a model for reforming community services as well as residential care. Normalisation or *social role valorisation* promoted the idea of enabling people who use services to lead 'normal' lives of participation in the community by revolutionising the way services were delivered. The key question of the normalisation approach was to ask whether you would choose a particular service arrangement for yourself or a valued family member, and if not, to change the service rather than the person. The aim is to create socially valued roles for devalued people so that they gain opportunities to secure resources and services to live a valued life style. The two strategies for social role valorisation are to improve the image and competences of devalued individuals in society. People with learning disabilities, for example, experience deprivations arising from their devalued status, and were viewed negatively as sub-human, segregated from 'normal' society, and often subjected to abuse.

Wolfensberger provided guidelines (Box 5.14) for putting social role valorisation into practice by considering the kinds of people who are devalued, identifying the elements of a valued life style, and specifying the targets for intervention. Problems are attributed to the structures and culture of society rather than to the individual. Social role valorisation respects the individual, but has developed a more sophisticated focus for helping activities. Biestek emphasised individual adjustment, but Wolfensberger requires that society changes.

Box 5.14: Social Role Valorisation (adapted from Wolfensberger, 1982, 1992)		
The kinds of people who are devalued	*The elements of a valued life style*	*Targets for intervention*
People who are institutionalised	Dignity, respect, acceptance, belonging	The individual
People at risk of being institutionalised	Development and exercise of personal capabilities	The individual's family
Users of services	Family and friends	Neighbourhood
People who experience social exclusion	Community participation	The community
	Acceptable standard of living	Service provision
Poor people	Living in the community	Society as a whole
	Education, work, support	

O'Brien's (1987) *five accomplishments* for service delivery, intended primarily to address learning disabilities, are similar to social role valorisation, emphasising the individual's choice and control and providing goals for service provision. The five accomplishments are:

- *Community presence,* where individuals can use mainstream activities instead of separate services.
- *Choice,* where individuals exert some meaningful decisions about day-to-day matters and major life events.
- *Competence,* which involves providing opportunities for skills development so that people can reach their full potential.
- *Respect,* which means recognising that individuals have a right to carry out a valued role within networks of reciprocal roles.
- *Community participation,* where individuals become part of a network of friends.

Modernisation and Care Standards

By the mid-1990s, social care had developed values, standards, and criteria for improving the quality of provision. Currently the modernisation agenda seeks to raise social care standards through regulatory frameworks. The CSCI in England and care councils in Scotland, Northern Ireland, and Wales are responsible for inspecting social care establishments in accordance with statutory regulations of the Care Standards Act 2000 and National Minimum Standards (CSCI, 2005). National Minimum Standards are available for:

- care homes for older people;
- adult placements;
- adults 18–65;
- adult placement schemes;
- domiciliary care;
- nurses' agencies;
- children's homes;
- adoption;
- residential family centres;
- fostering services;
- boarding schools;
- residential special schools; and
- accommodation of students under 18 by further education colleges.

Service standards and care standards incorporate many of the values promoted by Wagner, O'Brien, and Wolfensberger, which in turn drew on the individual values of social work. This is evident when considering the minimum standards for care homes for older people and for domiciliary care (Box 5.15). Although minimum standards help to improve practice, they will not be effective unless social care staff 'own' the standards as part of their practice values rather than viewing the standards as a tool of external inspection.

Box 5.15: Minimum Care Standards (adapted from CSCI, 2005)	
Minimum care standards for care homes for older people	*Minimum care standards for domiciliary care*
Choice of home	User focused services (including confidentiality)
Health and personal care (including privacy and dignity)	Personal care standards (including privacy and dignity)
Daily life and social activities (including choice and autonomy)	Protection (including risk assessment)
Complaints and protection (including rights)	Management and staff
Environment	Organising and running a business (including complaints and quality assurance)
Staffing	
Management and administration (including ethos of creativity and diversity)	

Permeation of Individual Social Work Values across Social Care

Individual values of social work have permeated social care, prompted first by a desire to maintain the existence of residential care by improving its status, and now by the realisation that social care encompasses more than residential care, and can provide choices. In the UK, social care is now recognised as a major industry of which social work is a part, although this relationship is disputed internationally where social care is viewed as part of social work. The individual values and the values that promote the quality of life are similar in many respects, but quality of life values are more concerned to promote rights and living standards than the individual values, and they draw attention to implicit oppressions in the individual values. Social care adopted social work's individual values but rejected Biestek's implicit emphasis on adjustment. Quality of life values now provide a rallying call to change services and raise standards.

Structural Values

During the 1960s, the civil rights movement in the USA, the growth of feminism and the student revolts in Europe signalled a challenge to the dominant values of society, which had traditionally categorised individuals on the basis of being in or outside the dominant power base, and in Western society the dominant group were white middle-class males. People excluded from the dominant power structure were subject to professional decisions that negatively affected their life chances. The Beveridge reforms tried to counteract the devastating effects of poverty and class in the UK, but did not address the effects of gender, age, sexuality, disability, religious belief, and (most particularly) ethnicity, race and culture. Because of structural inequality, some individuals were socially excluded and unable to develop their potential. The concept of exclusion/inclusion was not understood at the time. Widespread inequality among particular individuals continued to be a feature of society.

Social work's reliance on the values of individual practice was exposed as oppressive. The relationship-building skills of psycho-dynamically trained social workers were deployed to help users of services adjust to inequality, rather than to challenge the sources of the inequality. Dominelli (1988: 48–9) argued that 'casework professionalism portrays social work as a liberal profession graced with mutual tolerance and encourages white social workers to treat prejudice and discrimination as a matter of interpersonal dynamics … but prejudice and discrimination feed off social conditions and their sanctification and legitimation in legal, political, social and cultural institutions'. Social workers were mainly white middle-class women who were criticised for being too distant from the people they were trying to help. Radical social workers drew attention to socio-economic and political factors that negatively affected the life courses of people using services. Casework suffered a credibility crisis.

In 1989 the CCETSW (1989: 16) promoted a structural values approach that led to a requirement for anti-discriminatory and anti-racist practice. Social work students were required to 'combat racism', an expectation that put them in the position of challenging the authority structures of their placement agencies. The requirement to combat racism led to disagreements among social workers, some arguing that the strategy was ineffectual, and others arguing that social work had strayed too far from its core skills. Students were expected to lead the change in social work values, yet they were only beginning to acquire skills and knowledge and were relatively powerless as change agents. Criticism of social work's anti-discriminatory policy led to its modification in 1995. Instead of combating racism, the new values for social work practice, as well as requiring social workers to be respectful, trustworthy, and reliable, committed them to 'identify, challenge and deal with discrimination, racism, disadvantage, inequality and injustice, using strategies appropriate to role and context; and practise in a manner that does not stigmatise or disadvantage either individuals or groups' (CCETSW, 1995: 4). Subsequently, social work gained recognition as the profession that had the courage to recognise structural discrimination before other professions did. Structural values support values concept 3 (the importance of environmental context), while values concept 2 (the belief in change and development) bridges the individual and structural approaches.

The basis of structural values is to acknowledge the ineffectiveness of treating everyone as if they were exactly the same. The more appropriate response is to acknowledge differences in a positive way, and respond with appropriate policies and practices to redress the power imbalances. The principle of *individualisation* is helpful in recognising the particular dilemma of the individual who has to deal with structural inequalities. The strategy of valuing differences draws on the quality of life value of *social role valorisation*, leading to the conclusion that it is society that must change, not the individual.

The conceptual danger is that the different forms of discrimination may be viewed separately as competing processes. In early discussions of discriminatory practice, social workers vied with each other to reject one form of discrimination in favour of championing another form of discrimination. When racism was the topic under discussion, a participant might try to draw attention to disablism as the more pressing problem. When sexism was being discussed, a participant would argue the case for racism being the real problem. The recognition that individuals tend to face not just one but also a range of discriminatory experiences, which share certain features, led to the use of the term *oppression* (Ward and Mullender, 1993). *Oppression* is increasingly used to express the shared nature of experiences that result from being on the receiving end of different forms of discrimination, of living on the margins of society and being subject to power wielded by others. It is better expressed as *multiple oppressions*. To deal with multiple oppressions, social workers recognise the factors that link together the experience of racism, sexism, ageism, and other forms of discrimination, and develop strategies for reducing the effects of multiple oppressions. Thompson (2001) provides a maxim for understanding the different levels of discrimination (Box 5.16), explaining that discrimination takes place at three levels that interact with and reinforce each other. This concept is simply expressed, but illuminates an issue that caused British social work to lose confidence in itself in the 1980s and 1990s as a consequence of internal and external criticisms of its stance on anti-racist and anti-discriminatory practice. Structural values pose difficult and sensitive issues for practice. Sometimes a policy that seems fair in principle can discriminate against particular individuals (Case Study 5.2).

**Box 5.16: Maxim for Understanding Levels of Discrimination
(adapted from Thompson, 2001)**

Personal (P) level of discrimination: individual thoughts, actions, feelings and attitudes of prejudice and bias.

Cultural (C) level of discrimination: common values and shared ways of seeing, thinking and doing, often reinforced by group solidarity and allegiances.

Structural (S) level of discrimination: a society's established social order and social divisions.

Case Study 5.2 – An Early Years Centre's Policy on Admissions

Jack is a four-year-old boy with a learning disability. His development is delayed and he is not yet toilet trained. His parents want him to attend a playgroup at a nearby early years centre, because they believe its activities will encourage Jack's social development. He is the only child in his neighbourhood not to attend some kind of early learning group. However, the centre's policy for admission requires that all children must be toilet trained. They refuse to accept Jack. Jack's parents argue that Jack should be accepted and that the policy discriminates against children with delayed development.

? Question for Reflection

What response should a social worker make to this situation?
    This is a situation that calls for advocacy, but you may wish to consider whether the social worker's role is to support the parents' own advocacy, or to speak on their behalf. Another case study illustrates that discrimination can take place between service users (Case Study 5.3).

Case Study 5.3 – A Black Older Woman Rejects Homosexuality

Mrs L was a woman in her 80s who emigrated from Jamaica to the UK. She confided in her social worker that she had experienced discrimination when she first came to Britain. She wanted to study medicine but failed her course and then was unable to find any work other than office cleaning. Now she lived alone in a suburban area. Mrs L needed community support as she was becoming more frail and isolated. She began to attend a weekly activities group. Mrs L learned that Mr T, an older man who had joined the group, was homosexual and she expressed hostile views about homosexuality whose vehemence upset other participants at the activities group. The staff considered telling Mrs L that she could no longer attend the group as she was expressing discriminatory attitudes, but they recognised that she had experienced discrimination herself.

?   Question for Reflection

How should the staff deal with Mrs L's discriminatory behaviour? If they prevented her attending the group, she would be isolated and would become more vulnerable, but clearly her behaviour was distressing others.

You might consider the possibility that Mrs L might respond positively to the staff setting some ground rules for attendance that would apply to all members, including herself. Resolving situations like these requires negotiation, mediation, and balancing rights and responsibilities. Another example of structural discrimination is based on lack of communication (Box 5.17).

Box 5.17: Refugee Women Are Unable to Discover What Services Might Be Available

A number of refugee families (some from Africa, some from Asia, and some from Eastern Europe) were relocated to an urban area of Scotland. The women did not speak English and few of them shared a common language. They were interested in learning English. The local adult education college provided language lessons, but had not translated the publicity that advertised the lessons into the languages that the women spoke and read. Consequently, the women did not learn about the lessons, the college wondered why the take up was low, and the women decided that no one was interested in helping them.

?   Question for Reflection

How could this situation have been prevented? After the event, what could be done to remedy the situation and encourage the women to participate?

You might consider how easily trust is shattered when individuals are faced with what appears to be non-communicative bureaucracies that do not consider the cultural contexts of service provision. Structural values bring a widened understanding of different kinds of inequality. Emancipatory values (that include empowerment) provide a logical progression from structural values to a more action-oriented strategy.

Empowerment and Emancipatory Values

Empowerment began to attract attention as a conceptual basis for practice during the 1960s civil rights movements and the 1960s' and 1970s' efforts to promote quality of life values. Its origins are not located in social work theory, although its conceptual orientations support social work's perspectives. Arnstein's (1969; and Box 5.18) ladder of citizen participation provide a tool for understanding the principles of empowerment. Arnstein portrayed different rungs on a ladder of citizen participation of people in their communities. Here we note empowerment's connotation with citizenship, one of the concepts discussed in Chapter 3:

Box 5.18: A Ladder of Citizen Participation (adapted from Arnstein, 1969)

Degrees of citizen power: Citizen control
                                         Delegated power
                                         Partnership

Degrees of tokenism: Placation
                                         Consultation
                                         Informing

Non-participation: Therapy
                                         Manipulation

- The ladder's lowest two rungs represent *non-participation*. *Manipulation* is the selective use of public relations techniques to 'educate' the citizen about what is best for the organisation rather than the individual, while the *therapy* rung tries to cure whatever is deemed wrong.
- The third, fourth and fifth rungs represent *tokenism*. The third rung, *informing*, moves towards some participation, but the flow of information is usually from the top down, rather than listening to what citizens have to say. At the fourth rung, *consultation* takes place through meetings and surveys, but this rung may still be considered tokenism. *Placation,* the fifth rung, may allow certain citizen representatives to advise and contribute as committee or board members, but the majority has the right to reject the advice.
- The sixth and seventh rungs represent *citizen power*. For *partnership*, the sixth rung, citizens and those who hold the dominant power plan and make decisions together. Negotiation becomes an important tool for redistributing power. At the seventh rung, *delegated power*, citizens hold the majority of seats on committees and boards and assume decision-making powers, so that they can ensure that programmes are accountable to them.
- The highest rung, *citizen control*, represents *citizen power*. *Citizen control* denotes a situation where formerly excluded people take control of planning, determine policy, and manage programmes.

Barbara Solomon (1976), a Black American social work academic, was one of the first to use the concept of empowerment within social work, arguing that empowerment moved practice beyond the social work goals of insight and understanding towards helping service users to gain control of their own lives. Empowerment began to be understood as one of the purposes of social work so that its extension to other practice disciplines is attributed to the influence of social work (Jordan, 2004). Currently, empowerment has become a mainstream strategy for promoting partnership and collaboration. The shift in thinking towards empowerment was triggered by an underlying belief in the humanity, inherent strengths, and capacity for growth and development of people who use services. They were no longer viewed as needing moral guidance, but instead, appropriate support to overcome structural disadvantages. The concept of empowerment compels social workers to work collaboratively and facilitatively with people who use services. Leadbetter (2002: 100–1) compares empowerment to the requirement for good customer care at the beginning level of a professional relationship. The concept of empowerment shares some of the characteristics of social capital because it also promotes people's capability to take control of their lives. Empowerment tries to create strengths.

Social workers who seek to empower people demonstrate a belief in working for social justice but Solomon argued that social workers could not support service users to make choices if a lack of resources meant that there were no choices available. She therefore advocated a dual approach to empowerment, in which empowerment in its totality is not just about enhancing self-esteem or improving skills, but addresses structural inequalities and injustice. Empowerment that takes place only at the personal level will not be effective; infrastructural constraints must be dealt with by addressing the three levels of discrimination – personal, cultural, and structural (Thompson, 2001). Empowerment is intended to be a community strategy, not merely an individual strategy. Social workers who practise empowerment will use a range of intervention strategies, including community development as well as individual casework.

The key feature of empowerment is collaborative working between service user and social worker to address relevant aspects of the user's situation, including the socio-economic context. Empowerment is not difficult to understand but is a challenging concept to apply in practice. Social workers have to demonstrate their professional skills in a less obvious way, because they are asked to give up power and share power with service users. Leadbetter (2002: 206) identifies impediments to empowerment:

- Diluting the concept to 'enablement'.
- Delegating budgets to team managers but simultaneously imposing severe resource restraints.
- Practitioners handing responsibility to service users without supplying the required resources.
- Practitioners taking necessary action to protect individuals from harm.

In contrast, Harris (1997) doubts whether empowerment has a clear purpose or ideology in professional practice because of its moral neutrality. A social worker could discover that individuals express racist and xenophobic views as a chosen outcome of their empowerment. The social worker's role as a guardian of values would have to be called into action to refute those views. Harris (1997: 33) suggests that an alternative to empowering individuals is to use social workers' power to develop 'a proper philosophy and practice to express and meet the needs of disadvantaged or oppressed people'.

Means and Smith (1994; drawing on Hirschman, 1970: 71–103) portrayed three approaches by which adult service users can demonstrate empowerment within the policies and practices of community care (Box 5.19). They (1994: 102) argue that the *voice* and *exit* approaches to empowerment are compatible with the quasi-market model of community care, where the state purchases care from independent providers and the market is mediated through provision of a care manager, quality standards, contracts, and a consumer voice within the system. They warn that if the quasi-market model is to succeed in empowering users of services and carers, it should:

- Stimulate diverse providers to offer choice; provide advice, information and advocacy to assert claims for a quality service.
- Develop service quality standards in conjunction with users and carers.
- Enable service users to develop their own services and have a say in existing services.
- Develop ways for user and carer groups to participate in planning community care.

Box 5.19: Three Approaches to Empowerment (adapted from Means and Smith, 1994)	
Empowerment through voice	The service user is able to influence the planning and delivery of services.
Empowerment through exit	The service user is able to switch services and move to alternative providers.
Empowerment through rights	The service user is entitled by law to receive services, and to pursue his/her own goals and meet his/her needs with the minimum state interference.

Emancipatory Values

The third approach to empowerment (*rights*) requires an emancipatory approach that is consonant with values concept 4. Emancipatory values propose a more active approach for applying values to practice. They require the social worker to confront injustices that individual values cannot address satisfactorily (Case Study 5.4).

Case Study 5.4 – Oppression of an Older Single Woman

Francesca Michelini is an older single woman who is entitled to only a very small pension because of the poorly paid work that was available during her working life. She took years out from paid employment caring for her parents who are now dead. After a lifetime of having to make do with little, her old age is beset with worries about money. She has become disabled with arthritis, and finds that the available community care support is insufficient to compensate for her lack of family support because she has no living family members. She is called 'dear' by members of the public and by members of the caring services. When she walks, she uses a cane and progresses with difficulty. She has been subject to jeers from young people about her stooped appearance and slow moving gait. Despite this unwelcome attention, Francesca faces the oppression of invisibility. Like many older women, who by culture are not likely to 'make a fuss', she is invisible because she is so uncomplaining. She accepts her oppression of poverty, ageism, and disablism. Francesca would like to feel in control of her life because she values her independence, but doesn't have anyone to talk to about this. She is isolated. She also fears that the 'caring services' might put her into a home.

?   Question for Reflection

How might a social worker begin to address Francesca Michelini's situation?

You might consider assessing the practical needs but also the underlying gender and age dis-crimination. Establishing trust and rapport will require good communication skills to begin to understand her hopes and fears and offer appropriate information. In the case of Francesca Michelini, emancipatory values would question the basis of employment and pensions arrange-ments for women that have resulted in financial disadvantage in old age compared to men, even though women live longer than men and therefore are likely to draw their pensions longer. Although these inequalities may diminish as more women develop careers in better-paid jobs, older single women are likely to be poor. Emancipatory values suggest that a collective approach might help Francesca. Alone, she lacks confidence and does not know how to look systematically at how her life could be improved, but this could be tackled through an emancipatory approach that establishes some commonality with others experiencing similar situations.

An International Context: Pedagogy of the Oppressed

An example of emancipatory values in action is Freire's (1970) pedagogy of the oppressed. Paulo Freire was a Brazilian community organiser and educator who died in 1997. Freire's knowledge of the conditions of Brazilian landless peasants led him to recognise the dehumanisation of indi-viduals within oppressed communities. Freire describes an objectification process where the oppressors make everyone the objects of their purchasing power, reducing their humanity, and forcing them to live in a culture of silence. People must become aware of their objectification in order to fight for their liberation. He argued that the 'banking system' of education delivers knowledge as a gift transmitted from knowledgeable experts to people that lack knowledge (1970: 74). 'Bankable knowledge' requires oppressed people to adjust to their situations (an echo of the Bowers' [1949] definition of social work used by Biestek), and therefore become more easily dom-inated by experts (1970: 77). The process of bankable knowledge teaches a standard curriculum as a narrative of fixed 'truth' that requires rote memorisation. Freire (1970: 71) calls this kind of learning 'narration sickness'. Bankable knowledge is part of the oppression of the poor.

In contrast, Freire's pedagogy promotes a problem-solving style of learning – it is a method of participatory adult education that uses a dialogue of mutual respect between the facilita-tor/teacher and the learner, where each participates equally in the learning process and learns from each other. Freire's method of teaching is designed to raise the consciousness of mar-ginalised individuals and communities so that they become aware of their oppressions, and therefore attaining literacy in the fullest sense of the word (e.g. emotional, social, and politi-cal literacy) becomes a political action.

Freire's pedagogy seeks to develop critical thinking, dialogue, and reflection on each individ-ual's personal role and their relationships to others, with learning emerging from questioning and identifying problems to be solved. Dialogue between individuals identifies the changing and transitory nature of different realities rather than one fixed reality. Freire argued that this method of experiential learning led to group awareness, personal development, community action, and eventually, freedom from oppressions. People are able to mobilise themselves towards action when they join together as a community, because they need to reflect together if they are to free themselves of the false narratives of the oppressive structures of reality. Therefore action must be preceded by critical reflection on the consequences of action. (Here we see elements of the Biestek individual value of respect for persons contributing to the pedagogy.) Participative learning leads to values-based actions that empower oppressed groups and build social capital (Putnam, 1993, 2000; discussed in Chapter 4).

Freire believes that human beings have the capacity to attain a self-actualised individual and collective life. He also expresses faith that every individual is capable of participating in critical dialogue, reflection, and critical appraisal to transform their life. Freire can be criticised for naïve assumptions about the human capacity for self-actualisation and for ignoring the tendency for power imbalances in every society (including disagreements that take place among different groups of oppressed people), but his thinking influenced strategies for social justice. Emancipatory values honour the diverse and distinctive organisations and communities that make up contemporary society, and seek to combat processes that lead to discrimination, marginalisation, and social exclusion by empowering and emancipating individuals, groups, and communities. Emancipatory values embody all of the four values concepts, but emphasise concept 4. The emancipatory approach to values embodies the Benchmark Statement's explanation (QAA, 2000: § 2.4) that 'Social work is a moral activity that requires practitioners to make and implement difficult decisions about human situations that involve the potential for benefit or harm … at their core, social work values involve showing respect for persons, honouring the diverse and distinctive organisations and communities that make up contemporary society and combating processes that lead to discrimination, marginalisation and social exclusion.'

Applying Emancipatory Values to Individual Practice

Pease and Fook (1999) suggest an emancipatory theory and practice for social work that draws on critical realism traditions (Archer et al., 1998) in which emancipatory practice begins to develop from social workers' and service users' narratives that describe how each uses, recognises, and reacts to their different areas of knowledge, diversity, and power. Emancipatory practice requires social workers to recognise injustice, inequalities, and oppressive relationships, and to base their actions on constructively challenging individual, institutional, and structural discrimination, an approach to theory and practice that recognises the moral purpose of social work, in consonance with the Benchmark Statement (QAA, 2000: § 2.4).

Jordan (2004) casts some doubt on social work's emancipatory potential for promoting individual autonomy and choice, arguing that collective action by social movements must counter-balance the market economy's control of individual opportunities. Portraying social work practice as having moved from being 'at the cutting edge' (2004: 6) of welfare state reforms in the mid-20th century to a contemporary emphasis on implementing government policies that restrict choice and ration resources, he claims that social work has not challenged detrimental policy changes. The government emphasis on enabling people to realise their potential through building self-esteem represents 'technologies of the self' (2004: 9), while the emphasis on citizenship represents 'projects of the self' (2004: 9). Social work assists in the coercion of poor people into externally imposed self-improvement strategies, where they will fail in the competitive task of attaining excellence (2004: 10).

Jordan's view of poor people is protective. He argues that their vulnerability will cause them to fail in open competition, because strategies for empowerment based on knowledge and skills acquisition are designed to benefit the more able members of society. Globalisation, in his view, allows citizens to use *exit* strategies (withdrawing from jobs, moving house, ending associations) rather than using *voice* to protest against injustice – the kinds of empowerment noted by Means and Smith, who like Jordan, draw on Hirschman (1970) – but poor and disadvantaged people at the margins of society are citizens who lack choices for exit and voice. Jordan suggests that social work must align itself with new collective movements and that the future of emancipatory social work may lie in a community development approach. The classic dilemma for social workers is that their advocacy for individuals is conducted from within organisations that often can oppress or restrict people's freedoms and opportunities.

?   Question for Reflection

Do you agree with Jordan's view that current social policy which seeks to develop skills will only cause vulnerable poor people to fail? How would you develop emancipatory practice with people who are 'at the margins' of society?

A key issue in your response is whether you believe that skills development and training programmes can help service users who are poor and oppressed. You could consider the possibility of a community development approach – but how would you engage with users of services?

What Do Service Users Say about Social Work Values?

The consultation for the NOS in Social Work (2002; discussed in Chapter 2) engaged people who use services, their carers, and their organisations to identify expectations of social workers. Box 5.20 presents what they said about social work values.

**Box 5.20: Service Users' Expectations of Social Work Values
(Topss UK, 2002)**

Social workers must:

- Have respect for users and carers regardless of their age, ethnicity, culture, level of understanding, and need; and for the expertise and knowledge users and carers have about their own situations.
- Empower users and carers in decisions affecting them.

(Continued)

Box 5.20: *(Continued)*

- Be honest about the power invested in them, including legal powers, their role and the extent of resources available to meet need.
- Respect confidentiality, and inform users and carers when information needs to be shared with others.
- Be able to challenge discriminatory images and practices affecting users and carers.
- Put users and carers first.

The NOS adopted these expectations, broadening the designation of *users and carers* to *individuals, families, carers, groups, and communities* and drawing attention to individual values of respect for persons and confidentiality as well as values of empowerment and emancipation. The emphasis on honesty about social workers' power and the availability of resources is an indication that people who use services recognise social workers' balancing dilemma.

Values Dilemmas

Values dilemmas are likely to occur when different individuals have conflicting needs. Examples include:

- A carer of a person with a mental health problem has reached a state of exhaustion and feels that they can no longer continue their caring role, but the family member continues to need care and would experience feelings of rejection if he or she were asked to move away from home. The probable feelings of guilt and ambivalence, mixed with concern, can lead to tense angry situations into which the social worker enters.
- The parents of a person with learning disabilities are afraid to let go of their adult child who wants to establish a more independent life.

The most difficult values dilemma is when a social worker has to judge whether the need to protect individual safety and well-being outweighs the individual's desire for emancipation and independence (Case Study 5.5).

Case Study 5.5 – Mr Gupta

Mr Gupta, an older single man with uncontrolled diabetes living in a hostel, has a history that includes offending, prison, homelessness, and heavy alcohol consumption; his spoken English is not fluent. He asks for re-housing in the community but Jeff Albert, the social worker, is aware of Mr Gupta's previous lack of success in addressing his drinking, diet, medication, and finances. Jeff is faced with the dilemma of deciding whether the risk of living independently will be life-threatening or whether independence would be a reasonable risk.

? Question for Reflection

What are the specific issues that Jeff will need to consider, and how will he communicate these to Mr Gupta?

You may want to consider whether Mr Gupta might need an interpreter, the possibility of a resources shortfall that might limit the kinds of support that could be offered; and more positively, the possibility of agreeing an informal 'task contract' with Mr Gupta that would help him address some of the issues and be supported to reach his goal. Freire's emancipatory approach identifies values dilemmas through raising awareness of issues of freedom, independence, conflicting needs, choice, risk, and safety. Awareness-raising will expose lack of resources, inappropriate resources, or inappropriate policies that social workers cannot ignore. When this kind of process cannot be undertaken because participants reject the process, Freire suggests that action must be preceded by critical reflection on the consequences of action. Jeff Albert, the social worker, will need to think carefully about the values dilemma and the consequences of making one decision over another and discuss the choices in an honest way with Mr Gupta.

Social Work's Failure to Champion Social Care

It can be argued that British social work, in its search for professional recognition and identity, has ignored the historically disadvantaged plight of its social care colleagues employed as care assistants, community care assistants, and domiciliary workers. As discussed in Chapter 3, the social care workforce is comprises mainly part-time women with no qualifications who work for low wages to provide services to vulnerable people, the majority of whom are older women. When social work expanded its understanding of values to questions about the quality of life, structural values, and emancipatory values, it did not draw attention to the lack of skills and opportunities offered to social care workers. Social work instead felt uncomfortable about being linked with a largely unqualified, unskilled workforce (Roche and Rankin, 2004).

The need to improve the quality of social care by addressing the qualifications and roles of social care staff escaped social work notice, except for some social workers who qualified after rising through the ranks of social care and who still worked in social care. Now social work is viewed (controversially) as the professional wing of British social care, and cannot ignore social care, which is recognised as a large workforce needing qualifications and better career structures. The argument is that better qualified workers will offer better quality services. The relationship of social work to social care still needs consideration – social workers have much to offer social care workers through mentoring and developing practice quality, and the establishment of skill mix teams may further this kind of relationship.

Codes of Practice and Social Care Registers

Social care registers and social care codes of practice for workers and employers have been introduced in the four UK countries in September 2002 to raise practice standards and protect the public. The GSCC in England and the care councils in Wales, Scotland, and Northern Ireland collaborated to ensure that the final codes (GSCC, 2002) were similar and that a registered worker taken off the register in one country would not be able to re-register in another country of the United Kingdom. The social care registers provide a public record that registered workers have met the requirements for entry to the register and have agreed to practice according to the standards in the code of practice for social care workers. Social workers were the first occupational group to be put on the social care register as a requisite for professional practice. Over time, all social care workers will be registered. 'Social worker' is a registerable title, and the intention is that no one who is not registered can call himself or herself a social worker. The codes and the register will place social workers and social care workers on a similar regulatory basis to doctors and nurses. Employers will enforce the code of practice for social care workers, including social workers. A breach of the codes' standards could result in a registered worker being removed from the register and being unable to practice. The GSCC in England, the Scottish Social Services Council (SSSC), the CCW, and the NISCC will take account of the code's standards when considering issues of misconduct referred to them by employers, and decisions about whether a registered worker should remain on the register. In England, the CSCI will enforce the code of practice for employers.

Employers and workers are encouraged to use the *Codes of Practice* (Box 5.21) to monitor their own practices and standards. There are two complementary codes, one for employees and one for employers: the employers' code requires them to support the code's standards, help social care workers meet their code and take action when workers fail to meet standards of conduct. Employers' duties combine a regulatory function with a developmental responsibility for their workers. The code of practice for social care workers makes them responsible for ensuring that their conduct does not fall below the code's standards and that they do not harm service users' well-being through any action or omission of action (Box 5.22). The codes emphasise employers' and workers' mutual responsibilities for developing their own knowledge and skills. Unlike the BASW code of ethics and other interpretations of values, the codes of practice are mandatory. They build on existing good practice and social work values by including themes of rights and responsibilities, promoting independence, and protecting from harm, but are not synonymous with social work values, as discussed at the beginning of the chapter, and should not be used to avoid personal and professional values dilemmas and conflicts. The requirement for improved standards suggests that social workers must reflect on the implications of the codes for their practice, but individual reflection, although helpful, is not sufficient to improve practice. Practice supervision and the support of experienced qualified social work mentors are essential features for dealing with values dilemmas and developing higher standards of practice.

Box 5.21: Employers Code of Practice (GSCC, 2002)

Social care employers must:

- Make sure people are suitable to enter the workforce and understand their roles and responsibilities.
- Have written policies and procedures in place to enable social care workers to meet the *Code of Practice* for Social Care Workers.
- Provide training and development opportunities to enable social care workers to strengthen and develop their skills and knowledge.
- Put in place and implement written policies and procedures to deal with dangerous, discriminatory or exploitative behaviour and practice.
- Promote the ... codes of practice to social care workers, service users and carers and co-operate with [care council or GSCC] proceedings.

Box 5.22: Social Care Workers Code of Practice (GSCC, 2002)

Social care workers must:

- Protect the rights and promote the interests of service users and carers.
- Strive to establish and maintain the trust and confidence of service users and carers.
- Promote the independence of service users while protecting them as far as possible from danger or harm.
- Respect the rights of service users while seeking to ensure that their behaviour does not harm themselves or other people.
- Uphold public trust and confidence in social care services.
- Be accountable for the quality of their work and take responsibility for maintaining and improving their knowledge and skills.

？ Question for Reflection

Can you identify values dilemmas that might arise in practice?

You may identify values dilemmas that arise when a family whose members are users of services cannot agree on the best course of action to take, perceiving all possible outcomes as oppressive. The regulatory aspects of practice (child protection and placement, compulsory mental health admission to hospital) involve difficult decisions that apparently can leave everyone dissatisfied with the outcomes, including the practitioner. Sometimes there is no decision that appears 'right' according to social work values. In situations like these, the social worker needs to be supported by good practice supervision.

▶▶| **Conclusion**

Four observations can be made about social work values. First, under the codes of practice, the social worker carries an individual responsibility for applying values to their practice and ensuring that their conduct falls within the code; however, one of the key elements for promoting values-based practice is the availability of good practice supervision to support the social worker's inevitable values conflicts and dilemmas. Employers must provide access to professional practice supervision from a social work mentor, particularly when the social worker is part of a multi-professional team.

Second, social work has played an important part in promoting wider acceptance of essential values by importing new perspectives from other disciplines (for example, the social model of disability, the pedagogy of the oppressed, and social role valorisation) and then adopting these values perspectives, absorbing them into the culture of social work, and championing them as social work values. Significantly, social care has adopted the same values.

Third, social workers enter their names on a social *care* register, not a social *work* register, and eventually, all social care workers will join the register and will profess the same codes of practice as social workers. Although codes of practice should not serve as a substitute for social work values and ethics, their shared ownership by social work and social care will create a more powerful alliance and stronger identity for both social work and social care.

Fourth, social work successfully expanded from individual values to concerns about the quality of life in social care environments, oppression, and discrimination. Individual values as expressed by the casework principles should not be abandoned entirely, but adapted to align with contemporary expectations of empowerment and emancipation.

📖 **Further Reading**

Banks, S. (2003) *Ethics, Accountability and the Social Professions*. Basingstoke: Palgrave.
The second edition presents an updated overview of values and ethics for practice.

Hugman, R. (2005) *New Approaches in Ethics for the Caring Professions Taking Account of Change for Caring Professions*. Basingstoke: Palgrave.
This book examines different kinds of ethical theories from the perspectives of liberalism, feminism, ecology, postmodernism, and constructivism.

Smith, R. (2005) *Values and Practice in Children's Services*. Basingstoke: Palgrave.
This book explores key debates about values in children's services within their legislative, policy and practice contexts.

6 KNOWLEDGE FOR PROFESSIONAL PRACTICE

The Benchmark Statement requires that: *during their degree studies in social work, honours graduates should acquire, critically evaluate, apply and integrate knowledge and understanding' in five core areas*

- *Social work services and service users.*
- *The service delivery context.*
- *Values and ethics.*
- *Social work theory.*
- *The nature of social work practice.* (QAA, 2000: §§3.1.1–5)

Introduction

Professional judgement depends on social workers having appropriate knowledge to shape their practice, and although SCIE's electronic library (eLSC) and knowledge summaries help social workers keep up to date, accessing knowledge is not enough – social workers must sort through different kinds of knowledge, think about knowledge in relation to values, adopt their own particular 'take' on knowledge and values, and then apply their understanding to practice. Rather than attempting to cover every area of knowledge (an impossible task), this chapter considers particular aspects of the various fields of knowledge relevant for contemporary practice and relates these to the Benchmark Statement and the Occupational Standards' Key Roles. Selecting from different concepts of social work and social care is a difficult task. Gergen (1978) argues that no theory should be taken as a complete account, but should be evaluated for its potential for generating new ideas and new questions. Social work knowledge has to take account of changes in social workers' relationships with service users and carers and changes in social work's organisational structures that lead to new perceptions and new understandings, but as well as discovering these, social workers should reflect on and adapt old 'knowledges'.

Values, knowledge, and skills are interrelated and must be considered in juxtaposition – that is why perspectives on particular themes important to social work can be presented alternatively as belonging to a debate on social work values, or as part of social work knowledge, or belonging to practice skills. Social workers use different knowledges and skills and draw on research findings to make sense of complex situations and guide their judgement on which actions to take in carrying out multiple roles.

Chapter Structure

The chapter explores different knowledges for social work and social care, identifies tools for examining critically different 'knowledges', and explores research-informed practice, theories of human growth and development, attachment, loss, and resilience; the social model of disability; knowledges for adult services (older people, mental health, and disability); children and young people; criminal justice social work and probation; and carers.

Where Does Knowledge for Social Work and Social Care Come From?

The Benchmark Statement (QAA, 2000: §2.1) asserts:

> At honours degree level, the study of social work involves ... a critical application of research knowledge from the social and human sciences (and closely related domains) to inform understanding and to underpin action, reflection and evaluation.

The professional social worker has to learn how to select and use different knowledge in a discerning critical way, evaluating their fitness for purpose. A review of the sources and purposes of knowledge in social care, commissioned by the SCIE (2003), provides a basis for considering different areas of knowledge for practice, and a way to evaluate their relative usefulness. The review asked:

- Where does knowledge come from?
- Who does knowledge belong to?
- How do we judge the value of knowledge?

The review team categorised knowledge for social care according to the knowledge source. They identified five sources of social care knowledge: organisations; practitioners; the policy community; researchers; and users and carers.

In considering the purpose of the knowledge sources, the review team took the values-based stance that all types of knowledge deserve equal respect and attention, but not all knowledge is equally 'good' or useful. They recognised the need to find ways to judge the quality of the knowledge and suggested the importance of asking if the knowledge demonstrated:

- Transparency: are the reasons for the knowledge clear?
- Accuracy: is it honestly based on relevant evidence?
- Purposivity: is the method(s) used suitable for the aims of the work?
- Utility: does it provide answers to the questions asked?
- Propriety: is it legal and ethical?
- Accessibility: can you understand it?
- Specificity: does it meet the quality standards already used for this type of knowledge?

Research-based Knowledge

Research plays a significant role in identifying new knowledge from organisations, practitioners, the policy community, users and carers, and previous research findings. Social workers should be *research aware*, knowing how to draw on research findings to guide their practice; and *research minded*, knowing how to use research to understand and illuminate practice situations, evaluate their practice, provide explanations of social phenomena, and supply evidence for decision-making. Practice itself should be *research informed*. Some social workers will become *research active*, learning how to undertake and publish research.

The choice of methodological approach for doing research is determined by the nature of the research topic, the questions it wants to ask, its underlying values, and whether it views the world as consisting of social structures or alternatively, as needing to capture the views of 'social actors' who shape the world in which they live (Mead, 1934). The 'world as social structure' view is usually linked with positivist quantitative approaches to research such as social surveys and randomised controlled trials. The 'world as social actors' view is usually associated with interpretivist qualitative approaches such as interviews, observation, and focus groups. The traditional divide between qualitative and quantitative approaches has been superseded by the view that both approaches are needed for better knowledge, and that it is possible to combine both approaches (Blaikie, 1993; Bryman, 1988; Layder, 1993). Researchers' choices of approach are socially determined and values driven; research findings need to be critically examined to understand the assumptions underlying the way research has been conducted and analysed.

Social work research, whose remit for enquiry encompasses the wider domain of social care, has begun to claim a distinctive place in informing practice. Professional social work is, similar to medicine, both a practice discipline and an academic research discipline. In contrast to medicine, social work struggled to achieve its identity as a research discipline despite the existence of research active social work professors in British universities. Social work research has embraced new approaches that draw on Foucaultian (1980) perspectives of power, and Freire's (1972; discussed in Chapter 5) emancipatory ideas. Feminist understandings of methodology argue against rigid boundaries between the researcher and participants and seek to bridge the distances between knowledge, its uses, thoughts and feelings (Fee, 1986). Feminism requires research to be based on women's experiences; to deal with what women regard as problematic; and to relate to the people and issues being researched (Harding, 1987).

The social model of disability has influenced social work research as well as practice. Beresford (2000) and Oliver (1983, 1989, 1996) turned their attention to academic research; challenging academics' power and professionalism, criticising traditional research methodology, and the uses to which research is put. They demand that at the very least, research with users and carers should be consultative: participative research is better in their view, and most desirable is emancipatory research which addresses inequalities and oppression and recognises service users as co-researchers and commissioners of research rather than subjects or objects. Social work academics now promote emancipatory research with other service user groups, including people with mental health problems, children, families, and older people.

The social model research perspective recognises that it is usually relatively powerless people who are chosen as 'subjects' of social research. The willing consent of people who lack power may not be freely given, because service users may perceive that continuation of their services is contingent on their willingness to participate in research, or they may not understand fully the implications of giving their consent. They may find that after participating in a research enquiry they are not told what use the researchers will make of the information they gave. A partial solution to this dilemma may be to form research partnerships with service users that engage fully in service users' own agendas for research (Case Study 6.1).

Case Study 6.1 – Where Is the Voice of Service Users?

A group of social care managers, trainers, and professional bodies met together to consider recommendations arising from its report on future training strategies for staff in children and young people's services. A service user representative, who was an adult with a disability, was present. When the group considered a recommendation that the voices of children, young people, and their carers should be clearly represented, the service user pointed out that there were no children or young people present. The service user said that children and young people were able to join the group only through the gate keeping of organisations who purported to represent the voices of children but who in fact controlled the selection of representatives and controlled what was said. The service user claimed that young people were getting 'fed up' with researchers asking their views on what changes should be made to service provision because no one told them what use had been made of their contributions and whether any changes had been made. They felt that the same questions were being asked over and over again but no action was ever taken.

? Question for Reflection

The case study presents an example of well-meant intentions not carried out in practice, and arguably causing more harm than good. How would you seek to remedy the situation described above? Would an individual social worker be able to change the relationships with users?

You may want to reflect on the importance for social work practice of formal and informal channels of communication, and of a social work role in supporting effective communication.

Adopting a participative stance may lead to uneasiness about the methodological use of randomised controlled trials. Macdonald and Macdonald (1995) express a dissenting voice. While sharing concerns for protecting the rights of vulnerable people participating in research, they do not reject the use of large-scale surveys and randomised controlled trials, arguing that researchers' empowerment and participation concerns are ethically unsound because they prevent technically better research that will bring about better results to benefit service users.

Research practice is becoming subject to increased regulation designed to protect the public. The NHS Research Governance Framework for Health and Social Care (DH, 2001) imposes requirements on universities and employers of staff engaged in research. DH (2004b) guidance proposed a timetable for extending the Governance Framework to cover all social care/social work agencies by the end of 2006, which will make it more difficult for researchers, including social work students, to gain permission to undertake empirical research in health and social care.

Legislation on data protection and human rights must be noted by social work research practice (Clements, 2004). The Data Protection Act 1998, the EU Directive on Data Processing 95/46/ (European Commission [EC], 1995), the Human Rights Act 1998, and the Freedom of Information Act 2000 promote principles governing the processing of personal data:

- Researchers have a duty to ensure that data are not collected or processed without the informed consent of the data subject.
- Data must be collected only for specified purposes and not processed for purposes incompatible with those purposes.
- The privacy of the data subjects must be adequately protected so that data should, where at all possible, be stripped of personal identifiers before they are stored or re-used.
- Data should be kept in a form that permits identification of data subjects for no longer than is necessary for the purposes for which they were collected.
- The Data Protection Act states that data subjects have the right not to be exposed to unwarranted distress and have the right to rectify errors, or block the processing or keeping of inaccurate records.

The Code of Ethics for Social Work Research (Butler, 2000) recognises researchers' different relationships with service users and their carers. The Code seeks to empower service users, promote their welfare, and maintain a primary concern for vulnerable subjects' welfare by protecting them from harm and paying attention to issues of consent, by avoiding covert research, and acknowledging service users' participation. Researchers:

- must not tolerate any form of discrimination;
- should exclude any unacknowledged bias; and
- should ensure that the legitimate interests of service users are not compromised.

Box 6.1: *CSCI Code of Practice* (CSCI, 2004b)

Legislation introduced in 2003 gave the CSCI in England powers to enter and inspect social care services and to access a wide range of confidential personal information held by those services, provided the Commission produced a Code of Practice to explain the principles that govern how and when it will access confidential information. In 2004 CSCI consulted with stakeholders prior to introducing a Code of Practice in Relation to Confidential Information that would provide some safeguards for people subject to inspection.

?   Question for reflection

Is the *Code of Practice* a sufficient safeguard of the privacy of people who use services?

You may reflect that CSCI did not introduce the *Code of Practice* until a year after it began inspection – presumably no safeguards were in place for those involved in previous inspections. Another point to consider is whether a voluntary *Code of Practice* can be effective. The CSCI *Code* illustrates the power of governmental bodies to intrude in people's lives and become an unintentional oppressive tool, even when their overall purpose is to benefit service users. Humphries and Martin (2000) argue that ethical codes do not guarantee ethical research practice. Social work research design must confront the ethical issues of user involvement and the tendency of social workers to conflate informed consent for participation in research with receiving services. A service user may not feel able to refuse to participate because of the unequal power relationship. Social work research must also be aware of the possible risk to the researcher when investigating particular topics and using particular methodologies. Lee-Treweek and Linkogle (2000) identify the categories of researcher risk as physical, emotional, ethical, and professional danger. When service users are engaged in collaborative research as co-partners or commissioners of research, they will join in the process of evaluating risk factors to themselves and others (including academics and research students) who carry out research.

Human Growth and Development

Knowledge of human growth and development helps social workers to understand an individual's unique personality and strengths in relation to the context of culture and society, and to appreciate how people's past experiences influence their present and their future. Children's and young people's services (organised separately from adult social care in England) identified 'child and young person development' as one of the six common core of skills, knowledge and competence for building a children's workforce (DfES, 2005: 8). A belief that individuals, including people who use services, are capable of growth and development throughout their lives underpins social inclusion programmes that emphasise training and skills.

Human growth and development theories share overlapping concerns. Some theories address particular aspects of development that others omit, and others explore the same aspects using substantially different questions. Some historic studies do not consider how gender, class, and race and other inequalities influence processes of development, so that conclusions drawn from these studies will be limited in their potential application to practice. The Benchmark Statement (QAA, 2000: §3.1.4) requires knowledge of:

> the relevance of sociological perspective to understanding societal and structural influences on human behaviour at individual, group and community levels … the relevance of psychological and physiological perspectives to understanding individual and social development and functioning and social science theories explaining group and organisational behaviour, adaptation and change.

This overview of human growth and development selects theories from psychology and sociology that emphasise ongoing development into old age and fit with values concept 2:

Belief in change and development throughout human life, prompting the practitioner to understand the present within a context of change, and draw on knowledge of past influences.

Diachronic and Synchronic Perceptions of Human Growth and Development

Academic traditions of psychology and sociology adopt different perceptions of development. Bertaux (1982) identifies a *diachronic* perspective that studies processes across time based on biological and psychological perspectives. The second perception is *synchronic*, studying processes linked to particular moments in time based on sociological perspectives (Box 6.2).

Box 6.2: Two Contrasting Perceptions of Human Growth and Development		
The diachronic perception	Considers the life course in outline, and studies processes taking place over time	Biological and psychological perspectives
The synchronic perception	Looks closely at particular aspects of development at particular moments in time	Sociological perspectives

Diachronic Perceptions from Psychology: Piaget, Freud, Jung, Erikson, Kohlberg, Gilligan

Diachronic perceptions from developmental psychology argue the importance of early childhood experiences for shaping adult personality, with biological developmental processes influencing these perceptions. Piaget (1932) studied the development of cognitive intelligence, which may explain why teacher education emphasises his theory. He argued that children develop through four different stages and levels of reasoning (the *sensori-motor*, *pre-operational*, *concrete operational*, and *formal operational* periods) in response to their interaction with the environment, and he viewed intelligence as a process of adaptation to the environment. The child uses two interrelated processes: *assimilation*, adapting the environment to his or her own needs; and *accommodation*, accepting and incorporating environmental demands into his or her own existence. Implied in Piaget's theory is the need for balance and reciprocity in making and resolving demands on or from the environment. Piaget stopped short of developing the stages beyond the point of biological maturity, because of the influence of biological perspectives on his thinking.

Freud (1985) also stops short of considering adult development, but suggests that unconscious motivations shape human behaviour and to understand the adult, one must first understand the child. The *oral*, *anal*, and *phallic* developmental stages of early childhood up to the ages of five or six years are said to determine elements of adult personality. The most important relationships in infancy are those formed with the parents, in which Freud theorised that the child expresses sexual instincts and aggressive drives. As the child develops, frustrations and conflicts arising from these relationships are resolved through identification with another person, and displacement of the original identification onto another person or object. Feminists attacked Freud for attributing penis envy to women and for failure to acknowledge child sexual abuse (Mitchell, 1974). Freud's psychoanalytic theories have crept into popular understanding of human development, and influenced social work's direction towards psycho-social casework that sought psychological change and adjustment in the service user rather than tackling problems of poverty and inequality.

Jung (1969), initially a follower of Freud, portrayed development that continued into the adult years, theorising that each individual personality incorporates a collective cultural history: the *collective unconscious*. The *individuation process* seeks to integrate the *animus* (male) and *anima* (female) that are *archetypes* (prototypes or patterns) within the personality. Jung suggested that the goal of development is *self-actualisation*, with the personality characteristics of reflection and introspection assisting in developing the *transcendent self*. The drive of the personality towards the transcendent self suggests a changed pattern of relationships sought by men and women as they grow older.

Erikson (1963 [1950]; Erikson et al., 1986) based his theory on Freudian principles of psycho-sexual development, but like Jung, was concerned with development throughout the adult years. Drawing on Shakespeare's seven ages (*As You Like It*), Erikson portrayed the ages of 'man' as eight developmental crises (Box 6.3). Individuals resolve each crisis by choosing either psycho-social growth or decline. The stages occur in an ordered sequence, that Erikson calls *epigenetic*. The way an individual resolves each crisis lays the groundwork for resolving the next crisis. As Erikson himself grew older, he began to emphasise old age as a search for coherence with the wider world and the environment, in which the individual tries to achieve a balance between integrity and despair, at the same time re-working some of the earlier themes of previous stages. The favourable outcome of the last stage is wisdom, 'truly involved disinvolvement' (1986: 51).

Box 6.3: Eight Ages – Developmental Crises and Favourable Outcomes (adapted from Erikson et al., 1986)		
Age	*Developmental crisis*	*Favourable outcome*
Infancy	Basic trust vs basic mistrust	Hope
Early childhood	Autonomy vs shame, doubt	Will
Play age	Initiative vs guilt	Purpose
School age	Industry vs inferiority	Competence
Adolescence	Identity vs confusion	Fidelity
Young adulthood	Intimacy vs isolation	Love
Adulthood	Generativity vs self-absorption	Care
Old age	Integrity vs despair	Wisdom

Erikson takes account of the cultural contexts of each age, the impact of historical events, and the particular environments that affect individuals, suggesting that *reflective detachment* will be a strong feature of relationships in older adults. Similarly, Maslow (1987) suggests that motivational needs exist in a hierarchy, with *self-actualisation* (echoing Jung) or *self-fulfilment* at the top of the hierarchy. Self-fulfilment is embodied in the notion of the autonomous individual, rather than in features of the social structure. Rogers (1961), who influenced the development of person-centred counselling, also promotes the idea of personhood. Erikson notes a tendency in older people towards *pseudo-integration*, the deliberate omission from life reviews of earlier discontent in an attempt to construct a satisfactory view of one's life.

Erikson's theory is popular with social workers, because it suggests the possibility of development and change throughout life. Erikson valued the intimacy of marriage, parenting, and grandparenting above other kinds of relationships, seemingly excluding single people, childless people, and homosexual people. Buss (1975) criticised Erikson for naïveté in his acceptance of the conventional family, and for suggesting that psychological well-being is possible only when an individual is conforming to the conventional expectations of society.

Kohlberg's (1969) theory of moral development also suggested a stage of *self-realisation*, with the highest morality being that of independent behaviour and views, when the individual is able to take a moral stand different from that expressed by the crowd. Kohlberg's concepts are rooted in Western culture that emphasises individual choice rather than family and social cohesion. Gilligan (1982) criticises Kohlberg's assumptions that moral values are equated with autonomy and identifies a gender difference in moral development, with women valuing the connectedness of relationships above the predominantly male value of autonomy, while men have constructed theories that promote the importance of autonomy, which she sees as an essentially male characteristic. She accepts that social contexts affect development and argues that women demonstrate a distinctive, different moral development in three stages (Box 6.4). Gilligan derives much of her thinking from Jung's ideas of an emotional change taking place in midlife. The importance of Gilligan's views, like those of Jung, is to alert us to the likelihood of gender differences in the kinds of relationships that men and women develop throughout the life course. A further application of Gilligan's ideas could be theorised: that old age, and particularly advanced old age reprises the first stage of self-survival; physical dependency in advanced old age may, of necessity, make self-centredness the motivating force.

Box 6.4: Gilligan's Stages of Moral Development for Women (adapted from Gilligan, 1982)

1. The individual cares for her own survival, and seeks relationships in which being cared for is paramount.
2. The individual cares for others, assuming nurturing responsibilities.
3. The individual cares for her own integrity, recognising the need to balance care for self and others.

Synchronic Perceptions from Sociology: Ageing as a Social Problem, Ageing as Discovery, and Ageing with a Social Structure

A review of synchronic perceptions within selected sociological theories explores the individual's relationship to family, group, community, and wider social structures with snapshot views of particular aspects of life experience. The study of human growth and development in the adult years becomes a study of ageing. Social gerontology, the multi-disciplinary study of ageing, argues that ageing comprises three inter-active processes, biological, social, and psychological (Silverman, 1987). In infancy and childhood, the outcome of the ageing process is biological growth leading to physical maturity – beneficial processes that are called *development*. In adult life, the processes of biological change are called *senescence*, indicating the physical deterioration and decline that end in death (Bond et al., 1993). A biological definition of development precludes the possibility of development in adult life and denies recognition of possible psychological, cognitive, and social changes, but Baltes (1979) argued that biological change represents 'strong' development because it unfolds in a uni-directional, sequential, and irreversible pattern. In contrast, psychological, cognitive, and social environmental factors can bring about behavioural change in adult years, representing more variable, unpredictable, and flexible development. Social workers who practise with adults will find social gerontology's view that development is possible in adulthood a helpful concept.

Three dominant themes influence *synchronic* perceptions (Box 6.5). The theme of *ageing as a social problem* that takes a pessimistic view of adult development includes the political economy perspective and disengagement theory. The second theme, *ageing as discovery*, adopts an optimistic view. Some synchronic perceptions occupy a neutral middle ground that imposes neither a pessimistic nor an optimistic view of development, but locate the individual within a *social structure* that allows both positive and negative interpretations to be made.

Box 6.5: Three Themes of Synchronic Perceptions		
Ageing as a social problem	*Ageing as discovery*	*Ageing within a social structure*
Political economy approach	Third Age	Age stratification
Disengagement theory	Activity theory	Socialisation
	Reciprocity theory	Sub-culture
		Labelling
		Minority group
		Continuity

Ageing as a Social Problem: the Political Economy Approach

The *political economy* perspective (Walker, 1980, 1983) analyses the effect of economic and political policies on cohorts rather than on individuals, and a linked concept is *structured dependency* that associates old age with deprivation (Townsend, 1981; Walker, 1981). Older people are viewed as being disempowered and structurally dependent because of their limited access to resources, particularly income.

Phillipson (1982) and Townsend (1986) argued that structured dependency, the key components of which are institutional care, compulsory retirement, and inadequate pensions, contributed to the growth of residential care for older people in the 1980s where the perceived need to minimise risk of accidents led relatives and social workers to pressure older people to trade independence for the safety of residential care. Johnson (1978) criticised the assumption that structured dependency applies to all older people, arguing that occupational pensions provide many older people with economic choice and security. Bebbington (1991) argued that occupational pensions, better health and increased life expectancy result in a more prosperous old age for many.

Disengagement Theory

Cumming and Henry (1961) concluded that ageing leads to a mutual *disengagement* or withdrawal from contact between the older person and others in his or her social system, a withdrawal seen as inevitable and independent of variables such as poverty or illness. Before the ultimate disengagement of death, the individual gives up many of the relationships that have made up the fabric of individual life, so that disengagement from the social world serves as a preparation for death. Disengagement theory fails to account for ambivalence in human motivation, or for the possible substitution of different kinds of involvement when withdrawal from other activities takes place. The social pressures exerted by ageist attitudes in society must be taken into account when deciding whether disengagement is voluntary. Coleman (1994) suggests that two under-appreciated positive contributions of disengagement theory are its attention to personality changes in midlife, and respect for reminiscence as an activity of old age.

Ageing as Discovery: the Third Age, Activity Theory, Reciprocity, and Exchange

Ageing as discovery is a thematic perception that tries to redress some of the extremes of the social problem approach. Discovery takes place on two levels: first, acknowledging and exploring the different individual experiences of old age, and second, viewing old age not as a necessary adjustment to social problems but as non-pathological and a time to discover new experiences and meanings. Silverman (1987) viewed old age as pioneer territory and older people as new pioneers, thus supporting the discovery theme. Coleman (1993: 94–5) discussed ageing as a time of change and new beginnings, a perspective of later life that the theories of

Jung, Maslow, and Levinson promote. Four concepts of the discovery theme are compatible with the aims and values of contemporary social work (Box 6.6).

Box 6.6: Concepts of the Discovery Theme

- Understanding complexities of development and senescence processes without relying on stereotyped explanations.
- Empowering older people as consumers of services and seeking their opinions and views.
- Re-configuring social and economic environments that work to the disadvantage of older people.
- Disseminating research as an advocacy tool to promote a new concept of old age.

The Third Age (Laslett, 1996) is a phase of life that begins when people conclude their parenting roles and retire from work and ends after 15 or 20 years when the individual enters the Fourth Age of increased physical dependency. The Third Age provides people with potential opportunities for self-realisation and personal satisfaction, with examples seen in the increased amount of travel, study, hobbies, and social relationships undertaken by older people.

Activity theory (Havighurst, 1963) asserts the importance of activities for defeating the social problem of old age, thus enabling people to spend old age happily. Bond et al. (1993) criticise its unrealistic expectation that older people can ignore increasing physical frailty and maintain their middle-aged lifestyles, claiming that activity theory's denial of the influence of economic, social, and cultural factors on older people's activity choices is naive.

Exchange and reciprocity theory is concerned with the exchange of tangible and non-tangible goods and services in people's social relationships (Mauss, 1965). Simmons (1945) suggests that older people preserve their status in society to the extent of their ability to continue reciprocal relationships with others, in which power is more or less evenly balanced. Dowd's (1975) exchange theory argues that as people become older (and enter the Fourth Age) they lose more and more of their reciprocal power as their social roles diminish, so that finally they have only the power to decide whether to comply with others' wishes.

Ageing within a Social Structure: Age Stratification, Socialisation, Sub-culture, Labelling, Minority Group, Continuity

Age stratification (Neugarten and Neugarten, 1986; Riley et al., 1972), the first sociological theory to consider the implications of age, divides society into strata according to the boundaries of age, linking it with other stratifications of social class, ethnicity, and race. *Socialisation* (Rosow, 1974) is the process through which individuals learn the values, customs, roles, and skills expected within their culture. Rose (1965) argued a *sub-culture theory* of ageing, suggesting that some older people were beginning to form a distinct, although limited, sub-culture within society because they interacted more with each other than with other groups, and therefore were excluded from full participation in society. Increased longevity, postponement of frailty to the Fourth Age, compulsory retirement, and the growth of retirement communities support the sub-culture of ageing. Fischer (1978) found the concept ambivalent, simultaneously supporting new roles in old age but emphasising age segregation, and suggested that the approach should be called a 'partial culture'.

Labelling theory (Becker, 1963; Berger and Berger, 1976) argues that certain groups of people whom others perceive as different or deviant are subjected to negative interactions and expectations. Older people are labelled as deviant because age is associated with unattractiveness, dependency, and death, thus setting up chain reactions of decreased self-esteem and de-humanisation. The process of *negative stereotyping* (Goffman, 1963) erects a barrier between individuals and groups of people. The remedy, according to Bengtson and Kuypers (1984), is to re-define the status of older people by giving them better economic positions and more power to improve services and environments, a strategy that fits well with social work's emancipatory goals.

Continuity theory (Victor, 1994) emphasises stability in personality and life style. As individuals grow older, they remain essentially the same kind of people they always were, and respond to old age by attempting to preserve their previous personality and lifestyle patterns. Continuity theory recognises differences of class, gender, ethnicity, health, sexuality, spiritual beliefs, and income within the adult population. The *cohort effect* recognises that people born at a certain period in time experience the effects of, and in turn influence, the historical, social, and economic events of their lifetimes. Continuity theory does not impose a single strategy for achieving successful ageing, as do disengagement and activity theories, and it dispenses with moralistic judgements about what constitutes successful ageing (Hughes, 1990). At another level of analysis, it falls into the trap of measuring individuals' 'adjustment' to old age according to previous life styles.

A Theory that Bridges Diachronic and Synchronic Perceptions: Levinson

Instead of stages, Levinson et al. (1978) and Levinson and Levinson (1996) describe diachronic *eras* based on a view of humanity that integrates the contributions of biology, psychology, and sociology. Within each era, individuals build synchronic *life structures* based on societal context, social interaction, and personality. Transition periods lasting up to five years bridge the eras. These are *early adult transition*, *mid-life transition*, and *late life transition*. Influenced by Freud, and more particularly by Jung and Erikson, Levinson suggested that the individual must keep the drive of their youth within each new structure by balancing the needs of the self and the demands of society.

Levinson initially studied men, resulting in gender specific conclusions that described the central components of a man's life as occupation, marriage and family, friendship and peer relationships, ethnicity, religion, and leisure, and a mentor relationship where a young man is guided and inspired by an older man in the work setting. Levinson claimed that it was less likely for women to have a mentor, but later, when Levinson and Levinson (1996) studied women's transitions, they acknowledged that traditional gender influences on women's development were changing as more women sought career choices. Women's eras of development took somewhat different patterns from those of men, with career choices emerging later. Levinson described his eras as universal rather than culturally specific, although his discussion of men seeking to attain 'the dream' is grounded in Western values. Levinson argued that adult development can be undermined by poverty and despair, advocated more flexible patterns of work and leisure, and criticised the excessive masculinity of men.

The Life Course as a Unifying Perception of Human Growth and Development

The flexible concept of the *life course*, which recognises that individuals develop differently throughout their lives and adopt different roles within changing contexts, has supplanted the 'life cycle' approach to development. Studying the life course draws on psychological, sociological, biological, and economic knowledge for an integrated view of development. Blaikie (1992) advocates stitching together ideas from social and behavioural sciences into an interdisciplinary design that emphasises dimensions of time across the life course, the effect of which is to move the study of ageing away from its connotation with social problems. Two types of change take place within the life course: *transitions* over short time spans and specific life events; and *trajectories* that represent longer term changes (Elder and Pavalko, 1993). Neugarten and Datan (1973) identified three different dimensions of time (Box 6.7). These dimensions give the social worker a template for understanding individuals within wider social situations that is consonant with contemporary social work practice.

Box 6.7: Three Dimensions of Time (adapted from Neugarten and Datan, 1973)

- *Life time*, or *individual time* – the chronological age of an individual, closely linked to biological changes.
- *Social time* – the age grading and age expectations established by social systems, including the social system of the family.
- *Historical time* – the succession of social, political, economic and environmental events that take place during the lifetimes of individuals and cohorts of individuals.

Ecological Development Theory

The concept of ecological development fits well with the life course and is also consonant with contemporary practice. Lewin (1936, 1948) conceptualised the person and the environment as interdependent areas of the *life space*. Bronfenbrenner (1979), using Lewin's concepts and Brim's (1975) terminology, presented a model of development called the *ecological paradigm*, described as the configuration of the *person-in-environment*, each influencing the other and portrayed in four interrelated dimensions like a set of nested Russian dolls:

- The micro-system of dyadic and family relationships and social networks.
- The meso-system of relationships between an individual and institutions, functioning as a complex of micro-systems.
- The exo-system of the relationships of an individual with concrete; distant organisations with which there may be no direct contact.
- The macro-system of the over-arching cultural institutions of a society.

Social work practice adopted this theory as an ecological approach to practice (Germain and Gitterman, 1996; Jack, 1997) in which the social worker notes the importance of environmental layers on individual development.

Attachment

Bowlby's (1951, 1969) theory of attachment enlarges on certain aspects of Freud's work and highlights the importance of attachment between mother and child for healthy development, arguing that mother-child attachment needs to be established in early infancy and maintained to ensure psychological well-being. Bowlby theorised three phases of attachment: *the safety phase*, the *secure* base for exploration, and the *emotional relationship* between the child and the mother. By 18 months, *monotropy* or the close attachment relationship with the mother would be established. Bowlby suggested that these initial attachment patterns would probably be repeated in relationships in later life. Later, Bowlby was criticised for emphasising the mother as sole caregiver. Rutter (1972) modified Bowlby's findings, concluding that the constant nurturing figure necessary for the infant's optimum development could be a caregiver other than the mother.

Ainsworth et al. (1978) further developed the theory of attachment with the 'strange situation' experiment, identifying three types of attachment:

- *Secure attachment*: in which the infant feels distressed when the constant caregiver is away but recovers on their return.
- *Insecure* or *anxious avoidant attachment*: in which the infant shows few signs of distress when the caregiver is not there and on their return, does not seek contact with the caregiver.
- *Insecure resistant* or *anxious ambivalent attachment*: in which the infant is distressed when the caregiver is away, and when reunited, resists contact but does not avoid the caregiver.

Main and Soloman (1986) theorised a further type:

- *Disorganised attachment*: in which the infant does not play freely or respond to contact, demonstrating a mixed pattern of approach to, and avoidance of, the caregiver.

Attachment theory was extremely influential in changing social work practice with children. In the 1950s and 1960s James Robertson, a psychiatric social worker, and Joyce Robertson, a psychotherapist, filmed the reactions of very young children to brief separations from their parents (Robertson, 1967–71). These films convinced professionals of the validity of the theory of attachment, which led to the closure of residential nurseries that up to the mid-1960s were standard provision for infants looked after by the local authority, and changed policies for sick children in hospital to permit more contact between parents and children. Attachment theory changed social workers' decisions for the placement of children resulting from their increased understanding of the effects of separation from the constant caregiver.

? Question for Reflection

Try to use the SCIE (2003) template (discussed at the beginning of the chapter) to attribute the sources of knowledge of the theory of attachment. Did the theory originate with organisations, practitioners, the policy community, researchers, or users and carers, or a combination of these? Then evaluate the attachment theory according to the SCIE criteria (also discussed at the beginning of the chapter) of transparency, accuracy, purposivity, utility, propriety, accessibility, and specificity.

Cultural Specificity or Universal Theory?

The child development theories that were developed in Western Europe and America are recognised as culturally specific. To what extent are these theories applicable to the rest of the world? Kagitcibasi (1996), an American-educated Turkish psychologist, conducted an ambitious research project that explored attachment, child development, and cultural factors within the Turkish Early Years Enrichment Project, which provided educational, health, and social enrichment programmes for young children and their parents (resembling aspects of Head Start in the USA and Sure Start in the UK). She theorised that in bringing up their children, working-class Turkish mothers living in urban centres promoted the cultural values of a society that had a high degree of 'relatedness', valuing close family bonds. The mothers did not recognise their children's need for autonomy and development of individual capability, with the result that their children were falling behind in attaining cognitive competence.

Kagitcibasi recommended a programme of home-based enhanced environmental support for these young children to encourage 'emotional interdependence' between mothers and children rather than passive compliance to externally defined child rearing practices. By empowering the mothers rather than using a deficit model, the children's cognitive development was better supported as mothers began to recognise their children's developmental needs and encourage different kinds of behaviour. The findings that emerged from her study support some Western child rearing theories (perhaps because she studied parents and children whose lives were experiencing transition to an urban society). Kagitcibasi suggested ways in which traditional Turkish cultures of child rearing could be enhanced by adapting new ideas. Her study recognises shared themes that bridge cultural specificities – an important finding for social workers who work in cross cultural communities.

Loss

Bowlby was concerned with loss as the opposite of attachment. Kubler-Ross (1969) illuminated understanding of death, dying, and reactions to loss, theorising that although doctors and family members typically avoided discussing the onset of death with a mortally ill patient, the patients themselves wanted to share their feelings and be given truthful information about their conditions. She identified five stages through which dying people pass: *denial* of impending death; *anger* at having to die; *bargaining* with fate or God; *depression;* and *acceptance* of death. The stages do not always appear in this sequence, some stages may not be evident, or the stages may repeat. Other contributors to theories of loss include Worden (1991), who conceptualised mourning as tasks through which the mourner must work: acceptance of the reality of the death; suffering the pain of grief; and adjustment to the new situation.

Parkes' (1998) stages of bereavement include reactions of shock that result in:

- *Numbness or denial* when the bereaved individual seems to show no emotion.
- *Yearning, longing, and searching* for the lost person.
- *Depression and despair* as the loss is realised, often accompanied by confused thoughts; and
- *Acceptance and recovery*, when the loss is accommodated and the mourner is ready to move forward with their life.

Parkes argues that people construct an assumed world about life and death, and do not want to face the fact that we all have to die. When expressions of grief are suppressed, which happens frequently in contemporary society, ripple effects can affect individual and family functioning. Anniversary reactions may take place on the date of the loss. Individuals who work through their emotions may become more reflective and receptive to human emotions. This understanding can be transferred to situations of loss other than the death of a loved one. Stroebe and Schut (1999) developed a concept of processing grief by asking bereaved individuals to keep diaries, which revealed that the bereaved individuals swung backwards and forwards between loss-oriented positions (bad days) and restoration positions (good days) without needing to go through all the stages. Pitt-Aikens and Thomas Ellis (1986, 1989) promoted a different understanding of loss (Box 6.8). The perceptive social worker recognises that feelings of loss are triggered not only by death but also by events that may include divorce, unemployment, retirement, and ended relationships. Situations involving sexual abuse of children can trigger reactions akin to mourning and loss. Bradbury (1986) suggests that the principles of grief counselling can be adapted for work with children who have been sexually abused and their families, because abused children lose their trust in adults and also experience loss of their known family structure. The child and family caregivers may feel shocked and first deny that abuse took place; then feel responsible and guilty. Anger may be suppressed; individuals are likely to blame each other; the child may continue to idealise the perpetrator unrealistically, and behaviour may regress to irrational and confused actions. Sadness and depression may persist, but with skilled help and support, the child and the family caregivers can gain the strength to face their myriad emotions, including expressing their anger, and acknowledge the reality of what has happened to their family (Case Study 6.2).

Box 6.8: A Different View of Loss

Tom Pitt-Aikens, a child psychiatrist, and Alice Thomas Ellis, a novelist, collaborated on two books (1986, 1989) that provided a different explanation of the concept of loss. They conceptualised the *good authority* as a complex presence in family and organisational life exerting benign controls that play a conscious and unconscious part in individuals' lives by protecting them from pressures to distort perceptions of self and behaviour. Because unacknowledged loss of the good authority might be a factor in the delinquent behaviour of young people, restoring the 'good authority' could be the key to resolving behavioural problems.

Case Study 6.2 – Marilyn, an Abused Child

Marilyn, an eight-year-old child, lived with her mother Karen and Karen's partner Mick. Marilyn's father had left the family some years ago when Marilyn was six months old and has not maintained contact. Mick moved in with Karen and Marilyn a year ago. After six months together, Marilyn's behaviour changed from being an outgoing sociable child to a withdrawn worried looking little girl. Marilyn's teacher at school, whom Marilyn trusted, became concerned. Marilyn told the teacher about Mick's behaviour towards her, and the teacher realised that Mick was sexually abusing Marilyn on a regular basis. The social services department was contacted, and a social worker assigned to investigate. As the details of the allegations of abuse emerged, Mick left the relationship. Karen's emotional reactions to the revelations were at first denial and disbelief, then anger and blame. Then she became immobilised with depression as she realised the impact of the abuse on her daughter Marilyn and the shattering of her own relationship with Mick. She looked back with regret but also seemed to idolise and mourn the loss of the happy days she remembered. Marilyn in contrast displayed a numbness and lack of emotion.

The social worker's approach to this case should be informed by awareness of stages of grief and loss expressed by Karen and Marilyn: denial, anger, depression, searching, numbness. Intervention should help mother and daughter work through their emotional suffering and move towards emotional acceptance of the reality of the situation and eventual recovery.

Resilience

Social workers have become interested in the concept of resilience to help explain why some children and adults do not make the best use of opportunities that might help them to overcome earlier deprivation, and why other children do use available opportunities and develop well. Grotberg (1997) defined resilience as a capacity allowing either a person, a group, or community to prevent, minimise, or overcome damaging effects of adversity.

Werner (1989) and her colleagues (1982) undertook a 30-year longitudinal study of all the children born in 1955 on the 'Garden Island' of Kauai, in Hawaii – a total of 698 children from multi-ethnic backgrounds. She focused on high-risk children from poor families who had experienced pre-natal stress, and whose parents were experiencing problems that included poverty, alcoholism, and mental health issues so that she could explore the effect of early disadvantage on the children's progress to adulthood. Werner discovered that many (but not all) of the children, despite initial problems associated with difficult births and their families' poverty, grew up to lead successful adult lives.

Over time, the effects from the stress of difficult childbirth diminished, depending on the quality of the continuing environment. Those who experienced beneficial environments on the whole did better; however, one third of the children whose day-to-day childhood environments continued to reflect poverty, conflict, mental illness, and other disadvantaging conditions grew up to be competent adults who formed positive stable relationships, found success in employment, and were interested in improving themselves and caring for others.

To explain the progress of the successful children, Werner identified certain *protective* factors:

- The children's personalities were sociable, active, alert, and responsive, and the children were able to ask for help when they needed it.
- The children came from families who had fewer children born at relatively widely spaced intervals.
- The children had established a close bond with at least one caregiver in their first years.
- The children found sources of emotional support outside the family from teachers, youth leaders, and peers.

These children grew up believing that they could influence their destinies and that life had meaning. In contrast to these resilient children, the vulnerable children who remained so as adults had a sense of meaninglessness about life and felt powerless to control their destinies. Werner's study remains important for identifying factors of resilience. Social workers and other workers can use this and similar studies to inform their practice decisions. The Bowlby concept of attachment is affirmed but also modified because studies of resilience point to the importance of additional factors in the children themselves and in their environment.

Kindertransport Children: a Study of Loss and Resilience

Social workers can learn about responses to loss and resilience from the historical accounts (Gershon, 1966; Leverton and Lowensohn, 1990) of children brought to Britain from Nazi Germany on the Kindertransport programme. The World Movement for the Care of Children from Germany, a British initiative, sent trainloads of children up to 17-years-old to the UK for refuge. The first transport of 320 children arrived in early December 1938 and by September 1939, 9354 children had come, of whom 7482 were Jewish. Some of the children were sponsored and placed with relatives or friends but most were placed with strangers – foster parents who were chosen without much prior investigation of their suitability. The children had to learn a new language, their clothes and manners were a source of amusement to British people, and they did not know what had happened to their parents. Years later after the war, they learned that most of the parents had perished in the Holocaust. Some of the children remained in the UK; others emigrated eventually to the USA and Israel.

In 1966, Gershon, a former Kindertransport child, collected individual testimonies from the adults who had been Kindertransport children and who were then in their late 20s to early 40s.

Leaving

- I remember crying bitterly and saying: 'Please, Mummy, please don't send me away'. I was eleven years old at the time.

Becoming

- I went to university and began at last to feel that I was responsible for what I made of my life, an exciting discovery. It had taken a long time to accept that my parents were dead, and that family life as it had been would never return, and once this fact was firmly established it seemed possible to make a new start.

Identity

- For a long time, I found saying that I was Jewish just as difficult as saying that I was German.

Belonging

- I am no longer a refugee because I no longer feel the need of physical and moral help. I do have problems, both physical and spiritual, but I feel more ready to grapple with them than I once did, and am no longer as willing to relapse in self-pity, to blame external circumstances and long for outside help to extract me from my difficulties. To me one of the greatest dangers and tragedies of being a refugee is that one loses one's identity, one's self-respect and the ability to cope with new situations. (1966: 19, 121, 132, 167)

Other Kindertransport children wrote about their experiences. Leverton and Lowehnsohn (1990), former Kindertransport children, present later reminiscences. Kramer's poetry (1994a, 1994b, 1997) expresses feelings of loss arising from the experience of being a Kindertransport child. Novelists have explored the Kindertransport's impact: Sebald (2001) portrays a middle-aged man searching for his identity after growing up as a refugee placed in a loveless foster home. Knowledge of his earlier identity is denied him, and his foster parents die without providing any information about his origins. Lively (2001) wrote an autobiographical account of her youth during the Second World War that portrays her aunt's work as a volunteer social worker resettling refugees including some Kindertransport children.

The testimonies of the Kindertransport children can help social workers understand responses to loss, and children's experiences of foster homes and hostels at a time when there was little available help from professional social workers. Issues include their struggle to understand why their lives were disrupted, and what had happened to their parents. The Kindertransport children's efforts to establish a new identity in a new country depended on receiving help from strangers, and on gaining acceptance for their blended identities developed from their Jewish and European heritage and their British experiences. Social workers will recognise themes of attachment, loss, resilience, and the importance of giving appropriate help.

Law

Knowledge of law is specified by all the countries of the UK in their requirements for social work education (CCW, 2004; DH, 2002b; NISCC, 2003; SE, 2003), and by the Benchmark statement (QAA, 2000) and the National Occupational Standards (Topss UK Partnership, 2002). Howe (1986) argued that the state controls social work practice through the operation of the law, but there are areas for debate and development due to the changing nature of the law and different views of the relationship between social work practice and law. Law for social workers includes knowledge of: legislation about human rights; provision and regulation of benefits and services; protection from harm; criminal justice.

Social workers who work outside statutory agencies may not themselves exercise statutory powers and duties, but need to be familiar with regulations and statutes. Statutes of law that are specific to each country of the UK supply a framework for the tradition of common law. Acts of Parliament state what has to be done; statutory instruments supply details, and some Acts have schedules or rules that explain implementation, assisted by circulars and codes of practice.

Braye and Preston-Shoot (2005) present an overview of the position of law within social work knowledge, arguing that social workers need to reflect on the relationship between social work and the law and respond appropriately as the relationship changes over time. Complexity potentially can confuse: laws are constantly changing; new legislation is added to old; and some new Acts incorporate and 'tidy up' previous legislation. Social workers should appreciate the basic tenets of the law in relation to social work before they begin to practise, and learn how to use legal knowledge effectively. Acquiring and updating knowledge of law must be part of social workers' continuing professional development (Reder et al., 1993). An overview of a range of socio-legal knowledge and skills useful to social workers is presented in Box 6.9. To these must be added the caveat that social workers' socio-legal knowledge and skills must take into account the balancing dilemma of having to consider control as well as empowerment issues in making decisions.

Box 6.9: An Overview of Socio-legal Knowledge, Skills, and Transferable Skills		
Socio-legal knowledge (Cull and Roche, 2002)	*Socio-legal skills*	*Transferable skills for socio-legal practice*
A critical perception of: • legal language • key legal concepts • knowledge of how laws are made • discretionary areas in decision-making • policy issues behind legislative change	Competence to: • argue cases • challenge decisions (Jankovic and Green, 1981; Madden, 2000) • research legal issues to assist with individual decision-making and collective campaigning (Madden, 2000; Madden and Wayne, 2003)	• advocacy • problem solving • report writing • analysing and synthesising information • providing evidence • negotiating and decision-making (Madden and Wayne, 2003)

Human rights legislation (discussed also in Chapter 3) is important for practice. Morris (2000) recognises the implications for disabled people of the Human Rights Act's provision for the right to liberty, respect for private and family life, freedom of thought and expression, and freedom from inhuman or degrading treatment when she criticises social exclusion agendas for focusing on educational achievement and paid employment and ignoring prejudice, harassment, and denial of dignity. The Disability Rights Commission and the Disability Discrimination Act have begun to address issues about human rights and entitlements, but Morris argues that disabled people still live in a *disabling society* that denies human and civil rights.

Butler (2004) argues that although the Human Rights Act 1998 (in force from 2000 and based on the European Convention on Human Rights) can help to promote social justice and protect the rights of disadvantaged people (to liberty, right to life, fair hearing, private and family life, freedom of conscience, religion, expression and association, and freedom from degrading treatment and discrimination), little attention has been given to encouraging community based voluntary organisations to use the Act for improving service provision. Many voluntary organisations do not recognise the Act's relevance for promoting social justice, and find the Act difficult to use.

From 2007, the Commission for Equality and Human Rights will provide information and advice on how to apply the Act, and it could do this by working with voluntary community-based agencies to link the Act's implementation with social justice goals of dignity, respect, equality, empowerment, and participation. A human rights framework would give the voluntary sector tools to lobby for changes in policy and practice, and empower individuals. The professional social worker could play a part in promoting this emancipatory agenda.

Older People, Mental Health and Disability

Older People

Social services designate people who use services as being 'old' at the ages 60 or 65, sometimes shifting service provision to older people from one resource to another when 'old age' is reached, which takes no account of the continuity of the life course and the uniqueness of individuals. Within the overall designation of *adult services*, mental health, disability, and learning disability are usually made specific, while older people are not considered so precisely.

Demographic changes have resulted in larger numbers of people surviving into the 'old-old' Fourth Age. The majority of disabled people are older people who become disabled as they reach old age, but some older people have lifelong physical disabilities, or learning disabilities and mental health problems that span the life course. Dementia is a particular issue for some older people. The challenge of acquiring knowledge for practice with older people is to avoid stereotyping old age.

As well as knowledge of human growth and development, particular knowledge for practice with older people might include a review of older people's contributions to society, and an examination of the practitioner's personal values and attitudes to old age. Does the social worker believe that older individuals can learn, develop, change, and contribute to society? If so, then the social worker will be more likely to want to develop rehabilitative services and new alternatives to care that promote independence and respect. If the social worker holds a view that all older people are vulnerable, he or she will think first of services that protect them and keep them safe. Both kinds of services are needed for different situations.

Mental Health

Mental health used to be taught within social work qualifying programmes as the classification of mental illnesses. Over time, questions were raised about the arbitrary nature of diagnoses. For example, an alternative explanation for the cluster of behaviours known as 'borderline personality' might be: difficult behaviour triggered by adverse social circumstances. The author, who worked in the USA, recalls the chief of psychiatry at a regional hospital in Pennsylvania in the late 1970s announcing that the American Medical Association had agreed by a majority vote to remove homosexuality from the list of psychiatric illnesses, an example that illustrates how an explanation can be socially determined and therefore be subject to change.

The conventional treatment for severe mental illness used to be institutionalisation in locked wards, but this convention changed irrevocably with the introduction of drugs that could control symptoms and thus increase the feasibility of community-based care. This change also resulted from the attacks mounted by the literature of dysfunction, and the moral imperative to promote freedom. The anti-psychiatry movement of the 1960s is typified by Szasz' (1960) attack on psychiatric illness as a myth, and his assertion that people considered 'mentally ill' were individuals whose behaviour indicated that they did not share a consensus view of society. Szasz was a Hungarian born opponent of fascism who survived the Second World War, emigrated to the USA, and possibly as a consequence of his life experiences, subsequently opposed governmental powers and the medical profession's power over patients.

Mental health problems, often linked with problems of poverty, isolation, discrimination, homelessness, and unemployment, are more widespread than the public cares to admit. Mental health is a priority for the NHS's strategic reforms, yet Butler (2004) argues that mental health has not made particularly good progress in raising standards because of lingering attitudes of stigma towards mental illness, lack of trust towards professionals, and underfunding of services. The influence of the social model with its demands for emancipatory practices, combined with the intentions of the NHS and Community Care Act 1990 to move towards demand-led services, led to goals for more user involvement in service decisions (Bracken and Thomas, 2001) and inclusion strategies for people with multiple problems.

Human rights policies are being implemented, but the public remains concerned about the risk to public order. These clashes of concerns do not help the development agenda for mental health improvement. Although user and carer groups are being set up to promote participation, Rankin (2004) claims that not much progress has occurred in involving service users in decision-making about their own care, and not all users have a care plan as promised by the National Service Framework for Mental Health (DH, 1999a). As noted in previous chapters, the take up of direct payments by service users, including users of mental health services, has been low. Plans for improving mental health services recognise the need to eliminate discriminatory treatment of ethnic minorities (who are more likely to be poor and be diagnosed with mental health problems), to provide more woman-centred services, more support for carers, and to tackle multiple needs.

Early intervention teams, crisis intervention teams, and assertive outreach are some of the new approaches designed to reach people with untreated or incipient psychosis in the early stages and offer effective treatment that will prevent future decline. The social worker's role as approved social worker/mental health social worker contributing to decisions about compulsory admission to mental hospital will change with new legislation. New roles for proposed intervention raise issues about the future of community mental health teams, within which social workers play an essential part.

Disability

The social model of disability, which originated within the disability movement, is one of the most important conceptualisations for practice to emerge within the last 25 years. Academics who are disabled (Barnes, 1991; Finkelstein, 1980, 1981; Oliver, 1989, 1996) began to formalise, research, and disseminate the social model, so that disability studies with strong links to sociology is now an established field of academic learning in many UK universities (Barnes and Mercer, 2003). 'Disability' comprises both physical disabilities and learning disabilities, although learning disabilities are usually designated specifically and should not be considered within a designation of mental health. Social work has been strongly influenced by the social model, and has adapted its principles as a *social model of intervention* that accords with basic human rights. The social model is important not only to disabled people, but to other service users. As discussed in Chapter 2, the social model locates causal factors of problems (impairment) within society rather than within the individual; and therefore the remedy is not to pathologise individuals but to demand that society changes. The British Council of Organisations of Disabled People (BCODP) (2005: 18) described impairment and disability:

> Impairment is when a person has an injury, condition or a disease for some time. It can affect the brain or body. It can also cause pain, make a person feel tired, affect the way the person talks or mean they may not remember things very well. Impairment does not cause disability and impairment does not make discrimination alright.
>
> Disability is a disadvantage or restriction on doing things that is the fault of society and the way it is run. The world takes little account of people who have impairments and leaves them out and stops them doing things other people do. Disability is discrimination very much like racism and sexism.

The success of the disability movement can be attributed to its willingness to adopt a collective approach, to give voice to disabled people, and to conceptualise and disseminate issues through academic studies and research. The collective approach began in 1976 when UPIAS (Union of the Physically Impaired Against Segregation) began to promote the social model. Then in 1981 the BCODP was established as a UK-wide umbrella organisation of many smaller organisations that each represent a particular disability. It now provides a collective organisation for 126 groups with a membership of 350,000 disabled people, and is part of the international Disabled People's Movement that promotes full equality and participation in society.

Morris (2000) discusses a framework (used in her research with disabled children and their families 1998) whose four principles reflect the disability movement's aims for the inclusion of disabled people: rights and entitlements; social model of disability; needs-led approaches; and promoting choice and control. She argues that the disabled people's movement wants the social justice of *rights* and *entitlements* for citizens (who include disabled people) rather than *care* or *social welfare*. The designation of *social care* as an embracing identity for social services and social work appears an unfortunate designation in the light of Morris' comments.

Research provides evidence of practice shortfalls. Dearden and Becker (2000) found that disabled children were not receiving an assessment under the Chronically Sick and Disabled Persons Act 1970 that would establish entitlements to practical assistance in the home, and they were not receiving a full assessment of needs under the Community Care Act 1990 and the Disabled Persons Act 1986. Morris (1998) revealed that social workers assessing the needs of disabled children usually did not take into account children's needs and wishes, one of the requirements of the Children Act 1989, because they claimed that the children's level of disability prevented communication, a finding replicated by Abbott and Morris' (2000) research about the placement of disabled children in residential schools.

Feminist writers, including Morris (2000), Crow (1996), French (1993, 1994) and Thomas (1999) explored different effects of various kinds of impairment on disabled people's lives. Morris (2000) claims that by focusing on external barriers, disabled people seemingly ignore their experiences of sensory, physical, and intellectual impairments and deny the reality that most disabled people are women over 60 with a chronic or progressive painful condition like arthritis, or have learning disabilities or mental health problems. In similar vein, Shakespeare and Watson (2002) examined the British academic and political debates about the social model and argued the timeliness of moving beyond the social model because its success as a virtually unchallengeable ideology is actually a weakness. The social model is a modernist theory seeking a meta-explanation, but for contemporary society, a post-modern approach that acknowledges complexity would be more appropriate.

Shakespeare and Erickson (2000) argue that a social theory of disability should include all the dimensions of disabled people's experiences: bodily, psychological, cultural, social, and political. Shakespeare and Watson's alternative view is an *embodied ontology* that considers *impairment* and *disability* as different locations on a continuum of experiences, accepting all human beings as impaired, frail, and vulnerable, but acknowledging that not all humans are oppressed by impairment and illness. They argue the appropriateness of exploring the link between *impairment* and *embodiment* that comprises the experiences of the body.

Children and Young People

Services for children and young people lie at the heart of social work. Social work with children and families will take place within new partnerships that involve education. The social pedagogue (discussed in Chapter 3) practises an alternative form of social work. As in the instance of disability, social workers need to note these new developments and position themselves appropriately. An interpretation of 'social work' that is broader than *care* and *control* could provide a unifying approach to the new roles and approaches being developed outside social work, as long as responsibility for child protection remains clear. The transfer of responsibility for services to children and families in England away from the DH to the DfES symbolises the shift in thinking from *care* and *control* to the wider purpose of *promoting children and young people's development*. This change in thinking is present in other countries of the UK that have avoided the administrative divide of children's services and adult social care. The maxim of *care* and *control* is now set within a wider aim of *development* which has made a change in terminology necessary. Social work with children and young people used to be known as *child care*, a historical reminder of the legacy of the Children's Departments whose social workers were known as *child care officers*. *Child care* now refers to the work of child minders, foster parents, and other staff who provide physical and emotional care to children.

An example of a successful partnership arrangement is the UK-wide Early Years Development and Child Care Partnerships (Box 6.10). A different kind of partnership has been found necessary for improving the educational attainment of children who leave care, where social care's record of achievement has not been impressive. Young people who left care were unprepared to manage money, lacked support, and were not provided with the means to continue with their education and training. Too high a proportion of these young people experienced substance misuse, homelessness, and mental health problems. To help remedy this situation, the Children (Leaving Care) Act 2000 came into effect in October 2001, and applies in England and Wales only (Box 6.11).

Box 6.10: Partnership Arrangements: Early Years Development and Child Care Partnerships

Early Years Development and Childcare Partnerships (EYDCPs) evolved out of the National Child Care Strategy launched in 1998, when all local authorities were directed to set up EYDCPs. Partnerships aim to ensure that affordable, accessible child care is available to all children aged 0–14 (up to 16 for disabled children and children with Special Educational Needs) through increasing provision that includes breakfast clubs, after school clubs, holiday playschemes, extended care in pre-school wrap around care childminder networks. The broader aims are to ensure that every three- and four-year-old child can access a high quality free education place; increase the skills of the existing child care workforce; provide information and training for people wanting to work in early years and child care; make information on children's services more readily available; and offer specific support in developing care for children with disabilities, special educational needs and those who are most disadvantaged.

EYDCPs conduct an annual audit to identify and map the child care provision across their area and highlight any gaps that may exist within particular age groups, communities, social groups or at particular times of the year. This information is used to develop an annual local Implementation

(Continued)

Box 6.10: *(Continued)*

Plan for the DfES. Partnerships typically comprise local government children's services, education, and community services, brought together in a partnership board whose members include parents and representatives from local communities. The staff's professional identities include nursery nurses, social workers, teachers, and community development workers. Because the purpose of EYDCPs is strategic rather than directly operational, partnerships are more likely to avoid rivalries and build successful interdisciplinary approaches.

Box 6.11: Care Leavers

The Children (Leaving Care) Act 2000 aims to ensure that a local authority will provide help until a young person reaches the age of 21 and in some cases 24. The Act seeks to ensure that young people do not leave care until they are ready, and that they receive more effective support once they have left. The Act defines eligible, relevant, and formerly relevant children who may be covered by the provisions of the Act, and provides support stepped according to the young person's age. The support includes assessment of needs, a pathway plan, accommodation, financial assistance, and assistance with education, employment, or training, co-ordinated by a designated personal adviser, who does not have to be social work qualified, but must have close links with the Connexions service.

Youth work is a specialist universal caring service separate from social work whose main professional roles are carried out by youth workers, careers guidance officers, and in England, Connexions personal advisers. Children's Trusts are likely to bring together staff working with young people in statutory and voluntary organisations to implement the Green Paper (DfES, 2005) on youth. The Green Paper's three strands cover:

- 'Places to go and things to do' including providing opportunities for volunteering and mentoring.
- Better support for those who have more serious problems, including an integrated package of support with a designated lead professional as a single point of contact.
- Better information, advice and guidance on issues that matter to them, delivered in the way they want.

The National Youth Agency and the National Association of Connexions Partnerships, who have convened reference groups, promote the view that young people should have the potential to arrive at solutions and opportunities by working in partnership with stakeholders.

Social work practice with children and young people will continue to focus on child protection, but the wider pictures of intervention will place more emphasis on supporting children and families with new programmes that emphasise development. Legislation will regulate the exchange of information and the creation of new ways of working in partnership, the two weaknesses of child protection work that were revealed in a succession of enquiries that followed the deaths of vulnerable children who were let down by the protection systems (Reder et al., 1993). The demands for multi-professional practice will lead to partnerships where social workers practise alongside other workers, including child care workers, education welfare officers, youth workers, careers guidance officers, learning mentors, health visitors, and school nurses in children's trusts and children's centres. Partnerships with parents will become an established way of working.

Social work skills will be required for direct work with children and working in partnership to undertake assessments. Knowledge for working with children and young people will emphasise law, theories of attachment, loss, and resilience, but also should include a focus on combating substance misuse, and strategies for preventing teenaged pregnancies. The balancing of control and regulation with empowerment will continue to be a challenging feature of practice with children and young people. The professional social worker may be expected to take the lead responsibility for child protection, while other caring services take the lead in developing the more empowering forms of intervention. Social workers' ability to adopt multiple roles may not be fully utilised if specialist responsibilities become the predominant mode of multi-professional practice.

Criminal Justice Social Work and Probation

Criminal justice social work and probation practice with offenders have a long history in the UK. In England and Wales, probation services remained separate from the social services departments that were established following the Seebohm Report in 1970. In 1992, National Standards for probation officers were introduced in England and Wales. The Criminal Justice and Court Services Act 2000 abolished separate probation services in England and Wales and created a national probation service organised to be coterminous with police authorities. The National Offender Management Service will bring the Prison and Probation Services together. In Scotland, probation officers ceased working in a separate service after 1970 and became part of social work departments, where they are known as criminal justice social workers rather than probation officers. The Scottish Office directly funds criminal justice social work in contrast to other specialisms in social work.

Scotland introduced Children's Hearings in 1971 with the Social Work (Scotland) Act 1968, now incorporated in the Children (Scotland) Act 1995. Hearings replaced juvenile courts with a more informal system of decision-making for children and young people under 16 who commit offences or are in need of care or protection. Referrals from the police or other agencies are made to an official Reporter on children and young people who makes an initial investigation. If the Reporter decides that the referral should go further, they may set up a Children's Hearing, which is a lay tribunal comprising three trained male and female volunteers who meet with the child and the child's parents in a private informal meeting and then decide on the kinds of supervision required.

In 1991, Scotland introduced National Standards for criminal justice social work. In Northern Ireland, a non-governmental public body called the Probation Board is responsible for the work of probation officers who carry out risk assessments, provide pre-sentence reports to the courts, and provide statutory supervision of offenders in the community and a welfare service to prisoners.

As discussed in Chapter 4, the probation officer's guiding maxim was to 'advise, assist, and befriend'. Traditionally, the probation officer has always had to balance *care* and *control*, with their main focus on preparing pre-sentence reports that assist the court in its sentencing decisions; and to supervise probationers and parolees in the community. Since 1990, probation in England and Wales has been transformed by new reforming legislation that some probation officers did not entirely welcome. In England and Wales, probation officer training was made separate from social work in the 1990s, unlike criminal justice social workers and probation officers in Scotland and Northern Ireland, who qualify as social workers. Following recruitment and selection processes, trainee probation officers in England and Wales are appointed to particular areas and are paid a salary while they study two years part time for the Diploma in Probation Studies that leads to the Community Justice NVQ Level 4 and an undergraduate degree.

Since 1982, a flood of legislation (The Criminal Justice Act 1982, 1991, 1993; the Criminal Justice and Public Order Act 1994; the Crime [Sentences] Act 1997; and the Criminal Justice and Court Services Act 2000) has led to an increased emphasis on supervision, risk management, surveillance and electronic tagging, enforcement of court orders and licences after prison, cognitive behavioural interventions, and restorative justice in place of the casework approach that had been practised by probation officers. During this period, the prison population rose. The 1998 Crime and Disorder Act in England and Wales introduced the concept of multi-agency partnerships, set up the YJB as a separate agency, and established multi-professional YOTs, whose members include social workers.

Smith (2002) argued that prevention of crime and public safety are issues that criminal justice social workers and probation officers need to address, and notes the success of social inclusion initiatives such as Sure Start that have long range outcomes. Because of the high attention devoted to crime and offending by public opinion, criminal justice policy is volatile and has abandoned the 'nothing works' philosophy that dominated the mid-1970s to the end of the 1980s. The focus of probation changed to a less social work specific mission, while during the same period, criminology became a highly popular area of academic study.

Carers

'Carers' are individuals who provide care on an unpaid basis for a relative or a friend who needs ongoing support because of age, disability, or illness. Carers may be parents of a disabled child or parents of an adult with a mental health problem, whose caring roles are more demanding and protracted than many other parents because of the particular circumstances affecting their child, or they may be the spouse, child, or sibling of a frail older person. A 'young carer' is defined as an individual under 18 who supports another family member who is disabled or ill. According to the National Carers Strategy (DH, 1999b):

- One in eight people in Britain (almost 6 million people) is a carer.
- Women are more likely than men to be carers.
- Some 855,000 carers provide support for over 50 hours per week.
- Three-fifths of carers provide support to a disabled individual.
- Three-fifths of carers receive no regular visitor support services.
- Two-thirds of working-age carers work in paid employment as well as carrying out their caring roles.

Growing awareness of the importance of carers, especially since the implementation of the National Health Service and Community Care Act 1990 in 1993, led to research, raised awareness, and then legislation to provide more support and a national carers strategy. Carers provide essential help and without this support many more vulnerable individuals would need to enter residential or nursing care. The Carers (Representation and Services) Act 1995 provided carers with the right to have their ability to care assessed. The National Service Framework for Mental Health (DH, 1999a) stipulated that carers would receive their own care plan to assess their individual caring, physical, and mental health needs. A 2003 survey of carers who were in touch with the organisation Rethink claimed that almost half thought that carers' support had improved, but one in six stated that they had lacked local support (Pinfold and Corry, 2003).

Morris (1998) argued that the identification of children of disabled parents as 'young carers' undermines disabled lone parent mothers' statutory rights to practical assistance in the home including required adaptations and equipment; and that praise for young carers diverts attention from the way disabled parents' rights have been overlooked. The social model of disability's view is that disabled parents should not have to rely on their children for help. Subsequent to Morris' research, the Carers and Disabled Children Act 2000 provided for assessment of the needs of young carers aged 16–17, to be certain that caring is in their best interest and is not a substitute for the right to support of the person being cared for. Under this legislation, assessments can be offered to the carer even when the person being cared for has refused an assessment, and the parents of a disabled child have the right to an assessment. Local authorities can make direct payments to carers, including parent carers and young carers as well as to persons being cared for.

The National Strategy for Carers (DH, 1999b) recognises that many carers are in paid employment and therefore employers need to adopt more flexible 'carer-friendly' employment policies. The Strategy calls for better *information, support*, and *care* to be provided for all carers, urging a cultural change so that carers are respected rather than pitied. Carers may feel responsible for, and perhaps guilty about the disability or mental illness of their relative, but they are a potential source of information about the well-being of the family member who is being cared for, and professionals should view them as such.

Arksey (2002) argued that the services that carers want will vary and a single model of service provision will not suit all carers. Crossroads, an established national charity that provides in-home care and breaks for carers to reduce the stress that arises from the caring role, is one example of carer support.

▶▶| **Conclusion**

This chapter has selected certain areas of knowledge, but lack of space prevents coverage of all the important fields of knowledge for social work. Knowledge for practice consists of a kaleidoscope of information with constantly evolving understandings, so that professional social workers must update their knowledge continuously and scrutinise new information with critical reflective eyes. As well as adopting multiple roles, social workers also need to adopt multiple 'knowledges' to inform their practice. For contemporary practice, those knowledges will need to consider the principle of partnership.

A note of caution must be sounded about the link between knowledge and power. Hugman (1991) argues that the caring professions construct knowledge about people's situations that prevents professionals from becoming aware of people's real concerns, and Foucault believed that knowledge is used to subjugate others and that no one escapes from submitting himself or herself to some form of this subjugation (Parton and O'Byrne, 2000: 51–2). Certain kinds of knowledge (usually those of people who use services and their carers) have tended to be marginalised and discredited, and their communications are not heard. Social workers have a part to play in challenging accepted understandings of 'knowledge' by listening to the experiences of service users and carers as well as drawing on knowledges for practice drawn from formal research, the policy community, practice itself, and the service delivery context (SCIE, 2003).

📖 **Further Reading**

Brayne, H. and Carr, H. (2005) *Law for Social Workers,* ninth edition. Oxford: Oxford University Press.
This established social work law textbook has been updated to reflect changes in law on domestic violence, community care, mental capacity and children. The book is supported by a companion web site.

D'Cruz, H. and Jones, M. (2004) *Social Work Research: Ethical and Political Contexts.* London: Sage.
The book provides an in-depth discussion of contemporary methodological issues for social work research, including emancipatory approaches.

Howe, D., Brandon, M., Hinings, D. and Schofield, G. (1999) *Attachment Theory, Child Maltreatment and Family Support: A Practice and Assessment Model.* Basingstoke: Palgrave.
This book explains how social developmental perspectives and attachment theory can inform child protection and family, work, and provides a practice and assessment model.

7 SKILLS FOR PRACTICE AND CONTINUING PROFESSIONAL DEVELOPMENT

The Benchmark Statement requires that social workers become *accountable, reflective and self-critical* by learning to:

- *Work in a transparent and responsible way.*
- *Balance autonomy with complex, multiple and sometimes contradictory accountabilities (for example, to different service users, employing agencies, professional bodies and the wider society).*
- *Acquire and apply the habits of critical reflection, self-evaluation and consultation, and make appropriate use of research in the evaluation of practice outcomes.* (QAA, 2000: §2.5)

Introduction

Skills develop from a process of learning. The Benchmark Statement (QAA, 2000: §4.2) argues that learning involves, *inter alia*, raising of awareness and acquiring knowledge; developing conceptual understanding; gaining practice experience; and reflecting on one's performance in practice. Professional practice requires skills to be based on, and emerge from, social work values and knowledges. Informed by social work values and knowledges, the practitioner's next step is to learn how to select, combine, and apply particular skills, which involves thought and reflection, and with experience, becomes part of the use of self. The newly qualified social worker begins to move from *competence* that relies heavily on maxims for practice to *expertise* where situations are grasped holistically and almost intuitively (Benner, 1984). Experience alone does not guarantee the acquisition of expertise; critical awareness is also required. The challenge for busy social workers who are immersed in practice is to find effective ways to continue building a purposeful use of knowledges, values, and skills in practice.

Chapter Structure

This chapter considers skills for practice, beginning with transferable skills that can be applied to different situations and the *social work process* that provides a framework for assessment, and then discusses selected theories, methods, and models that collectively comprise approaches to practice:

- psycho-social interventions;
- cognitive behavioural approaches;

- task-centred practice;
- crisis intervention;
- advocacy;
- person-centred dementia care;
- constructive and narrative based practice; and
- multi-professional practice.

The chapter concludes with a discussion of continuing professional development and future issues for professional social work.

Transferable Skills: Communication, Information Sharing, and Numeracy Skills

Skills that can be transferred from one situation and environment to another enable social workers to develop new roles and approaches. The Benchmark Statement (QAA, 2000: §3.2) identifies transferable skills that include: communication skills, information technology, and numerical skills (§3.2.1); problem solving skills (§3.2.2); and skills in working with others (§ 3.2.4).

Communication

Being able to communicate effectively requires technical competence but also sensitivity to others and a commitment to social work values. This was a concern identified by people who use services (Box 7.1). The social worker's knowledge should be used to enable rather than to overwhelm – and that means adopting an approach to practice that recognises the power imbalance between the social worker and the individual who uses services. People who use services require honesty from their social workers. This requirement casts into doubt social workers' use of psychoanalytic interpretations (for example, the social worker interpreting a service user's expression of anger as evidence of a longstanding hostility to parental figures) unless these interpretations are discussed openly and the service user is able to reject the interpretation. Demonstrating the technical skill of using complex theory to explain service users' behaviour can create a barrier to honest communication by overpowering the service user's confidence and creating mistrust.

Box 7.1: Statement of Expectations from People Who Use Services (adapted from Topss UK, 2002)

Social workers must:

- Explain their role and the purpose of contact, e.g. assessment; and their legal and other powers in a way that can be understood by all involved.
- Inform individuals, families, carers, groups, and communities about what steps they are going to take.

(Continued)

Box 7.1: *(Continued)*

- Give information to individuals, families, carers, groups, and communities about their rights and entitlements.
- Be open and honest about what they can and cannot do.
- Be honest if they cannot offer the resources needed.
- Inform individuals, families, carers, groups, and communities about what is available beyond the brief of their organisation.
- Listen actively to what individuals, families, carers, groups, and communities have to say.
- Talk to those requiring and using services, and their carers, with due respect for their age, ethnicity, culture, understanding, and needs.
- Involve individuals, families, carers, groups, and communities in decision-making.
- Offer individuals, families, carers, groups, and communities choices and options.
- Share records with individuals, families, carers, groups, and communities.
- Build honest relationships based on clear communication.

These expectations present the social worker with a blueprint for communication: *listen, explain, inform,* and *share* with *honesty, openness, and respect.* The social worker should be a facilitator who encourages others to communicate by using clear language and avoiding jargon, providing appropriate communication support for adults and children with particular communication needs, including language interpretation for deaf people and people who are not fluent in English, and communication through play for children. Communication includes essential skills for conducting interviews (Kadushin, 1972):

- listening;
- responding;
- expressing;
- clarifying;
- summarising; and
- ending.

The 'skills laboratories' that many universities have provided to social work students can help to develop these skills. After qualifying, social workers can further develop their communication skills through part-time counselling courses and access to good practice supervision.

Information Sharing

Communication skills include being able to use computer and information technology (CIT) (Benchmark Statement – QAA, 2000: §3.2.1). In an information society, CIT provides a channel for communication (http://www.isc.ie/). The different countries of the UK, the EC, the United Nations, and private bodies are using the power of these technologies to transform society through Internet banking, mobile phones, email, and computers which are increasing presences in day-to-day living. People who have access to information possess power and those who are excluded from such access will have less power. Because of their poverty and lack of skills people who use services are often excluded from the information society, or exclude themselves (Box 7.2). The advertisement implies that older people (and by implication, other individuals) are excluded or exclude themselves from the information society. Continued exclusion will exacerbate inequalities. Social workers must be able to use word processors, email, and spreadsheets for their own practice, but also should be concerned to advocate the acquisition of CIT skills for service users through low cost or no cost adult education classes, and free access to the Web in community centres and libraries. Users of services need to access information that will assist them to make the best possible choices and manage their own situations (Box 7.3).

Box 7.2: Example of Different Communication Tools

Consider two advertising leaflets sent through the post. One leaflet from a leading computer superstore advertises the latest laptops and 'hand-helds'. The other leaflet from a telephone mail-order firm advertises items including a blood pressure monitor, a garden weed grabber, a record player that played 45s, 33 1/3 and 78 rpm records, snuggle slippers, and an adjustable folding cane. By implication, the target audience for the second leaflet was older people. The second brochure did not advertise computers or hand-helds but the last page featured a manual typewriter for 'those who don't want to spend over a thousand pounds on a computer and then there's the electric bills' (UK Bright Life, August 2004).

Box 7.3: Information Giving as a Therapeutic Tool

A study of the needs of people with brain injury discovered three critical moments for intervention: first, when the person left hospital; second, when the period of rehabilitative care ended; and third, when carers died or were unable to continue in their caring roles. At each critical moment, the brain injured person and carer needed appropriate information about services and benefits to empower them to find the most appropriate support. Where brain injury was experienced before the introduction of care management and community care service, users and carers were given little advice, often were slotted into services designed for people with learning disabilities, and felt disempowered by the lack of knowledge and specialist care for brain injury. In contrast, those who received specialist care management assistance that included information felt more confident about their ability to self-manage their future (Higham, 1998).

Numeracy Skills

Numeracy skills are important for social workers who manage care budgets, a project's income and expenditure, or who may be asked to support service users who want to handle their own finances for care. As careers in social work develop, social workers may be expected to present a range of numerical skills if they are to be promoted.

The Social Work Process

The social work process (SWP) is a tool for learning how to assess and plan intervention activities in a logical, consistent manner, embodied in Key Role 1 of the National Occupational Standards. The Benchmark Statement (QAA, 2000: §3.1.4) states that social workers need to use models and methods of assessment, including factors underpinning the selection and testing of relevant information, the nature of professional judgement and the processes of risk assessment.

The SWP was developed by John Dewey, an American educator and philosopher, who proposed a five step process of logical thinking for effective enquiry (1933, 1938, 1997), which social work later adopted (Box 7.4). The five steps are neither chronological nor entirely separate from each other and Dewey did not supply lists of factors to take into account when assessing need but concentrated on explaining how to think through a problem and determine what to do about it. His five steps do not separate the contributions of thinking (logic) and intuitive feelings. Social workers use an adaptation of the five steps when assessing needs in partnership with service users and carers; they:

- identify the situations that require assessment;
- gather information;
- analyse the information;
- specify the desired outcomes;
- make a plan for intervention;
- carry out the intervention;
- evaluate the intervention; and
- end the contact or re-assess the situation.

Box 7.4: Dewey's (1933) Five Steps

1. *Identify a situation* where activities are disrupted and you are uncertain what to do.
2. *Specify the problems* within the situation by selecting, structuring, and specifying relevant data.
3. *Construct a hypothesis/suggestion* that, if correct, will solve the problem. Use imagination, self-control, skill, and precision to develop possible solutions through carefully analysing the data and avoiding emotional conclusions and wishful thinking.
4. *Explore, through reasoning, the possible consequences* of basing actions on the hypothesis/ suggestion by comparing it to other suggestions/hypotheses.
5. *Test the hypothesis/suggestion* by carrying out activities to see if the strategy works and whether the anticipated outcomes take place and therefore provide an explanation of the original situation.

Social workers are usually expected to use specific assessment frameworks for determining need. The DH's (2000) Framework for Assessing Children in Need and Their Families considers development needs, parenting capacity, and family and environmental factors. Other assessment frameworks (in England) include the Connexions (DfES, 2001) personal adviser APIR (Assessment, Planning, Intervention, Review) Framework for use with 13–19-year-olds, and the YJB's (2003) ASSET (Young Offender Assessment) Framework. The three frameworks are intended for different populations of children and young people, but are broadly similar. A family could conceivably encounter different workers conducting assessments that use different frameworks for different children in a family. In England, following the Green Paper *Every Child Matters* (DfES, 2003), the Change for Children programme has taken steps to develop a Common Assessment Framework (CAF) that would enable professionals to work together in co-ordinated systems for assessing needs and sharing information about children and families across different professions. The CAF is designed to assist the achievement of five priority outcomes for children:

- be healthy;
- stay safe;
- enjoy and achieve;
- make a positive contribution; and
- achieve economic well-being.

The introduction of a SAP for older people in the National Service Framework for Older People (DH, 2002a) requires health and social care to work together to promote person-centred care. The Green Paper (DH, 2005) suggests examining how the SAP could be linked with PCP to provide a means for assessing all people with complex needs.

Some service providers may separate the assessment process from intervention, using workers from one team to assess needs and workers from another team to undertake ongoing activities. Other agencies do not separate the two stages, and argue that 'intervention begins on day one' (Compton and Galaway, 1984: 427). Separating the two stages implies that social work contact will continue over a considerable period of time. The separate approach to assessment may be effective when social workers are certain that contact will be ongoing. The inevitable disruption to relationships caused by switching to another worker may actually bring about a premature ending of contact. Another approach might be for the social worker making the assessment to assume a co-ordinator role that ensures continuity but does not preclude other workers engaging with the service user.

Identifying need is not a simple task. Bradshaw (1972) devised a multi-perspective taxonomy to differentiate between different types of need:

- *Normative need* defined by a professional or expert.
- *Felt need* that people who use services feel that they want (but may not be able to express).
- *Expressed need* that makes the felt need explicit.
- *Comparative need* that is evident when particular users of services do not get the level of help that is given to others in the same circumstances.

This taxonomy can help to make sense of situations where the worker must assess complex needs. Everitt et al. (1992), writing from a social work practitioner perspective, supported criticisms by Foucault (1980), Illich et al. (1977), and Cousins (1987) that having professional control and power over service users leads to conformity in needs assessment, although Everitt acknowledges the skill of the professional worker in assessing need.

Social workers can identify needs with reasonable certainty only by asking service users and carers what their needs are. Social workers recognise empowerment (Solomon, 1976) and working in partnership (Marsh and Fisher, 1992; Monach and Spriggs, 1994) as the twin ideals of professional practice. Working in partnership requires skilled professionals to be prepared to listen carefully, gather evidence, mediate between different points of view (because people who use services and carers may not always agree), and disseminate the evidence that has been gathered jointly by the social worker, the user of services, and the carer. Increasingly, the service user will take the lead role in the assessment process to self-assess their needs, with the social workers assuming the role of mentor.

Risk Assessment

Risk assessment has acquired more importance for social workers because they are employed within a risk society (Beck, 1992), which searches for ways to identify and manage risk effectively. The positive aim of risk assessment is to improve decision-making by clarifying the nature of the risks and predicting behaviour as far as possible (Alaszewski et al., 1998). The social worker identifies factors in a situation that may pose a risk to the health, well-being, and safety of the service user, and the associated factors that might ameliorate or exacerbate the level of risk. In keeping with the value of empowerment, social workers should assess users' strengths that are likely to diminish the predicted risks. The social worker, together with the person who uses services, identifies the probable outcomes and potential risks of a particular action compared with outcomes that are consequences of taking no action or an alternative action. The presumed risks can be compared, and the comparison used as a tool to guide decision-making.

Risk assessments are partly 'guess-work' whose predictive capability must be based on research evidence, views of service users and carers, and knowledge of the particular individual situation. Risk assessments with people who have mental health problems may need to identify factors of danger to self and others that might warrant compulsory admission to hospital; risk assessment with older people may consider the probability of risk to health or the danger of accidents; and with children, the risk to well-being and safety that might justify removing a child from their caregivers. Assessment processes within the criminal justice system have to take into account the risk of re-offending and potential harm to others.

Organisations undertake risk assessments of the financial and legal implications of taking a particular course of action or not. The possible clash between organisational and individual risk assessments can pose ethical dilemmas. In Case Study 7.1, Fazia had taken a calculated risk in assessing Mr Bowman. His accident could have occurred in residential care, but that was scant consolation. Fazia's employers might conclude that the reputational and financial threat to social services from the circumstances of Mr Bowman's accident was not considered sufficiently. The choice between choosing calculated risks to preserve independence and playing safe is not easy, particularly when service user empowerment is the accepted ethos but organisations face criticisms for taking risks. An excessive avoidance of risk, resulting in action stalemate, can be a negative feature of a risk society.

🗋 Case Study 7.1 – a Risk Assessment

Social worker Fazia Ahmed assessed the care needs of Mr Albert Bowman, a man of 89, a widower who lived on his own. His Parkinson's disease had worsened; unsteady on his feet, he had problems in caring for himself. Despite considerable pressure from the GP and Mr Bowman's married daughter (who lived in a different part of the country) to place Mr Bowman in residential care, Fazia judged that the risk of Mr Bowman remaining at home could be managed with a package of supportive care. Mr Bowman was very motivated to remain at home. At first, all seemed to be going well, but then Mr Bowman fell down the stairs, fractured his skull, and died of pneumonia. Mr Bowman's daughter threatened to sue. The social services department was criticised publicly for not having properly assessed the health and safety risks to Mr Bowman.

? Question for Reflection

Can you think of any other way that Fazia might have approached the situation of taking a calculated risk?

You might consider undertaking prior work with Mr Bowman and his daughter to discuss choices and risks in making one decision over another, and the facts about Mr Bowman's right to make a decision, and after his death work with his daughter and her feelings of bereavement.

Langan and Lindow (2004) researched mental health service users' involvement in risk assessment and management, focusing on those considered by professionals to pose potential risks, and finding that some users wanted help to reduce the risk their severe illness might create for others. It could be argued that users have a right to know that they are considered to pose a risk, but alternatively the knowledge may further stigmatise and distress some individuals. The research recommended a format for assessing and managing risk that ensured the inclusion of service users' views; and suggested that looking holistically at a person's life experiences might lead to more effective risk management.

Making an Assessment

Relying on an approved assessment framework is not sufficient for a good assessment. The social worker must make sense of the process for him or herself, decide which questions to ask, how, when, and whom to ask, and check the risk implications of a situation. Diatonic perceptions of human growth and development suggest exploring stages of development, and systonic perceptions suggest examining the individual's relationships to their social environment. The life course perspective helps the social worker draw together separate diatonic and systonic perceptions. In the example presented in Case Study 7.2, the social worker assesses different layers and dimensions of the situation, but does not force explanations on the service user. In the situation, assessment and intervention appropriately merge into each other. To make a preliminary assessment, Jim drew on his knowledge of human growth and development, attachment and loss, and mental health, as well as considering practical issues of lack of income and employment. Jim used empathetic communication skills when he met with Carlo. Jim was careful to share his assessment with Carlo to find out whether Carlo would agree with the assessment and accept it. Professional status in the past has been associated with the social worker's skill in drawing together and analysing information for assessments of need. Psychiatric social workers like Jim used to take detailed social histories for assessment purposes but seldom gave feedback to service users.

Case Study of Assessment 7.2 – Carlo, a Young Man in Mental Distress

Late one afternoon a young man, Carlo Stefanacci, visited a crisis intervention centre, stating that he felt desperate and had considered taking an overdose because life was without meaning. The social worker, Jim O'Donnell, asked about Carlo's feelings, mood, and thoughts about suicide, and invited Carlo to talk about his work, friends, and activities (the systonic approach). He learned that Carlo lived alone, had been made redundant from his job, and no longer saw his former workmates. Lately, Carlo had incurred debt and was worried about being evicted for non-payment of rent, but spent most of his time sleeping or drinking in the pub. Carlo could not explain his feelings of hopelessness.

Jim invited Carlo to talk about his family and his background (diatonic perception). Jim learned that Carlo's family, originally from Italy, was a large one and Carlo had six younger brothers and sisters to whom he felt close. After Carlo's mother died six years ago, his father took Carlo's younger siblings with him back to Italy. Because Carlo was already working, he decided to stay in Scotland, and found a flat. Carlo had been engaged to be married twice before. The first engagement followed his mother's death, but his fiancée, whom he'd known since school, broke off the engagement because Carlo kept postponing the wedding. The second engagement was to a young woman who was a work colleague, and again his fiancée broke off the engagement because Carlo couldn't commit himself to a wedding date. Jim O'Donnell's risk assessment concluded that Carlo was probably depressed and needed medical assistance to alleviate some of his symptoms, and that his threats of suicide should be taken seriously. The problems of isolation, joblessness, and debts needed tackling. The family history and Carlo's account of his mother's death, two broken engagements, and difficulty in sustaining relationships suggested a pattern of loss and rejection that kept repeating itself.

Jim learned that Carlo had never been able to express any emotion about his mother's unexpected death, and wondered if Carlo might be 'stuck' at the stage of bereavement where feelings are numb, and whether Carlo's broken engagements echoed the loss of his mother. Jim considered whether Carlo's being made redundant was another important loss that, added to the other losses, had led to Carlo's seeming inability to overcome his difficulties. Jim gave feedback to Carlo, sharing his views in an exploratory way, having drawn a conclusion that Carlo was ready to listen and would not be unduly distressed by what Jim had to say. Carlo said that he felt better after talking through his situation – first, he wanted help in dealing with his practical issues but he also wanted to talk about the loss of his mother, relationships, and job.

Until relatively recently, social workers did not question the ethics of an unequal power balance between the assessor and the person being assessed, but the use of social work skill to determine eligibility in a scarce resource market is now questioned. Gillman et al. (1997) criticised social workers' gathering of life histories of people with learning disabilities as an appropriation of a precious possession – the story of a life – without recompense. In a similar exercise, Devore and Schlesinger (1991) evaluated different theories of social work for their consonance with ethnic-sensitive practice, concluding that theories in which the social worker engaged in an open transparent way by sharing information with the user were the most ethnic-sensitive.

The National Occupational Standards support the view that assessment must be a partnership with people who use services, rather than something that is done to them. The commentary for Key Role 1, unit 1 – Prepare for social work contact and involvement – states that service users want the social worker to prepare for the first contact, first by gathering all relevant information and then by evaluating the information to decide the best way to begin contact (QAA, 2000: §§ 1.2, 1.3). The social worker is expected to undertake assessment with families, carers, groups and communities (unit 2), by gathering information, enabling those who are partners in the assessment to express their 'strengths, expectations and limitations', and make 'informed decisions about their needs, circumstances, risks, preferred options and resources' (2000: §§ 2.3, 2.4).

Smale et al. (1993) described assessment in terms of:

- A *questioning model*, in which the social worker is the expert.
- A *procedural model*, in which the social worker relies on criteria set by expert managers to determine eligibility.
- An *exchange model* based on a citizen-to-citizen partnership between the social worker and user of services.

Smale advocates the exchange model, in which information is exchanged and the participants arrive at a mutual understanding of problems and how to tackle them. The exchange model relies on the social worker's use of self, good communication skills, and relationship building – all essential features of individual social work values. The values of empowerment are required: openness, authenticity, congruence and problem solving directed towards the social situation rather than to the individual (Smale et al., 1993: 99). Indirect work is required to develop the kinds of services that are effective in supporting people, and Smale et al. warn against colonising voluntary sector agencies through service contracts and thus sabotaging their advocacy roles (1993: 68). The general approach of the exchange model of assessment is to recognise the dependability of people in the community rather than their dependence (1993: 67). Smale et al. acknowledge that the exchange model takes more time and involves more people but this assessment model could be adapted to support self-assessments, direct payments, and individual budgets because it is based on a citizen-to-citizen relationship (1993: 17).

Empathy

Empathy (Davis, 1994) is partly a skill and partly an intrinsic quality that is enhanced through self-awareness – being able to see with another's eyes, hear with another's ears, feel another person's feelings without being overwhelmed, and then convey an understanding that is not simply intellectual but reflects a sense of shared humanity. Social workers who have to juggle many conflicting demands and are seemingly required to work in a process-oriented manner may not be sufficiently empathetic to service users' needs and may need to use conceptual tools for building empathy. One approach is to use vignettes from practice experience, literature, and autobiographical accounts to form *empathetic snapshots* (Case Study 7.3) that illuminate understanding, and enable the transfer of empathetic understanding from one situation to another. In the example, the social worker was able to transfer empathy from historic situations (Kindertransport) to current practice (asylum-seeking children) through the empathetic snapshot.

Case Study 7.3 – an Empathetic Snapshot (adapted from Boyd and Higham, 2001)

During Holocaust week, a social worker who worked with asylum-seeking families and unaccompanied minors attended a lecture given by a woman who had come to Britain as a child on the 1939 Kindertransport to escape Nazi persecution (Gershon, 1966; Leverton and Lowensohn, 1990; Sebald, 2001). Touched by the account of children who had to leave their parents and travel on their own from Germany to Britain, the social worker asked the speaker if there were any relevant messages for social workers working with children from asylum-seeking families. The social worker was given two messages: first, children need to feel a sense of belonging; and second, social workers need continually to question and examine their role within a state-led system. The speaker's account of her childhood experiences, and her two messages provided the empathetic snapshot that engaged the social worker in seeking a deeper understanding of children within asylum-seeking families. Social workers can reflect that before developing a true sense of social identity, all children need to feel safe and a sense of belonging.

? Question for Reflection

Is it possible to develop a sense of empathy or is empathy an innate quality that you either do or do not possess?

You might consider how in the past you gained insight and understanding through a process of learning. Your understanding of human nature may determine your response, according to whether you believe all individuals share a common humanity.

Theories, Models, and Methods

Social workers are urged to choose particular theories, methods, or models for their interventions, but how can they decide which ones to choose from the many examples? An overview of theories may help the practitioner decide on the two or more approaches that they will want to make a part of their practice expertise. As social workers carry out multiple flexible roles, they will need to use more than one theoretical approach, but developing expertise across the whole range of theories is impractical – expertise is acquired gradually over time and involves experience, study, reflection, and supervision – initially, two or three areas of expertise should be achievable.

Social work's search for professional status concerned the identification of an appropriate theoretical basis for social work practice. Although Goldstein (1973) proposed a unitary theory of social work that draws together different methods and models in a systems-driven approach, this failed to win widespread acceptance as postmodern influences drove social work theory towards a 'pick and mix' approach. Interest in classifying social work theory resulted in Howe (1987: 50) using a sociological framework of radical change to develop four theoretical categories: *raisers of consciousness*, *seekers after meaning*, *revolutionists*, and *fixers* and in Payne's (1991) analysis of the social construction of social work theories. Surrounded by many theories, social workers were apt to claim that they were eclectic in their use of theory. The introduction of a competence-based social work qualification (CCETSW, 1989) supported the trend towards an atheoretical approach to practice.

The Benchmark Statement (QAA, 2000: §3.1.4) requires: 'critical explanations from social work theory and other disciplines that contribute to the knowledge base of social work, including their distinctive epistemological status and application to practice'.

The variety of social work theories is attributed to the profession's roots in different epistemologies or theories of knowledge. Debates about the differences between a theory, a method, and a model are inconclusive: theory, model, and method can be viewed on a continuum of theoretical approaches – a *theory* is a logical construct that provides explanations, guides practice and ideally should help in predicting results; a *model* is a somewhat freer construct of social work practice with a more fluid approach to theory; and a *method* is a way of doing social work that is usually tied to a particular theoretical base. This chapter refers to theories, models, and methods as *approaches to practice* within a particular theoretical orientation.

Two epistemological polarities have dominated social work theory: first, individuals are shaped by the social structures of their environments; and second, individuals are social actors that shape their own worlds (Harvey, 1990) but postmodernism has led to social work abandoning a search for mutually exclusive approaches to research and theorising in favour of relativism and subjectivity. Lorenz (2000) discusses theoretical polarities, affirming the shift in power structure to previously silenced voices and a 'communicative community' beginning to articulate views of previously disempowered individuals. A potential contradiction is whether social work aims to foster lifestyles and behaviours that are the responsibility of service users themselves (empowerment and emancipation), or aims to support collective identities which do not allow for diversity (adjustment).

The Benchmark Statement (QAA, 2000: § 3.1.4) requires social workers to know and use approaches for intervention in a range of community-based settings at individual, group, and community levels and multi-professional practice. (Chapter 2 discussed group care as a guiding principle for individualising social care practice.) To illustrate the variety of approaches, this chapter presents a selective overview of psycho-social, cognitive-behavioural, task-centred, crisis intervention, advocacy, person-centred dementia care and constructive narrative approaches.

Psycho-social Casework   Psycho-social casework applied Freudian psychoanalytic theory to Richmond's casework method, and became almost synonymous with social work practice until the late 1960s. Three phenomena then contributed to its eclipse: first, social workers became interested in tackling social inequalities and accused psycho-social casework of ignoring the service users' poverty by inappropriately analysing emotional responses; second, in 1982, Barclay identified *counselling* as one of the two main roles of social workers, but did not explain or define counselling other than equating counselling with psycho-social social work, thus diminishing psycho-social casework's distinctive identity. Third, around this time counsellors took steps to become a separate profession aligned with psychology rather than with social work. The National Council for Voluntary Organisations' 1970 Standing Conference for the Advancement of Counselling (BACP, 2005) led to the founding of the British Association for Counselling in 1977. In 2000, the BAC became the British Association for Counselling and Psychotherapy (BACP) that accredits training courses, advises on setting up counselling services, and maintains standards. Although counselling plays a part in social work practice, as Seden (2005) demonstrates, counselling is an importation into social work rather than an integral part.

An examination of Hollis' theory of psycho-social casework (1972) shows its roots to be in social work. Hollis believed that social work needed a well-developed practice theory backed by research, and she developed psycho-social theory for that purpose (Box 7.5). Psycho-social casework uses the defence mechanisms (Hollis, 1972, Chapter 4) and the concept of the unconscious (Freud, 1986) to explain behaviour and interactions between the worker and the service user. Hollis (Chapter 5) classified casework 'treatment' into a *sustaining process* (support); *direct influence* (of the worker); and *ventilation* (of feelings). Although contemporary social workers may object to the use of *direct influence* that diminishes the power of the service user, Hollis urges caution, warning workers against assuming too much control and advising workers to encourage the service user's *reflective consideration* (Hollis, 1972, Chapter 7) of all the factors affecting their situation, and to build the service user's own strengths to tackle problems. She argued that the *environmental press* of poverty, unemployment, and homelessness, and the internal factors of emotions and relationships cause social problems (Chapter 1), and diversity of race, culture, class, and ethnicity are factors to be acknowledged (1972: 239).

Box 7.5: Five Distinctive Characteristics of Psycho-social Casework (adapted from Hollis, 1972: 288–9)

1. Works with the individual and the environment.
2. Encourages the service user to think through problems rationally rather than the worker trying to manipulate the service user.
3. Recognises that the person who uses services has the right to direct their own life.
4. Values the individual's well-being and gives warm acceptance.
5. Helps not only individuals but also families and others close to the service user.

Psycho-social casework traditionally conducts an assessment in a leisurely manner over several sessions, compiling a psycho-social study, making a diagnosis, and clearly separating assessment from intervention – a lengthy process that appears a luxury which does not fit well with contemporary social work. Other objections to Hollis' psycho-social casework include her belief in psychoanalytic concepts as causal explanations, and use of medical terminology (for example, diagnosis and treatment). Hollis urged psycho-social caseworkers to develop more skill in their practice, arguing (1972: 269) that 'any reading of ... case records will show a serious gap between what is known in the profession and what is actually being used by the average practitioner'. She urged more research to be undertaken on casework methods to develop new and more effective evidence informed approaches, and was interested in exploring sociological contributions to casework theory.

Perlman (1957, 1979), an advocate of psycho-social casework, developed the problem-solving approach, emphasising the importance of relationships without promoting psychoanalytic concepts to the same extent as Hollis. Her approach influenced the later development of task-centred work (Doel and Marsh, 1992; Reid and Epstein, 1972). Rather than *clinical diagnosis* classifying 'illness', which she did not see as the business of casework, Perlman used the concept of *dynamic diagnosis* that considered service users within a social context (pp. 168–75). Her '4 P' approach to practice analyses separately and then integrates data into a unified understanding about:

- the *person* or persons seeking help;
- the *place* (e.g. the agency of the social worker);
- the *problem* (s) presented by the person, and;
- the *process* of problem-solving social casework.

This approach now appears limited for contemporary practice priorities. Devore and Schlesinger (1991) criticised problem-solving for not placing enough emphasis on the 'ethnic reality', but acknowledged that the approach could be adapted to do so. The failure to modify the psycho-social approach for contemporary practice was a lost opportunity because social work could have adapted and developed the best principles of the Perlman version of psycho-social casework, rather than discarding the approach and now having to import counselling skills back into social work. The 4P approach can be adapted to a *6P approach* that places more importance on the underpinning statutory and legal *policy* basis for providing services, so that the *process* of giving help is tempered by awareness of boundaries, opportunities, and sometimes, insufficiencies in service provision (Box 7.6). Contemporary practice also requires the *process* of *partnership* between the *person* and the social worker, rather than a power imbalance where the social worker or other professional worker makes decisions without full regard for the wishes of the person who uses services. The *process* should include careful listening to the person's issues. Understanding the *person* means paying attention to the *place* where the person is situated – the environment consisting of family circumstances and relationships, ethnic identities and cultures, employment, education, health, income, leisure, housing, and other issues.

Professional social work practice – doing social work – integrates all these areas of knowledge, using social work values and skills to address situations that require resolution. Perlman's approach makes the point that the process of the agency should not subjugate the professional role: 'The [social worker], while representing [the] agency, is first and foremost a representative of [the] profession ... . The profession of social work ... upholds certain human values and standards. [The social worker] does so not in any parroting acquiescence or smug assumption that the term 'professional' automatically bestows grace but in constant alertness to measure … daily practice and that of [the] agency against what [the] profession knows or thinks to be good. Hopefully, too, at the same time as [the social worker] knows and acts on what he stands for, [the social worker] also stretches himself to seek to know more and to do better than he knows and does today' (1957: 51–2).

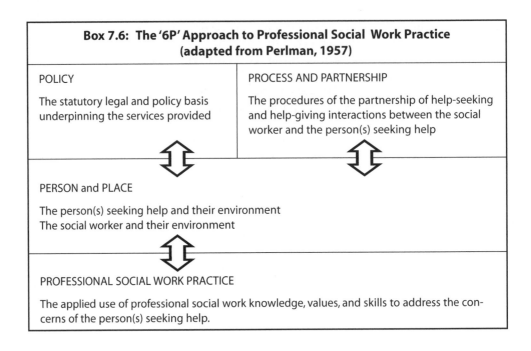

Box 7.6: The '6P' Approach to Professional Social Work Practice (adapted from Perlman, 1957)

POLICY	PROCESS AND PARTNERSHIP
The statutory legal and policy basis underpinning the services provided	The procedures of the partnership of help-seeking and help-giving interactions between the social worker and the person(s) seeking help

PERSON and PLACE

The person(s) seeking help and their environment
The social worker and their environment

PROFESSIONAL SOCIAL WORK PRACTICE

The applied use of professional social work knowledge, values, and skills to address the concerns of the person(s) seeking help.

Cognitive Behavioural Approaches

Cognitive behavioural therapeutic (CBT) approaches, which represent a linking together of cognitive learning and behavioural theory, became popular in social work practice after the eclipse of psycho-social approaches. Behavioural theory is based on Pavlov's (1927) concepts of conditioning behaviour researched in Russia by experimenting with dogs. *Classical conditioning* occurs when an *unconditioned stimulus* of food, presented with a *conditioned stimulus* of a bell, results in an *unconditioned response* of salivation. Eventually salivation occurs when the *conditioned stimulus* of the bell is presented on its own, thus becoming a *conditioned response*. The underlying principle is that behaviour is learned, and therefore a structured behavioural programme of rewards and reinforcements can help human beings to learn new behaviours.

Bandura's (1986) social learning theory suggested that the use of role models would be an effective learning tool for modelling new behaviour, while Skinner (1938) argued that changed behaviour is a function of learning that takes place in response to stimuli within the environment. The rewarding or reinforcing of a stimulus–response pattern, conditions the individual to respond in a particular way. Behaviour modification reinforces desired behaviours through rewards that include verbal praise or use of a token economy, and reduces the incidence of undesirable behaviour by ignoring behaviours that are not wanted.

CBT helps individuals change their patterns of thinking and behaviour, and arguably, changes the way they feel (Hawtin, 1989). The CBT approach concentrates on resolving here-and-now difficulties that are identified as behaviour requiring change; unlike psycho-social casework, CBT does not look to the past. Its focus is to help users of services develop solutions that are more helpful than their current behaviours through a structured programme, whose first step is when the worker and the user of services arrive at a shared understanding of the issues. Then the service user and the worker agree time-limited goals, a plan to tackle the behaviour and thinking, activities that will be monitored and reviewed on a continuous basis, and the number of sessions to take place. Analysing the *antecedents* of the behaviour, the *behaviour* itself, and the *consequences* of the behaviour, (known as the ABC process, Ellis [1962]) can help the worker and service user agree the most appropriate intervention. Assessment becomes a continuous activity, checking back with both service user and worker contributing, and the person who uses services usually being required to undertake 'homework' – trying out new behaviour – between sessions.

Social care providers have used CBT approaches to change service users' behaviour, and schools have used the techniques to modify pupils' behaviour and motivation, but some social workers raise ethical objections to using these approaches with service users who may not be able to give informed consent (Payne, 1991: 118). Contemporary CBT approaches advise giving more attention to the cognitive learning aspects of behavioural approaches, with the user of services and therapist agreeing shared goals. Examples of CBT influenced approaches include *transactional analysis* (discussed in Chapter 4), which uses behavioural responses of positive and negative *strokes* as a means of recognising behaviours; and *motivational interviewing* (Miller and Rollnick, 1991; Prochaska and DiClemente, 1982), which is a combined assessment and intervention approach that helps service users particularly in substance misuse programmes to overcome reluctance to engage with social work help. Motivational interviewing follows a staged sequence of encouraging the individual to talk, generating self-motivational statements, dealing with resistance, developing readiness to change and negotiating a plan, and developing determination and action. *Social skills training* and *assertiveness training* (Baer, 1976; Smith, 1975) are other applications of CBT.

CBT is a specialism practised in the NHS by qualified therapists who may be nurses, psychologists, doctors, social workers, or counsellors who have taken additional training. Social workers need to be cautious in claiming expertise in CBT unless they have taken further training. CBT is reputedly effective, *inter alia*, in addressing anxiety and panic attacks, phobias, obsessive-compulsive disorders, eating problems, sexual and relationship problems, anger, drug or alcohol problems, post-traumatic stress disorders, and sleep disorders. Sheldon (1982) and Hudson and Macdonald (1986) in the UK; and Gambrill (1983) in the USA have promoted behavioural social work approaches, while Goldstein (1981) developed social learning as a cognitive approach to practice. The British Association for Behavioural and Cognitive Psychotherapies (BABCP) was founded in 1972 as a multi-disciplinary interest group for practitioners and theorists of behavioural and cognitive psychotherapy (BABCP, 2005).

Task-centred Practice

Reid and Epstein (1972) popularised task-centred practice (TCP) as an attractive alternative when psycho-social casework incurred criticism for its lengthy process, unclear purpose and oppressive use of power (Mayer and Timms, 1970). Systems theory (Pincus and Minahan, 1973) shares characteristics with TCP, and became popular around the same time. TCP could be viewed as an adaptation of Perlman's problem-solving process: first known as task-centred casework, the approach rapidly won acceptance as TCP. Reid and Shyne (1969) developed TCP in the USA as a short-term structured intervention that moves through the phases of exploring problems, agreeing a goal, planning and carrying out tasks, and ending or exiting (Doel and Marsh, 1992). The structured stages of TCP correspond with aspects of cognitive behavioural approaches.

TCP requires organisation and planning for an iterative assessment process where the social worker and service user mutually explore problems. Usually there is a written agreement between the social worker and the service user, specifying the tasks that will lead to the attainment of the agreed goals, and stating who will undertake particular actions within a set timescale. TCP leaves no room for ambiguity about the reasons for the social worker's involvement, and the service user plays an important role in selecting the problems to be resolved. TCP can incorporate other approaches; its processes fit with a person-centred approach and the social work process.

Doel (2002) affirms Tolson et al.'s (1994) argument that TCP is a well-tested generic approach that can be used with all service user groupings and with individuals, families, groups, organisations, and communities. The pitfalls of using this approach lie in its apparent simplicity. TCP was never intended to be a universal remedy, and should not be used as a panacea for every kind of practice issue – Payne (1991) argues its unsuitability for ongoing psychological problems. TCP embraces partnership and emancipatory approaches, but with some slight modification, this could be true of other theoretical approaches. The written agreement or contract in most instances is not binding on the signatories. The approach requires careful negotiation and building of motivation, and needs to be used carefully to avoid becoming only a series of unconnected tasks.

Crisis Intervention

Crisis intervention is a multi-professional approach that is used extensively within mental health services, but is applicable to people's life situations across the life course. In crisis intervention (O'Hagan, 1991, 1986; Roberts, 2004) the worker intervenes as swiftly as possible after the crisis reveals itself, and takes control briefly to enable an individual to reduce anxiety, begin to think rationally, and find coping strategies to overcome the crisis. A crisis situation occurs when an individual's reactions to events result in a sense of being overwhelmed and unable to cope. Crises can be triggered by death, abuse, domestic and public violence, redundancy, and childbirth. The individual may become anxious, confused, incoherent, angry, depressed, and may threaten violence or suicide, or exhibit the numbness and denial that are part of the stages of loss and bereavement. Traumas in the form of natural disasters (the tsunami wave in southeast Asia), terrorism (the 9/11 attack on the World Trade Center in New York), or war (Kosovo, Iraq) can affect cohorts of people.

One of the most important requirements for the social worker is to be able to identify a crisis reaction and deal with it by both adopting a structured approach and then appropriately timing the handing back of control to the individual. Crisis intervention is short-term and intensive; supportive and cognitive behavioural approaches can help to reduce panic symptoms.

Advocacy

Many professions, including social work, have adopted an advocacy approach. The role of an advocate (discussed in Chapter 4) is to promote social justice by enabling excluded individuals to participate in decision-making, change the power relationships that determine policies and practices, and so improve the quality of individual lives. Stakeholders (including service users and carers), who contributed their views to the NOS consultation (Topss UK, 2002), have their views presented in Box 7.7.

Box 7.7: Advocacy (adapted from NOS Topss UK, 2002)

Social workers must be able to:

- Lobby on behalf of individuals, families, carers, groups, and communities to access services.
- Challenge their own organisations on behalf of individuals, families, carers, groups, and communities.
- Challenge injustice and lack of access to services.
- Challenge poor practice.
- Advise individuals, families, carers, groups, and communities about independent advocacy that can best meet their needs.
- Enable individuals, families, carers, groups, and communities to be empowered to represent their views.
- Help individuals, families, carers, groups, and communities to represent their views in all meetings affecting them.
- Involve independent advocates, where appropriate.

Bateman (1995: 4–15) discusses three advocacy approaches:

- *self-advocacy* that can be either an individual or collective activity;
- *citizen advocacy* (Ivers, 1994) that pairs a volunteer citizen advocate with a user of services to work for change; and
- *legal advocacy* as a role for the legal profession.

Bateman identifies counselling and negotiating as advocacy skills, to which Brandon and Brandon (2000) add listening skills. Advocacy practitioners will benefit from learning how organisations use power; they also need to develop skills of communication, group work, and team building that are associated with community development. As in all areas of practice, combining knowledge and skills appropriately is essential to be effective. Brandon and Brandon (2000: 16) link advocacy conceptually with social role valorisation, the social model of disability, welfare rights, empowerment, citizenship and whistle-blowing, but warn against the dictatorship of the articulate where only those who are confident and skilled enough to express their wishes gain a hearing.

Person-centred Dementia Care

Social care provides care for people with dementia, and social workers working as care managers in adult care undertake assessments with people with dementia and their carers. Person-centred dementia care is a powerful practice tool for social care that was developed from the observational research of Kitwood (1997) and his associates in the late 1980s. Similar to other social work and social care practice models, its origins lie in another discipline, psychology, but its widespread application and adoption as a practice model depend on social care's wrap around ability (Cozens, 2004) to embrace new ways of working.

Dementia is a progressive disease that hinders an individual's intellectual and emotional functioning, as well as their physical well-being, with Alzheimer's disease being the most frequently occurring form. There is no completely known cause of or cure for dementia, and it is estimated that over 750,000 individuals living in the UK have a form of dementia (Alzheimer's Society, 2005). The progression of dementia deprives an individual of their memory, language, concentration, and reasoning as the disease affects functional abilities. The individual and their friends and relatives will experience feelings of loss as the individual adopts different behaviours with apparently only the shell of their former personality intact.

Kitwood (1997), arguing that the person with dementia is an individual with personhood and that person-centred care which emphasises social interactions could maximise opportunities for quality of life, developed *dementia care mapping* (DCM) as an empathetic observational tool to assess the quality of care from the point of view of the person with dementia. Mapping is carried out as unobtrusively as possible, respecting the privacy and the emotional needs of the persons with dementia, as well as noting the emotional needs of mappers and care staff. Trained staff observe participants with dementia within the care setting for at least six hours, analyse data, and feed back the findings to staff who then plan changes in the care provision. Mapping uses two coding frames: the first frame records three-minute time frames of the individual service users' activities and inactivities on a scale of 'well-being' to 'relative ill being'; the second frame notes any episodes where the person with dementia is demeaned or depersonalised, on levels ranging from mild to extreme. The data gathered provide a detailed picture of the care environment.

Fox (1995) describes the mapping process in day centres for people with dementia, where she found generally high standards, but a prevailing culture of *convenient* rather than *personalised care*. Social divisions between care staff and management, and between care staff and family carers were observed, with managers providing little support to care staff members who needed daily briefing and debriefing to maintain personalised care. Staff preserved social divisions by wearing uniforms and not sharing mealtimes or social moments with users. There was little evidence of person-to-person contact between the staff and the users. A traditional *them and us* culture maintained a gap between management, care staff, and users, preventing trust from growing.

Service users offering to help with tasks were refused; the care staff did too much for the service users and failed to promote their independence. Staff members ignored users' momentary emotional distress or else tried to jolly them out of it. As well as unresponsiveness, staff sometimes made derogatory comments in front of service users, an example of *malignant social psychology* (Fox, 1995: 73). The purpose of DCM is to feed back the findings to the managers so that they can institute changes in care practice, but unresponsive management can sabotage efforts to get staff's commitment to work on the changes that DCM reveals as necessary.

Constructive and Narrative-based Practice

Power in social work, like power in society, operates through the culture of dominant knowledge and practices (Parton and O'Byrne, 2000: 53). As an alternative to perpetuating dominant power, Parton and O'Byrne argue (2000: 183) for a *constructive model* of social work that encourages a range of different discourses and uses 'a narrative process with real outcomes' that values individuals' resources 'within and around them'. The way resources are 'storied' is 'key to opening up new and more positive possibilities'; the *constructive model* values peoples' narratives as a means of telling their stories, with each lived experience constituting a kind of truth, so that knowledge becomes more inclusive and diverse.

The social worker within a constructive model of social work will focus on service users' different dialogues, listening, and acknowledging uncertainties (Parton and O'Byrne, 2000: 186–187), valuing users' participation and narratives and practising with artistry rather than seeking a definition of scientific truth. Goldstein (1992) thought there was an argument for social work to rediscover its connection with stories of people's lives rather than to focus on gathering of information or data about them. Constructive social work fits well with empowerment strategies and a feminist approach, but it describes a style of practice rather than a particular role. Perhaps constructive social work cannot be more specific, since its concern is with construction of different kinds of knowledge rather than certainties. Social workers who convey respectful honest communications in their relationships with people who use services will help to establish a new power sharing process that, in effect, constitutes constructive practice.

Research practice with older people, women, and other individuals has a tradition of valuing narratives within biographical interviews (Bornat, 1994; Gearing and Dant, 1990). Social work practice can borrow this approach and use narratives as a way of giving voice to disempowered individuals, as long as ethical objections to professional ownership of the narratives can be met and ownership remains with the originators of the narratives. Parton and O'Byrne (2000) explored constructions of narratives in social work practice, representing a return to a humanist tradition, and Barnett (2000), one of Kitwood's associates, adopted a consonant perspective by devising narrative analyses of *memory stories* with interpretive metaphors that enable older people with dementia to communicate their experiences. Pease and Fook (1999; discussed in Chapter 5) promote the importance of listening to service users' narratives as a starting point for emancipatory practice. Williams (1996: 62–3) argues that sociologists have begun to abandon the use of oppositional categories that contrast ruling class/working class and man/woman, in favour of listening to different narratives and constructions of reality. Chamberlayne et al. (2004: 184) explore international perspectives of using biographical methods in professional practice. Communication skills play a large part in narrative-based practice.

Putting Values, Knowledge and Skills Together for Practice

Social workers need to evaluate theoretical approaches for their helpfulness in promoting a particular aspect of practice in consonance with the purpose of their agency, and then use and combine the helpful aspects of certain theories. There are more theories and approaches than this book can cover; each one deserves careful detailed study and inevitably, adaptation to contemporary practice. Noticeably, the theoretical approaches that have won recent acceptance are modelled closely on the principles of the social work process – for example they use a planned sequential process. Contemporary theories focus on current behaviour and problems more than the past, and are designed as short-term interventions that lend themselves well to partnership with users and carers; however, a wider range of theories that take account of life-course events could be adapted for partnership working.

Theories are meant to be predictive and help the social worker choose an appropriate combination of values, knowledge, and skills for application to practice. Getting used to thinking systematically helps social workers organise their approach and be more effective. In selecting an intervention approach, social workers will first use the social work process for assessing the situation by drawing on agency assessment frameworks but should think more widely about the essence of assessment. The eight assessment steps (discussed earlier in the chapter) can be used in partnership with service users and carers, facilitating their participation, and adopting an empowering emancipatory orientation to practice (Box 7.8). Following assessment, the social worker will intervene by following a particular theoretical approach, backed up by values and knowledge, as a template for selecting and combining appropriate skills. Transferable skills of communication, numeracy, CIT, problem-solving, and working with others enable social workers to develop flexible responses and roles.

Box 7.8: Eight Steps for the Social Work Process and Working in Partnership

1. Identify the situations that require assessment *in partnership with the service user and carer.*
2. Gather information *in partnership with the service user and carer.*
3. Analyse the information *in partnership with the service user and carer,* by mentally sorting the different kinds of knowledge, thinking about the meanings of knowledge in relation to values and ethics, and drawing on your own and the service user's particular internalised 'take' on knowledge and values.

(Continued)

Box 7.8: *(Continued)*

4. Specify the desired outcomes *in partnership with the service user and carer.*
5. Make a plan for intervention *in partnership with the service user and carer* by selecting an intervention approach.
6. Carry out the intervention *in partnership with the service user and carer* by applying your understanding and the service user's and carer's understanding to practice.
7. Evaluate the intervention *in partnership with the service user and carer.*
8. End the contact or re-assess the situation *in partnership with the service user and carer.*

Multi-professional Practice

Chapter 1 established the importance of multi-professional practice for social workers with the example of a social worker employed in a Yot. This final chapter reiterates the significance of multi-professional practice. The Statement of Expectations from service users and carers (Topss UK Partnership/Skills for Care, 2002) claims that in *Working with other professionals,* social workers must:

- Be honest, clear and make sure all involved understand what happens to the information individuals, families, carers, groups, and communities give to the social worker, how it is kept, who it is shared with, and why, and how it might be used.
- Understand what information other organisations can offer and share with individuals, families, carers, groups, and communities.
- Work effectively with others to improve services offered to individuals, families, carers, groups, and communities.

The service user statement suggests that multi-professional work contributes to the future of social work practice because this is the approach most likely to raise the standard of services. Enquiries that followed failures of child protection (Reder et al., 1993) identified the inability of separate services to co-ordinate information and services. The NOS (Topss UK Partnership, 2002) mention likely future requirements for practice in multi-disciplinary settings and diverse structures, with Key Role 3 requiring social workers to: develop and maintain professional relationships within and outside the organisation, and to work within multi-disciplinary and multi-organisational teams, networks and systems (unit 22) and to establish and maintain effective working relationships within and outside the organisation (unit 23). The Benchmark Statement (QAA, 2000: § 3.1.1) refers to services provided in interdisciplinary contexts and the issues associated with working across professional boundaries and within different disciplinary groups.

Multi-professional teams usually adopt one of two models: either a *blurring of roles,* so that tasks and skills are shared across professional boundaries, or *retention of professional specialisms* with an implied division of tasks according to professional role (Brown et al., 2000; Buckley, 2005). Teams are likely to consist of a *skill mix,* where some team members will be higher-level technical assistants or assistant practitioners employed as social care workers, teaching assistants, or early years workers, and others will be qualified professionals. Because different teams may be organised according to different organisational models, the range of practice experiences is potentially wide. Membership of a multi-professional team requires confident articulation of well-considered, evidenced recommendations for, and evaluations of, practice. Creating an effective multi-professional team depends on team members' willingness to develop new ways of working that require sharing, trusting each other, and overcoming possible feelings of insecurity and professional rivalries about their own roles and contributions.

A good way to overcome these quite human reactions is to undertake joint staff development that establishes shared goals and expectations, and enables members to discuss their different perceptions and contributions. For example, the YJB in England and Wales provided members of its Yots with shared academically assessed in-service training to achieve team cohesiveness. Multi-professional team members need good supervision from a team leader who values each individual's contribution, but additionally, social workers will need a social work mentor to support their development of professional practice. The nursing profession has recognised the need for clinical supervision in addition to line management supervision; social workers' new professionalism should require the same kind of supervisory arrangements.

Improvement of mental health provision for children, adults, and older people and their families and carers is an NHS priority. The NHS wants to develop better multi-professional working (Baguley, 2005). The NIMHE was launched in June 2002 to improve the quality of life for people of all ages who experience mental health problems by developing more and different kinds of staff who will ensure that service users receive more continuity and contact time. The NHS vision is to design a mental health service embedded in social inclusion processes and based on the values, skills, and knowledge of a flexible workforce. Skills gaps have been identified for user-centred approaches, multi-disciplinary working, risk assessment and management, race equality, working with families, and evidence and values-based practice. Social workers could supply many of these skills gaps, but equally apparent is NIMHE's aim for all team members, including social workers, to develop 10 Essential Shared Capabilities across professional boundaries through a national education and training strategy (Box 7.9).

Box 7.9: Ten Essential Shared Capabilities for Multi-Professional Mental Health Practitioners (adapted from NIMHE et al., 2004)

1. Working in partnership
2. Respecting diversity
3. Practising ethically
4. Challenging inequality
5. Promoting recovery
6. Identifying people's needs and strengths
7. Providing service user centred care
8. Making a difference
9. Promoting safety and positive risk taking
10. Personal development and learning.

The Essential Shared Capabilities and the Skills Escalator (discussed in Chapter 3) open up the possibility of non-medical staff developing career pathways as consultants in their own specialisms.

Continuing Professional Development

The Benchmark Statement asserts that 'graduates in social work should be enabled to analyse, adapt to, manage and eventually to lead the processes of change' and requires social workers to become accountable, reflective and self-critical' (QAA, 2000: §§ 2.2.4, 2.5).

Continuing professional development (CPD) is the broad concept of ongoing post-qualification learning for developing and maintaining practice skills, updating for re-registration, attaining formal post-qualification (PQ) awards, and developing the level of professionalism suggested by the Benchmark Statement. CPD becomes important because now that British social work is officially recognised as a profession, all social workers will need to apply for enrolment on a social care register maintained by the GSCC in England, the CCW, the SSSC, and the NISCC, bodies which regulate social work qualifications and maintain registers. Each country in the UK is developing its own customised strategy for CPD and PQ study. Social workers will need to demonstrate that they have updated their skills and knowledge to maintain their name on the register. The care councils have introduced the concept of Post-Registration Training and Learning (PRTL) that represents the minimum CPD requirement for registration, but does not require attainment of an award. Registered social workers will be required to complete 90 hours or 15 days of study or training. The PRTL guidelines are more structured in Scotland, Wales and Northern Ireland than in England (GSCC, 2003).

Reviews of the UK PQ award framework in each country will result in changes from 2007 to the system of PQ awards first introduced in 1991. Future PQ and CPD arrangements will depend on effective partnership arrangements between employers who will be responsible for strategic regional workforce planning and development, university providers, practitioners, service users, and carers. Employers of social workers need to become *learning organisations* (Senge, 1990). CPD and PQ appropriately may start with consolidating, deepening, and broadening the social worker's values, knowledge, and skills beyond the beginning capability to practise. Then, drawing on Benner's (1984) adaptation of the Dreyfus model (discussed in Chapter 2), CPD and PQ will support social workers' practice development from competence to proficiency and then expertise. However, until social work and social care employers develop a social care career development framework and skills escalator (NHS Modernisation Agency, 2004) that provides a ladder for progression, the post qualifying awards may not provide a clear incentive for take up by practitioners.

At this time of writing, not all the countries of the UK have completed their PQ reviews, but CPD and PQ study are likely to be organised with the following characteristics:

- Modular programmes earning academic credits.
- Interprofessional and interdisciplinary content and learning.
- Emphasis on specialisms and research-informed practice.
- Requirement for consolidation of qualifying level knowledge, skills, and values.
- Requirement for mentoring and practice assessment skills.

In England, every social worker undertaking PQ study will be expected to learn how to support, mentor, and assess practice-based learning, so that they can help a student or a colleague to learn. In turn, they must secure suitable social work mentoring and supervision for themselves (GSCC, 2005). Social workers are expected to use research findings for evidence-informed practice, and they may find opportunities to undertake action research as part of their practice. They may benefit from undertaking a research methods course, or a part-time applied *professional doctorate* based on project work and a dissertation that develops an aspect of their practice. CPD embraces the idea that learning is life-long, and encourages practitioners to think reflectively. Belonging to a professional association can help to support continued learning and provide a collective voice for social work that can influence social policy in a way that an individual social worker would find difficult to achieve.

Reflective Practice and Mentoring

Social work and other caring professions have adopted the concept of *reflective practice* that Schon (1983) developed initially for professional architects as an appropriate tool for developing practice to higher standards. Becoming a reflective practitioner involves thinking about and becoming aware of aspects of one's practice, and then, based on that increased self-awareness, taking steps to improve practice. The concept is related to Dewey's (1933, 1997) logical process of assessment and Freire's (1972) pedagogy of the oppressed that also strive to create more self-awareness. Schon (1983) proposed two kinds of reflection: *reflection-on-action* that looks back at prior practice; and *reflection-in-action* that involves thinking about and understanding practice while it is taking place. Reflection is not meant to result in negative self-criticism; the process is intended to identify good aspects of practice as well as areas for improvement through developing self-awareness.

Reflection can help students avoid a 'scatter gun' approach to theories and knowledges and begin to piece together the different strands of values, knowledge, and skills because sharing strategies for addressing issues can help to overcome stalemates in practice and frustrations arising from the difficult demanding nature of social work. Reflection-on-action within an action learning set of trusted colleagues potentially yields more insight. An action learning set – that first has agreed ground rules for making constructive comments – provides opportunities for sharing experiences and gaining an understanding of the commonality of particular issues. An employer organisation that adopts the principles of a learning organisation (Senge, 1990) will use a collective process of reflection to examine its own processes and is likely to provide social work practitioners with regular practice supervision that encourages reflective practice.

The role of *mentor* can support CPD and reflective practice, and others' learning. Brooks and Sikes (1997) define a mentor as a *reflective coach, critical friend,* and *co-enquirer.* Coaching, a role similar to mentoring, is used typically for more specific short-term outcomes. Mentoring is widely used in education, careers guidance, business, and for personal development, but can play a role in social work and social care. Coaches and mentors combine elements of counselling, TCP and assertiveness training by observing, listening, questioning, and enabling mentees to work out their own solutions through personal growth and change. The National

Mentoring Network (NMN) (2005) in England and the Scottish Mentoring Network promote the development of mentoring and befriending by offering advice and support to mentoring programmes and providing an information forum and network (Box 7.10). Mentoring is a two-way process, although not necessarily involving the same practitioners in exchanging roles of mentor and mentee: the social worker may adopt a mentoring role in relation to a colleague, and be mentored by another social worker, or can mentor social care workers within a skill mix team. A trained volunteer can act as a mentor in direct practice with service users, and members of self-help groups can mentor each other to build confidence.

Box 7.10: Mentorship in Education

Student teachers are required to find a mentor who can offer practice wisdom, but who is not their line manager or assessor. The mentor is an experienced practitioner who develops a peer relationship with the mentee. The mentor and mentee mutually develop reflective awareness of the issues arising from the mentee's experiences.

▶▶ Conclusion and Summary: the Importance of Professional Social Work

The conclusion of this last chapter summarises the book's key messages. This book argues that social workers combine multiple roles (e.g. planner, assessor, evaluator, supporter, advocate, protector, and manager) that balance empowerment and emancipation with protection and support. The essence of professionalism lies in developing the capability to select and combine appropriate social work roles for particular situations. Social work's distinctiveness is found in its holistic practice with different situations and people, a valuable attribute for developing multi-professional partnerships, now required for better service provision. Braye and Preston-Shoot (2004) argue that social workers should not only be competent technicians who are *fixers*, but also *critical thinkers* – well-rounded professionals with knowledge and judgement to address strategy issues.

As discussed in Chapter 3, social workers and social care workers sometimes struggle to identify the skills they possess compared with other professions, and may overlook their own potential to develop 'whole systems' thinking about situations and people, rather than being limited to perceiving just a part of a situation. One of social work's most successful achievements is the way it reviews and adapts its values by drawing on new ideas from outside social work. British social work and social care promote participation, empowerment, and emancipation, and have adopted the social model of disability as a highly appropriate form of intervention. The social worker's role as a *guardian of values* keeps them at the forefront of practice.

Social work is becoming a protected title and an officially recognised profession throughout the UK and its recognised status as a profession places a responsibility on social workers to move beyond competence to expertise. Social care is modernising its workforce, training, and qualifications to promote higher practice standards. Over time, social care registers in the four countries of the UK will include all social care workers – a sign of social care's growing professionalism.

The large social care workforce and its professional arm, social work, benefit from their mutual alliance, although Britain's location of social work within social care, rather than placing social work in the dominant role, is internationally disputed. Through collaborating with each other in skill mix teams, the alliance will develop more effective practice. Social work has achieved considerable impact through its link with social care. Social care's workforce needs qualifications and better career structures; social workers can mentor social care workers to develop their practice. A newly recognised profession requires a critical voice that enhances practice knowledge. Social work research contributes evidence-informed, research-minded practice to social care, promotes social inclusion through its selection of research topics (TSWR, 2000), and identifies significant findings for social science research activity.

British social work has worried about its survival, in part because it depends on continued governmental support, a concern that impeded some workers from developing a broad vision of what social work and social care can become in the future. Social work (together with social care) needs to establish a non-governmental collective voice that can influence the direction of social policy. Social work practice is a difficult endeavour that can challenge practitioners' morale because of the all too frequent insufficiency of resources to deal with social inequalities. Reflection on practice both individually and within peer-led groups, supervision, and establishing a collective voice for social work and social care are tools for sustaining motivation.

The international definition of social work has gained support within the UK, but the definition of social work's purpose may change as it links more closely with social care. The concept of professionalism will change, particularly as people who use services and carers are empowered to express their views of what they want from service provision. Debates about what social work (and by implication, social care) are meant to be and do will probably never cease: 'Social work adapts and changes in response to social, political and economic challenges and the demands of contemporary social welfare policy, practice, and legislation' (QAA, 2000: §2.2.3).

Finally, if the newly qualified social worker asked for advice on how to begin, this might be a response:

- Be honest, trustworthy, and reliable in all aspects of your practice.
- Listen carefully to the views of people who use services and their carers.
- Communicate clearly and tactfully.
- Be knowledgeable, thoughtful, evaluative, reflective, and self-aware.
- Develop a support system for your practice through mentoring, supervision, and peer groups.
- Continue to learn and develop your practice.

📖 Further Reading

Dominelli, L. (2004) *Social Work Theory and Practice for a Changing Profession*. London: Polity Press.
The book explores the contested nature of practice and the concept of service users as citizens with human rights.

Tew, J. (ed.) (2005) *Social Perspectives in Mental Health: Developing Social Models to Understand and Work with Mental Distress*. London: Jessica Kingsley.

Skills for Practice and Continuing Professional Development

This book promotes a multi-professional holistic approach to mental health practice that explores social factors of power, abuse, ethnicity, gender and sexual orientation, and emphasises recovery and empowerment, building on the experiences of service users.

Weinstein, J., Whittington, C. and Leiba, T. (eds) (2003) *Collaboration in Social Work Practice.* London: Jessica Kingsley.
The book suggests ways for practitioners in social care, health and related sectors to work more effectively together and appraises both the benefits and challenges.

GLOSSARY

AHP	Allied Health Professions
APGSM	Association of Professional Geriatric Care Managers
APIR	Assessment Planning Review Framework (Connexions Personal Advisers, England)
Assembly	Assembly for Social Care and Social Work Education, Training and Research
ASSET	Youth Justice Board's Young Offender Assessment Framework (England and Wales)
BABCP	British Association for Behavioural and Cognitive Psychotherapies
BACP	British Association for Counselling and Psychotherapy
BASW	British Association of Social Workers
BCODP	The British Council of Organisations of Disabled People
CAF	Common Assessment Framework (children)
CBT	Cognitive Behavioural Therapy
CCETSW	Central Council for Education and Training in Social Work
CCW	Care Council for Wales
CIT	Computer and Information Technology
COS	Charity Organisation Society
CPA	Care Programme Approach
CPD	Continuing Professional Development
CSCI	Commission for Social Care Inspection

Glossary

CSS	Certificate in Social Services
CSWP NASW	The Commission on Social Work Practice of the National Association of Social Workers
CWP	Changing Workforce Programme
CWDC	Children's Workforce Development Council (England)
DCM	Dementia Care Mapping
DfEE	Department for Education and Employment
DfES	Department for Education and Skills
DH	Department of Health
DHSS	Department of Health and Social Security
DHSSPS	Department of Health, Social Services and Public Safety Northern Ireland
DWP	Department for Work and Pensions
EASSW	European Association of Schools of Social Work
EC	European Community
ESRC	Economics and Social Research Council
EYCCP	Early Years Child Care Partnership
EYDCPs	Early Years Development and Childcare Partnership
GC	The Guidance Council
GCM	Geriatric Care Manager
GSCC	General Social Care Council
HCSC	House of Commons Select Committee
HDA	Health Development Agency
HMIP	HM Inspectorate of Probation
IASSW	International Association of Schools of Social Work

Glossary

ICAR	Information Centre about Asylum and Refugees in the UK
Ippr	Institute for Public Policy Research
JRF	Joseph Rowntree Foundation
JUC SWEC	Joint University Council Social Work Education Committee
NASS	National Asylum Support Service
NASW	National Association of Social Workers (USA)
NGO	Non-governmental Organisation
NHS	National Health Service
NIMHE	National Institute for Mental Health (England)
NISCC	Northern Ireland Social Care Council
NMC	Nursing & Midwifery Council
NMN	National Mentoring Network
NOMS	National Offender Management Service
NOS	National Occupational Standards
NSF	National Service Framework
NVQ	National Vocational Qualifications (England and Wales)
PCP	Person centred planning
PQ	Post-qualification
PRTL	Post Registration Training and Learning
PSE	Poverty and Social Exclusion Survey
QAA	Quality Assurance Agency for Higher Education
RCN	Royal College of Nursing
SAP	Single Assessment Process, in National Service Framework for Older People

Glossary

SCA	Social Care Association
SCIE	Social Care Institute for Excellence
SE	Scottish Executive
SEU	Social Exclusion Unit
SiSWE	Standards in Social Work Education (Scotland)
Skills for Care Sector	Skills council for social care in England, formerly Topss England
Skills for Care and Development UK	Coalition of sector skills councils for adult social care and children and young people's workforce
SSI	Social Services Inspectorate
SSSC	Scottish Social Services Council
SVQ	Scottish Vocational Qualification
SWP	Social work process
SWSPD	Social Work Services Policy Division Scotland
TCP	Task Centred Practice
TA	Transactional Analysis
Topss England	National training organisation for social care in England, now Skills for Care
Topss UK	Partnership of UK-wide training organisations and care councils for care, now defunct
TSWR	Theorising Social Work Research seminar series
VQ	Vocational Qualifications
YJB	Youth Justice Board
Yot	Youth Offending Team

REFERENCES

Abbott, D. and Morris, J. (2000) *Disabled Children and Residential Schools*. Bristol: Norah Fry Research Centre, University of Bristol.

Addams, J. (1935) *Forty Years at Hull House*. New York: Macmillan.

Ainsworth, M.D.S., Blehar, M.C., Waters, E. and Wall, S. (1978) *Patterns of Attachment: A Psychological Study of the Strange Situation*. Hillsdale, NJ: Erlbaum.

Ainsworth, F. and Fulcher, L. (1981) 'Introduction: group care for children. Concepts and issues', in F. Ainsworth and L. Fulcher (eds) *Group Care for Children*. London: Tavistock. pp. 1–15.

Ainsworth, F. and Fulcher, L. (1985) 'Group care practice with children', in L. Fulcher and F. Ainsworth (eds) *Group Care Practice with Children*. London: Tavistock. pp. 1–20.

Alaszeweski, A., Harrison, L. and Manthorpe, J. (eds) (1998) *Risk, Health and Welfare*. Buckingham: Open University Press.

Alcock, P. (2003a) 'The subject of social policy', in P. Alcock, A. Erskine and M. May (eds) *The Student's Companion to Social Policy*, 2nd edition. Oxford: Blackwell. pp. 1–10.

Alcock, P. (2003b) *Social Policy in Britain*, 2nd edition. Basingstoke: Palgrave.

Aldgate, J., Jones, D., Rose, W. and Jeffery, C. (eds) (2005) *The Developing World of the Child*. London: Jessica Kingsley.

Alzheimer's Society (2005) www.alzheimers.org.uk/

Association of Professional Geriatric Care Managers (APGCM) (2004) *National Advice on Selecting a Geriatric Care Manager*. Tueson, AZ: Association of Professional Geriatric Care Managers.

Archer, M., Bhaskar, R., Collier, A., Lawson, T. and Norrie, A. (eds) (1998) *Critical Realism: Essential Readings*. London: Routledge.

Arksey, H. (2002) 'Combining informal care and work: supporting carers in the workplace', *Health and Social Care in the Community*, 10(3): 151–61.

Arnstein, S.R. (1969) 'A ladder of citizen participation', *Journal of American Institute of Planners*, 35: 216–24.

Atherton, J. (1989) *Interpreting Residential Life: Values to Practice*. London: Routledge.

Audit Commission, Commission for Social Care Inspection and Ofsted (2004) *Joint Inspection of Youth Offending Teams First Phase Annual Report*, September 2004. London: Audit Commission.

Baer, J. (1976) *How to be an Assertive (Not Aggressive) Woman*. Bergenfield, NJ: New American Library.

Baguley, I. (2005) 'The future mental health workforce', presentation to Leicestershire, Northamptonshire & Rutland Workforce Development Confederation Mental Health Skills Escalator Day, Leicester, 23 February.

Baldock, J. (1999) 'Culture: the missing variable in understanding social policy?', *Social Policy and Administration*, 33(4): 458–73.

Baltes, P.B. (1979) 'Life-span developmental psychology: some converging observations on history and theory', in P.B. Baltes and O.G. Brim, Jr. (eds) *Life Span Development and Behaviour*. New York: Academic Press. pp. 255–79.

References

Bamford, T. (1990) *The Future of Social Work*. London: Macmillan.

Bandura, A. (1986) *Social Foundations of Thought and Action: A Social Cognitive Perspective*. Englewood Cliffs, NJ: Prentice Hall.

Barclay, P. (1982) *Social Workers. Their Roles & Tasks*. London: National Institute for Social Work Bedford Square Press/NCVO.

Barnes, C. (1991) *Disabled People in Britain and Discrimination: A case for Anti-Discrimination Legislation*. London: C. Hurst & Company, University of Calgary Press, Calgary Alberta, in association with the British Council of Organisations of Disabled People.

Barnes, C. and Mercer, G. (2003) *Implementing the Social Model of Disability: Theory and Practice*. Leeds: The Disability Press, University of Leeds.

Barnes, J. and Connelly, N. (eds) (1978) *Social Care Research*. London: Policy Studies Institute, Bedford Square Press.

Barnett, E. (2000) *Including the Person with Dementia in Designing and Delivering Care. 'I Need to be Me!'*. London: Jessica Kingsley.

Barry, D.W. (1966) 'Programs to combat poverty in the United States', in M. Webb (ed.) *Wealth and Want in One World*. New York: Friendship Press. pp. 73–90.

Bateman, Neil (1995) *Advocacy Skills. A Handbook for Human Service Professionals*. Aldershot: Arena Ashgate/Gower.

Bauman, Z. (1993) *Postmodern Ethics*. Oxford: Blackwell.

Bebbington, P. (1991) 'The expectation of life without disability', *Population Trends*, 66: 26–9.

Beck, U. (1992) *Risk Society: Towards a New Modernity*. London: Sage.

Becker, H. (1963) *Outsiders: Studies in the Sociology of Deviance*. New York: Free Press.

Bengtson, V.L. and Kuypers, J.A. (1984) 'Toward competence in the older family', in T.H. Brubaker (ed.) *Family Relationships in Later Life*. Beverly Hills, CA: Sage. pp. 211–28.

Benner, P. (1984) *From Novice to Expert*. Menlo Park, CA: Addison Wesley.

Beresford, Peter (2000) 'Service users' knowledges and social work theory: conflict or collaboration?', *British Journal of Social Work*, 30(4): 489–504.

Berger, P. and Berger, B. (1976) *Sociology: a Biographical Approach*. New York: Basic Books.

Berne, Eric (1964) *Games People Play. The Psychology of Human Relationships*. New York: Grove Press.

Bertaux, D. (1982) 'The life course approach as a challenge to the social sciences', in T.K. Hareven and K.J. Adams (eds) *Aging and Life Course Transitions: An Interdisciplinary Perspective*. New York: Tavistock. pp. 127–50.

Beveridge, W. (1942) *Social Insurance and Allied Services (Beveridge Report)* (Cmd 6404). London: HMSO.

Biestek, F. (1961) *The Casework Relationship*. London: Allen and Unwin.

Biggs, S. (1989) *Confronting Ageing*. London: Central Council for Education and Training in Social Work (CCETSW).

Blaikie, A. (1992) 'Whither the Third Age? Implications for gerontology', *Generations Review*, 2(1): 2–4.

Blaikie, N. (1993) *Approaches to Social Enquiry*. Cambridge: Polity Press.

Boddy, J., Cameron, C. and Moss, P. (eds) (2005) *Care Work Present and Future*. London: Routledge.

Bond, J., Briggs, R. and Coleman, P. (1993) 'The study of ageing', in J. Bond, P. Coleman and S. Peace (eds) *Ageing in Society*. London: Sage. pp. 19–52.

Booth, T. (1985) *Home Truths: Old People's Homes and the Outcome of Care*. Aldershot: Gower.

Booth, C. (1889–1903) *Life and Labour of the London Poor* 1–17. London: Macmillan.

Bornat, J. (ed.) (1994) *Reminiscence Reviewed. Perspectives, Evaluations, Achievements*. Buckingham: Open University Press.

Boswell, G. (1997) 'The role of the practice teacher', in M. Davies (ed.) *The Blackwell Companion to Social Work*. Oxford: Blackwell. pp. 348–55.

References

Bowlby, J. (1951) *Maternal Care and Mental Health*. Geneva: World Health Organisation.

Bowlby, J. (1969) *Attachment and Loss, Vol. I: Attachment*. New York: Basic Books.

Bowers, S. (1949) 'The Nature and Definition of Social Casework: Part III', *Journal of Social Casework*, 30: 417.

Boyd, F. and Higham, P. (2001) 'The social work assessment framework and asylum-seeking families', draft unpublished paper Department of Health and Human Services, Nottingham Trent University, Nottingham.

Bracken, P. and Thomas, P. (2001) 'Post psychiatry: a new direction for mental health', *British Medical Journal*, 24 March.

Bradbury, A. (1986) 'Sexual abuse: a model of treatment', *Community Care*, 4 September. 24–5.

Bradshaw, J. (1972) 'A taxonomy of social need', in G. McLachlan (ed.) *Problems and Progress in Medical Care*, 7th Series. London: Oxford University Press. pp. 69–82.

Brandon, D. and Brandon, T. (2000) *Advocacy in Social Work*. Birmingham: Venture Press.

Braye, S. and Preston-Shoot, M. with Cull, L.A., Johns, R. and Roche, J. (2005) *Knowledge Review, Teaching, Learning and Assessment of Law in Social Work Education*. London: Social Care Institute for Excellence (SCIE).

Brayne, H., Martin, G. and Carr, H. (eds) (2005) *Law for Social Workers*, 9th edition. Oxford: Oxford University Press.

Brearley, P. (1990) *Working in Residential Homes for Elderly People*. London: Tavistock/Routledge.

Brim, O.G. (1975) 'Macro-structural influences on child development and the need for childhood social indicators', *American Journal of Orthopsychiatry*, 45(4): 516–24.

British Association for Behavioural and Cognitive Psychotherapies (BABCP) (2005) www.babcp.org.uk/

British Association for Counselling and Psychotherapy (BACP) (2005) *Profile and History*. Rugby: BACP. www.bacp.co.uk/about_bacp/profile_history.html

British Association of Social Workers (BASW) (2003) *A Code of Ethics for Social Workers*. Birmingham: BASW.

British Council of Organisations of Disabled People (BCODP) (2005) *Fighting Talk, Annual Review 2002–3*. Derby: BCODP.

Bronfenbrenner, U. (1979) *The Ecology of Human Development*. Cambridge, MA: Harvard University Press.

Brooks, R., Regan, S. and Robinson, P. (eds) (2002) *A New Contract for Retirement: Modelling Policy Options to 2050*. London: Institute for Public Policy Research.

Brooks, V. and Sikes, P. (1997) *The Good Mentor Guide*. Buckingham: Open University Press.

Brown, B., Crawford, P. and Darongkamas, J. (2000) 'Blurred roles and permeable boundaries: the experience of multidisciplinary working in community mental health', *Health & Social Care in the Community*, 8(8): 425–35.

Brunel University (Centre for Citizen Participation) and NISW National Institute for Social Work (1999) *National Debate on the Future of Social Work, Creating a New Agenda*, Briefing Paper 28. London: NISW.

Bruntland, G. (ed.) (1987) *Our Common Future: The World Commission on Environment and Development*. Oxford: Oxford University Press.

Bryman, A. (1988) *Quantity and Quality in Social Research*. London: Unwin Hyman.

Buckley, B. (2005) *Presentation to Strategic Work Based Learning Forum*. Leicester: Skills for Care.

Burrell, G. and Morgan, G. (1979) *Sociological Paradigms and Organisational Analysis*. London: Heinemann.

Buss, A.R. (1975) 'The emerging field of the sociology of psychological knowledge', *American Psychologist*, 30: 988–1002.

Butcher, H., Glen, A., Henderson, P. and Smith, J. (eds) (1993) *Community and Public Policy*. London: Pluto Press.

Butler, F. (2004) *Human Rights: Who Needs Them? Using Human Rights in the Voluntary Sector*. London: Institute for Public Policy Research.

References

Butler, Ian (2000) 'A code of ethics for social work and social care research', Theorising Social Work Research (TSWR) Seminar Series, seminar 6. *Researching the Social Work Process 11* Luton: Electronic Library for Social Care. www.elsc.org.uk/socialcareresource/ tswr/seminar6/butler.html

Butrym, Z. (1976) *The Nature of Social Work*. London: Macmillan.

Calouste Gulbenkian Foundation (1968) *Community Work and Social Change. A Report on Training*. London: Longman.

Cameron, C. (2004) 'Building an integrated workforce for a long-term vision of universal early education and care', Policy Paper 3, Leading the Vision series. London: Daycare Trust/Paul Hamlyn Foundation.

Cannan, C., Berry, L. and Lyons, K. (1992) *Social Work and Europe*. Basingstoke: BASW/Macmillan Press.

Care Council for Wales (CCW) (2004) *Approval and Visiting of Degree Courses in Social Work (Wales) Rules 200*. Cardiff: Care Council for Wales.

Carkhuff, R.R. (1971) 'Principles of social action training for new careers in human services', *Journal of Counseling Psychology*, 18: 147–51.

Carkhuff, R.R. (1984) *Helping and Human Relations*, 2 vols. Amherst, MA: Human Resource Development Press. (Originally published 1969)

Carkhuff, R.R. (1987) *The Art of Helping*, 6th edition. Amherst, MA: Human Resource Development Press.

Castles, S. and Miller, M.J. (1998) *The Age of Migration. International Population Movements in the Modern World*, 2nd edition. Basingstoke: Macmillan Press.

Central Council for Education and Training in Social Work (CCETSW) (1983) *A Practice Curriculum for Group Care*. London: CCETSW.

Central Council for Education and Training in Social Work (CCETSW) (1989) *Requirements and Guidelines for the Diploma in Social Work*, Paper 30. London: CCETSW.

Central Council for Education and Training in Social Work (CCETSW) (1992) *Expert Group Report Setting Quality Standards for Residential Child Care: A Practical Way Forward. Final Report of the Expert Group*. London: CCETSW.

Central Council for Education and Training in Social Work (CCETSW) (1995) *Paper 30. Rules and Requirements for the Diploma in Social Work*. London: CCETSW.

Centre for Policy on Ageing (CPA) (1984) *Home Life*. London: CPA.

Challis, L. (1990) *Organising Public Social Services*. London: Longman.

Chamberlayne, P., Bornat, J. and Apitzsch, U. (eds) (2004) *Biographical Methods and Professional Practice. An International Perspective*. Bristol: Policy Press.

Changing Workforce Programme (CWP) (2004) *Role Redesign: Review of Activities 2003/04*. London: NHS Modernisation Agency.

Clarke, J. (2003) *Creating Citizen-Consumers: Changing Relationships and Identifications*, Research project 2003–5. Milton Keynes: Open University.

Clements, L. (2004) *Community Care and the Law*, 3rd edition. London: Legal Action Group Books.

Cohen, D. and Prusak, L. (2001) *In Good Company. How Social Capital Makes Organizations Work*. Boston, MA: Harvard Business School Press.

Coleman, P. (1993) 'Psychological ageing', in J. Bond, P. Colman and S. Peace (eds) *Ageing in Society an Introduction to Social Gerontology*, 2nd edition. London: Sage. pp. 68–96.

Coleman, P.G. (1994) 'Reminiscence within the study of ageing: the social significance of story' in J. Bornat (ed.) *Reminiscence Reviewed. Perspective, Evaluations, Achievements*. Buckingham: Open University Press. pp. 8–20.

Commission for Social Care Inspection (CSCI) (2004a) *When I Get Older: What People Want from Social Care Services and Inspections as They Get Older*. London: CSCI.

Commission for Social Care Inspection (CSCI) (2004b) *Consultation on Draft Code of Practice, CSCI*. Newcastle-upon-Tyne: Customer Services Unit, CSCI.

References

Commission for Social Care Inspection (CSCI) (2005) *National Minimum Standards* London: Department of Health. www.csci.org.uk/information_for_service_providers/national_minimum_standards/default.htm – (accessed 5 March 2005).

Commission on Social Work Practice of the National Association of Social Workers (CSWP NASW) (1958) 'Working definition of social work practice', *Social Work*, 3: 5–8.

Compton, B. and Galaway, B. (1984) *Social Work Processes*, 3rd edition. Itasca, IL: The Dorsey Press.

Cornwall, A. and Gaventa, J. (2001) 'From users and choosers to makers and shapers: repositioning participation in social policy', working paper Institute of Development Studies University of Sussex, Brighton.

Corrigan, P. and Leonard, P. (1978) *Social Work Practice Under Capitalism: A Marxist Approach*. London: Macmillan.

Cousins, C. (1987) *Controlling Social Welfare: a Sociology of State Welfare Work and Organisation*. Brighton: Wheatsheaf.

Cozens, A. (2004) 'Our social secret', *Guardian*, 10 March.

Craig, G. (2002) 'Poverty, social work and social justice', *British Journal of Social Work*, 32(6): 669–82.

Cree, V. (ed.) 2003 *Becoming a Social Worker*. London: Routledge.

Crimmens, D. (2001) 'Comments in response to Pat Higham and Nol Reverda', *Social Work in Europe*, 8(1): 30–1.

Cropper, S. and Ong, P. (2002) 'How did "social capital" translate in Salford and Nottingham?', Social Action Research Project: findings of the process evaluation, unpublished presentation at the *Social Action for Health and Wellbeing Conference*, London, 20–21 June.

Cross, F.L. (1958) *Oxford Dictionary of the Christian Church*. London: Oxford University Press.

Crow, L. (1996) 'Including all our lives: Renewing the social model of disability', in C. Barnes and C. Mercer (eds) *Exploring the Divide: Illness and Disability*. Leeds: The Disability Press. pp. 55–73.

Cull, L.-A. and Roche, J. (2002) *The Law and Social Work*. Basingstoke: Palgrave.

Cumming, E. and Henry, W. E. (1961) *Growing Old: The Process of Disengagement*. New York: Basic Books.

Dale, J. and Foster, P. (1986) *Feminists and State Welfare*. London: Routledge & Kegan Paul.

Davies, M. (1994) *The Essential Social Worker: An Introduction to Professional Practice in the 1990s*, 3rd edition. Aldershot: Aldgate.

Davis, M.H. (1994) *Empathy: A Social Psychological Approach*. Madison, WI: Brown & Benchmark.

de Schweinitz. K. (1962) 'Official statement of curriculum policy for the Master's Degree Program in Graduate Professional School of Social Work', in R. Smalley (ed.) *Theory for Social Work Practice*. New York: Columbia University Press. p. 4.

Dearden, C. and Becker, S. (2000) *Growing up Caring: Vulnerability and Transition to Adulthood – Young Carers' Experiences*. Leicester: National Youth Agency.

Department for Education and Employment (DfEE) (2000) *Connexions. The Best Start in Life for Every Young Person*. Nottingham: DfEE Publications.

Department for Education and Skills (DfES) (2001) *The Connexions Framework for Assessment, Planning, Implementation and Review – Guidance for Personal Advisers*. London: DfES.

Department for Education and Skills (DfES) (2003) *Every Child Matters*, Green Paper. London: DfES.

Department for Education and Skills (DfES) (2004) *Five Year Strategy for Children and Learners*. London: DfES.

Department for Education and Skills (DfES) (2005) *Common Core Skills and Knowledge for the Children's Workforce*. London: DfES. www.teachernet.gov.uk/publications DfES/1189/2005

Department for Education and Skills (DfES) (2005) *Youth Matters*, Green Paper. London: DfES.

Department for Work and Pensions (DWP) (2003) *United Kingdom National Action Plan on Social Inclusion 2003–05*. www.dwp.co.ukUKnapsi

References

Department of Health (DH) (1994) *Report of the Brain Injury Rehabilitation Conference Peterborough.* London: DH.

Department of Health (DH) (1998) *Modernising Social Services.* London: DH.

Department of Health (DH) (1999a) *National Service Framework for Mental Health.* London: DH.

Department of Health (DH) (1999b) *Caring about Carers: A National Strategy for Carers.* London: DH.

Department of Health (DH) (2000) *Assessing Children in Need and Their Families.* London: DH.

Department of Health (DH) (2001) *Research Governance Framework for Health and Social Care.* London: DH.

Department of Health (DH) (2002a) *Quality in Social Care: The National Institutional Framework.* London: DH. www.doh.gov.uk/qualityin

Department of Health (DH) (2002b) *The Reform of Social Work Education. Standards for the Award.* London: DH. www.doh.gov.uk/swqualification/newrequirements.htm

Department of Health (DH) (2002c) *Learning from Past Experience – A Review of Serious Case Reviews.* London: DH.

Department of Health (DH) (2003) *Children's Health Task Group Recommendations.* London: DH.

Department of Health (DH) (2004a) *Choosing Health: Making Healthier Choices Easier,* Public Health White Paper. London: DH.

Department of Health (DH) (2004b) *Research Governance Framework for Health and Social Care. Implementation Plan for Social Care.* London: DH.

Department of Health (DH) (2005) *Independence, Well-being and Choice,* Green Paper for adult social care. London: DH.

Department of Health and Social Security (DHSS) (1974) *Maria Colwell Report.* London: DHSS.

Department of Health, Social Services and Public Safety Northern Ireland (DHSSPS) (2003) *Framework Specification for the Degree in Social Work.* Belfast: DHSSPS.

Devore, W. and Schlesinger, E.G. (1991) *Ethnic-Sensitive Social Work,* 3rd edition. New York: Merrill, Macmillan.

Dewey, J. (1933) *How We Think. A Restatement of the Relation of Reflective Thinking to the Educative Process,* revised edition. Boston, MA: D.C. Heath.

Dewey, J. (1938) *Experience and Education.* New York: Collier Books.

Dewey, J. (1997) *How We Think.* Mineola Long Island: Dover Books. (Originally published in 1910).

Dingwall, R. (1999) '"Risk Society": the cult of theory and the millennium', *Social Policy and Administration,* 33(4): 474–91. (Reprinted in N. Manning and I. Shaw (eds) (2000) *New Risks, New Welfare. Signposts for Social Policy.* Oxford: Blackwells. pp. 137–53.

Doel, M. (2002) 'Task centred work', in R. Adams, L. Dominelli and M. Payne (eds) *Social Work: Themes, Issues and Critical Debates,* 2nd edition. Basingstoke: Palgrave. pp. 191–9.

Doel, M. and Marsh, P. (1992) *Task-Centred Social Work.* Aldershot: Ashgate.

Dominelli, L. (1988) *Anti-Racist Social Work.* London: Macmillan.

Dowd, J.P. (1975) 'Ageing as exchange: a preface to theory', *Journal of Gerontology,* 30(5): 584–94.

Drake, R.F. (2001) *The Principles of Social Policy.* Basingstoke: Palgrave.

Ellis, A. (1962) *Reason and Emotion in Psychotherapy.* Secaucus NJ: Citadel.

Emerson, E., Robertson, J., Gregory, N., Hatton, C., Kessissoglou, S., Hallam, A., Knapp, M., Järbrink, K. and Netten, A. (1999) *Quality and Costs of Residential Supports for People with Learning Disabilities: A Comparative Analysis of Quality and Costs in Village Communities, Residential Campuses and Dispersed Housing Schemes.* Manchester: Hester Adrian Research Centre University of Manchester.

England, H. (1986) *Social Work as Art: Making Sense for Good Practice.* London: Routledge.

Erikson, E. (1963) *Childhood and Society.* New York: W.W. Norton. (Originally published in 1950)

Erikson, E. (1968) *Identity Youth and Crisis.* New York: W.W. Norton.

References

Erikson, E., Erikson, J.M. and Kivnick, H.Q. (1986) *Vital Involvement in Old Age: The Experience of Old Age in Our Time*. New York: Norton.

Estes, C.L. (1979) *The Aging Enterprise*. San Francisco, CA: Jossey-Bass.

Etzioni, A. (1969) *The Semi-Professions and Their Organisation*. New York: Free Press.

Etzioni, A. (1997) *The New Golden Rule: Community and Morality in a Democratic Society*. London: Profile Books.

European Community (EC) (1995) *EU Directive on Data Processing 95/46*. Brussels: EC.

Elder, G.H. and Pavalko, E.K. (1993) 'Work careers in men's later years: transitions, trajectories and historical change', *Journal of Gerontology: Social Sciences*, 48(4): 180–1.

Eurostat (2000) *European Social Statistics: Income, Poverty and Social Exclusion*. Luxembourg: Eurostat.

Everitt, A., Hardiker, P., Littlewood, J. and Mullender, A. (1992) *Applied Research for Better Practice*. London: Macmillan.

Fee, E. (1986) 'Critiques of modern science: the relation of feminism to other radical epistemologies', in R. Bleier (ed.) *Feminist Approaches to Science*. New York: Pergamon. pp. 42–56.

Finch, J. (1984) 'Community care: developing non-sexist alternatives', *Critical Social Policy*, 9: 6–18.

Finkelstein, V. (1980) *Attitudes and Disabled People*. New York: World Rehabilitation Fund.

Finkelstein, V. (1981) 'Disability and the helper/helped relationship: An historical view', in P. Liddiard, A. Brechin and J. Swain (eds) *Handicap in a Social World: A Reader*. Sevenoaks: Hodder and Stoughton. pp. 34–6. www.leeds.ac.uk/disabilitystudies/archiveuk/finkelstein/finkelstein.htm

Fischer, D. (1978) *Growing Old in America*. Oxford: Oxford University Press.

Flaherty, J., Veit-Wilson, J. and Dornan, P. (2004) *Poverty: The Facts*, 5th edition. London: Child Poverty Action Group.

Flexner, A. (1915) 'Is social work a profession?', *Proceedings of the National Conference of Charities and Correction*. Chicago: Hildemann. pp. 577–90.

Foucault, M. (1971) *Madness and Civilisation*. London: Tavistock.

Foucault, M. (1979) *The History of Sexuality*. London: Tavistock.

Foucault, M. (1980) *Power/Knowledge: Selected Interviews and Writings 1972–1977*, Gordon, C. (ed.). Pantheon: New York.

Fox, L. (1995) 'Mapping the advance of the new culture in dementia care,' in T. Kitwood and S. Benson (eds) *The New Culture of Dementia Care*. Bradford: Hawker Publication Bradford Dementia Group, University of Bradford. pp. 70–4.

Frankin County Children's Services (2002) *Country Kinship Navigator Program Resource Guide* JFS 08146 2 and Meigs County Kinship Navigator Program Brochure *Caring for Children*, Columbus Ohio. http://defiance.osu.edu/fcs/SH03Winter2.pdf.

Freire, P. (1970) *Pedagogy of the Oppressed*. New York: Continuum Books.

Freire, P. (1972) *Pedagogy of the Oppressed*. Harmondsworth: Penguin.

French, S. (1993) 'Disability, impairment or something in between', in: J. Swain, V. Finkelstein, S. French and M. Oliver (eds) *Disabling Barriers – Disabling Environments*. London: Sage. pp. 17–25.

French, S. (1994) 'The attitudes of health professionals towards disabled people. A discussion and review of the literature', *Physiotherapy*, 80: 687–93.

Freud, A. (1936) *The Ego and Mechanisms of Defense*. New York: International University Press.

Freud, S. (1986) *The Essentials of Psycho-Analysis*, selected by Anna Freud. London: Penguin.

Gambrill, E. (1983) *Casework: A Competency Based Approach*. Englewood Cliffs, NJ: Prentice Hall.

Gearing, B. and Dant, T. (1990) 'Doing biographical research', in S.M. Peace (ed.) *Researching Social Gerontology*. London: Sage. pp. 143–59.

General Social Care Council (GSCC) (2001) *Social Work Education Post Qualifying Training Handbook*. London: GSCC. www.gscc.org.uk/

References

General Social Care Council (GSCC) (2002) *Codes of Practice for Social Care Workers and Employers.* London: GSCC.

General Social Care Council (GSCC) (2003) *Post-Registration Training and Learning Level of Achievement.* London: GSCC. www.gscc.org.uk/

General Social Care Council (GSCC) (2003) *Registration Rules.* London: GSCC.

General Social Care Council (GSCC) (2005) *New Post qualifying Framework for Social Work Education and Training.* London: GSCC. www.gscc.org.uk/

Germain, C.B. and Gitterman, A. (1996) *The Life Model of Social Work Practice. Advances in Practice and Theory.* New York: Columbia University Press.

Gergen, K.J. (1978) 'Toward generative theory', *Journal of Personality and Social Psychology*, 36(11): 1344–60.

Gershon, K. (ed.) (1966) *We Came As Children. A Collective Autobiography of Refugees.* London:Gollancz.

Giddens, A. (1990) *The Consequences of Modernity.* Cambridge: Polity Press.

Giddens, A. (1991) *Modernity and Self-Identity: Self and Society in the Late Modern Age.* Cambridge: Polity Press.

Giddens, A. (1994) *Beyond Left and Right: The Future of Radical Politics.* Cambridge: Polity Press.

Giddens, A. (1998) *The Third Way: The Renewal of Social Democracy.* Cambridge: Polity Press.

Gilligan, C. (1982) *In a Different Voice.* Cambridge, MA: Harvard University Press.

Gillman, M., Swain, J. and Heyman, B. (1997) 'Life history or "case history": the objectification of people with learning difficulties through the tyranny of professional discourses', *Disability & Society*, 12(5): 675–93.

Glass, N. (1999) 'Sure Start. The development of an Early Intervention Programme in the United Kingdom', *Children & Society*, 13(4): 257–64.

Glennister, H. (1997) *Paying for Welfare*, 3rd edition. London: Harvester Wheatsheaf.

Goffman, E. (1961) *Asylums.* Coventry: Anchor Books Doubleday.

Goffman, E. (1963) *Stigma: Notes on the Management of Spoiled Identity.* Englewood Cliffs, NJ: Prentice Hall.

Golan, N. (1986) 'Crisis Theory', in F. Turner (ed.) *Social Work Treatment: Interlocking Theoretical Approaches.* New York: Free Press. pp. 319–21.

Goldberg, E.M. and Connolly, N. (1982) *The Effectiveness of Social Care for the Elderly.* London: Heinnemann.

Goldson, B. (2002) 'New Labour, social justice and children: political calculation and the deserving-undeserving schism', *British Journal of Social Work*, 32(6): 683–96.

Goldstein, H. (1973) *Social Work practice: A Unitary Approach.* Columbia, SC: University of South Carolina Press.

Goldstein, H. (1981) *Social Learning and Change: A Cognitive Approach to Human Services.* Columbia, SC: University of South Carolina.

Goldstein, H. (1992) 'If social work hasn't made progress as a science, maybe it is an art?', *Families in Society*, 73: 48–55.

Gramsci, A. (1971) *Selections from the Prison Notebooks.* London: Lawrence and Wishart.

Green, L. and Statham, D. (2004) *Scoping Report, East Midlands Learning Resource Centre Network.* Derby: Skills for Care East Midlands Regional Committee.

Greenwich London Borough Council (1987) *Kimberley Carlisle Report: A Child in Mind.* London: Borough of Greenwich.

Greenwood, E. (1966) 'The elements of professionalization', in H. Vollmer and D. Mills (eds) *Professionalization.* Englewood Cliffs, NJ: Prentice Hall. pp. 9–19.

Grotberg, E. (1997) 'The International Resilience Project: Findings from the Research and the Effectiveness of Interventions', in B. Bain et al. (eds) *Psychology and Education in the 21st Century: Proceedings of the 54th Annual Convention of the International Council of Psychologists.* Edmonton: IC Press. pp. 118–28.

The Guidance Council (GC) (2004) *Campaigning Agenda for Guidance.* Winchester: The Guidance Council.

References

Hadley, R., Cooper, M., Dale, P. and Stacy, G. (1987) *A Community Social Worker's Handbook*. London: Tavistock.

Hamilton, G. (1951) *Theory and Practice of Social Casework*, 2nd edition. New York: Columbia University Press.

Harding, S. (1987) *Feminism and Methodology*. Bloomington, IN: Indiana University Press.

Harris, R. (1997) 'Power', in M. Davies (ed.) *The Blackwell Companion to Social Work*. Oxford: Blackwell. pp. 28–33.

Harvey, L. (1990) *Critical Social Research*. London: Unwin Hyman.

Havighurst, R.J. (1963) 'Successful aging', in R.H. Williams, C. Tibbetss and W. Donohue (eds) *Processes of Aging*. New York: Atherton. pp. 299–320.

Hawtin, K. (ed.) (1989) *Cognitive Behaviour Therapy for Psychiatric Problems: A Practical Guide*. Oxford: Oxford University Press.

Health Development Agency (HDA) (2005) *Social Capital*. www.social-action.org.uk/hdaresearch/research.asp

Henwood, M. (1992) *Through a Glass Darkly: Community Care and Elderly People*. London: King's Fund Institute.

Heraud, B.J. (1970) *Sociology & Social Work. Perspectives and Problems*. Oxford: Pergamon Press.

Higham, P. (2001) 'Changing practice and an emerging social pedagogue paradigm in England: the role of the Personal Adviser', *Social Work in Europe*, 8(1): 21–8.

Higham, P.E. (1998) *Careers of Care. Survivors of Traumatic Brain Injury and the Response of Health and Social Care*. Aldershot: Ashgate.

Higham, P.E. (2005) 'Where credit's due', *Care and Health*, 109: 12–18.

Hillyard, P., Kelly, G., McLaughlin, E. Patsios, D. and Tomlinson, M. (2003) *Bare Necessities: Poverty and Social Exclusion in Northern Ireland*. Belfast: Democratic Dialogue.

Hirschman, A.O. (1970) *Exit, Voice, and Loyalty: Responses to Decline in Firms, Organizations, and States*. Cambridge, MA: Harvard University Press.

HM Inspectorate of Probation (HMIP) (1998) *Strategies for effective offender supervision*. Report of the HMIP What Works Project. London: Home Office.

Hollis, F. (1972) *Casework: A Psychosocial Therapy*, 2nd edition. New York: Random House. (Originally published 1964)

Holman, A. and Bewley, C. (1999) *Funding Freedom 2000: People with Learning Difficulties using Direct Payments*. London: Values Into Action.

Holman, B. (1998) *Child Care Revisited: The Children's Departments 1948–1971. How the Childcare Specialists of the Past Hold Lessons for the Future*. London: Institute of Childcare and Social Education UK.

Homans, G. (1974) *Social Behaviour*, 2nd edition. New York: Harcourt Brace.

House of Commons Select Committee (HCSC) (2004) *Report on Elder Abuse*. www.parliament.the-stationery-office.co.uk/pa/cm200304/cmselect/cmhealth/111/11101.htm

Howe, D. (1986) 'Welfare law and the welfare principle in social work practice', *Journal of Social Welfare Law*, May: 130–43.

Howe, D. (1987) *An Introduction to Social Work Theory. Making Sense in Practice*. Aldershot: Gower.

Hudson, B. and Macdonald, G. (1986) *Behavioural Social Work: An Introduction*. London: Macmillan.

Hughes, B. (1990) 'Quality of Life', in S.M. Peace (ed.) *Researching Social Gerontology. Concepts. Methods and Issues*. London: Sage. pp. 46–58.

Hughes, L. (2002) 'Services at the crossroads', *Community Care*, October 3–9: 36–7.

Hugman, R. (1991) *Power in the Caring Professions*. Basingstoke: Macmillan.

Hugman, R. (2005) *New Approaches in Ethics for the Caring Professions Taking Account of Change for Caring Professions*. Basingstoke: Palgrave.

References

Humphries, B. and Martin, M. (2000) 'Disrupting ethics in social research', in B. Humphries (ed.) *Research in Social Care and Social Welfare: Issues and Debates for Practice.* London: Jessica Kingsley. pp. 69–85.

Illich, I., McKnight, J., Zola, I.K., Caplan, J. and Shaiken, H. (1977) *The Disabling Professions.* London: Marion Boyers.

Information Centre About Asylum and Refugees in the UK (ICAR) (2005) www.icar.org

Ivers, V. (1994) *Citizen Advocacy in Action: Working with Older People.* Stoke-on-Trent: Beth Johnson Foundation in association with the European Commission.

Jack, G. (1997) 'An ecological approach to social work with children and families', *Child and Family Social Work*, 2: 109–20.

Jacobs, M. (1996) *The Politics of the Real World: Meeting the New Century.* London: Pluto Press.

Jacobs, B., Buschman, R., Schaeffer, D. and Dendy, R. (1973) *Counselor Training: Short-term Client systems. Training Manual for Counseling Skills.* Arlington, VR: National Drug Abuse Center for Training and Resource Development.

Jankovic, J. and Green, R. (1981) 'Teaching legal principles to social workers', *Journal of Education for Social Work*, 17(13): 28–35.

Johnson, P. (1978) *Structured Dependency of the Elderly: A Critical Note.* London: Centre for Economic Policy Research.

Jones, C. (1997) 'Poverty', in M. Davies (ed.) *The Blackwell Companion to Social Work.* Oxford: Blackwell. pp. 118–25.

Jones, C. (2002) 'Social work and society', in R. Adams, L. Dominelli and M. Payne (eds) *Social Work Themes, Issues and Critical Debates*, 2nd edition. Basingstoke: Open University/Palgrave. pp. 41–9.

Jones, C. (2003) *Social Work and Social Justice: A Manifesto for a New Engaged Practice.* Liverpool: University of Liverpool.

Jones, D. (2002) 'Questioning New Labour's Youth Justice Strategy: a review article', *Youth Justice*, 1(3): 14–26.

Jones, K. (1994) *The Making of Social Policy in Britain 1830–1990*, 2nd edition. London: Athlone Press.

Jordan, B. (1979) *Helping in Social Work.* London: Routledge & Kegan Paul.

Jordan, B. (2004) 'Emancipatory social work? Opportunity or oxymoron', *British Journal of Social Work*, 34(1): 5–19.

Jordan, B. with Jordan, C. (2000) *Social Work and the Third Way: Tough Love as Social Policy.* London: Sage.

Joseph Rowntree Foundation (JRF) (2004) *Findings. Monitoring Poverty and Social Exclusion 2004.* York: Joseph Rowntree Foundation. www.jrf.org.uk

Jung, C.G. (1969) *Collected Works.* London: Routledge.

Kadushin, A. (1972) *The Social Work Interview.* New York: Columbia University Press.

Kagitcibasi, Cigdem (1996) *Family and Human Development Across Cultures. A View from the Other Side.* Mahwah, NJ: Lawrence Erbaum.

Kant, I. (1996) *Practical Philosophy* M.J. Gregor (ed. and trans.) with introduction by A.W. Wood. Cambridge: Cambridge University Press.

Kerr, B. (1985) *She'd Be Better Off in a Home, Wouldn't She?* London: CCCETSW.

Kilpatrick, W. (1993) *Why Johnny Can't Tell Right from Wrong.* New York: Touchstone Books Simon and Schuster.

Kingston, P., Bennet, G. and Penhale, B. (1997) *The Dimensions of Elder Abuse.* Basingstoke: Macmillan Palgrave.

Kitwood, T. (1997) *Dementia Reconsidered. The Person Comes First.* Buckingham: Open University Press.

Knight, B., Gibson, M., Grant, S. and Tolladay, P. (1979) *Family Groups in the Community.* London: London Voluntary Service Council.

References

Kohlberg, L. (1969) *Stages in the Development of Moral Thought and Action.* New York: Holt, Rhinehart and Winston.

Kornbeck, J. (2000) 'Social work versus social pedagogy', *Professional Social Work* November: 12–13.

Kramer, L. (1994a) *Earthquake and Other Poems.* Ware: Rockingham Press.

Kramer, L. (1994b) *The Desecration of Trees.* Frome: Hippopotamus Press.

Kramer, L. (1997) *Selected and New Poems 1980–1997.* Ware: Rockingham Press in association with the European Jewish Publication Society.

Kubler-Ross, E. (1969) *On Death and Dying.* New York: Macmillan.

Ladyman, S. (2004) 'General Social Care Council conference speech', 24 November, London.

Laird, S. (2002) 'Imposing Best Practice', *Professional Social Work*, June: 18–19.

Laming, H. (2003) *The Victoria Climbié Inquiry.* London: DH.

Langan, J. and Lindow, V. (2004) *Living with risk: Mental Health Service User Involvement in Risk Assessment and Management.* Bristol: The Policy Press.

Laslett, P. (1996) *A Fresh Map of Life,* 2nd edition. London: Macmillan.

Layder, D. (1993) *New Strategies in Social Research.* Cambridge: Polity Press.

Leadbetter, M. (2002) 'Empowerment and advocacy', in R. Adams, L. Dominelli and M. Payne (eds) *Social Work Themes, Issues and Critical Debates,* 2nd edition. Basingstoke: Palgrave. pp. 200–8.

Lee-Treweek, G. and Linkogle, S. (2000) *Danger in the Field. Risk and Ethics in Social Research.* London: Routledge.

Leverton, B. and Lowensohn, S. (eds) (1990) *I Came Alone. The Stories of the Kindertransports.* Lewes, Sussex: The Book Guild Ltd.

Levinson, D. with Darrow, C., Klein, E., Levinson, M. and McKee, B. (1978) *The Seasons of a Man's Life.* New York: Knopf.

Levinson, D. and Levinson, J. (1996) *The Seasons of a Woman's Life.* New York: Knopf.

Lewin, K. (1936) *Principles of Topological Psychology.* New York: McGraw Hill.

Lewin, K. (1948) *Resolving Social Conflicts.* London: Souvenir Press.

Linton, R. (1936) *The Study of Man.* New York: Apple Century.

Lively, P. (2001) *A House Unlocked.* London: Penguin.

London Borough of Brent (1985) *A Child in Trust: the Report of the Panel of Inquiry into the circumstances surrounding the death of Jasmine Beckford.* London: London Borough of Brent.

Loney, M. (1983) *Community Against Government. The British Community Development Project 1968–78: A Study of Government Incompetence.* London: Heinemann.

Longmate, N. (1974) *The Workhouse.* London: Temple Smith.

Lorenz, W. (1991) 'Social work practice in Europe', in M. Hill (ed.) *Social Work and the European Community.* London: Jessica Kingsley.

Lorenz, W. (2000) 'Contentious identities – social work research and the search for professional and personal identities', *Researching Social Work as a Means of Social Inclusion: Theorising Social Work Research* ESRC Seminar series eLSC Electronic Library for Social Care. www.elsc.org.uk/socialcareresource/tswr/seminars.htm

Lorenz, W. (2003) 'The role of training in preparing socio-educational care workers to meet the challenges of social change', FESET Congress Conference paper. www.petersbroe.dk/feset/uk/congress/03traini.htm

Luft, J. (1970) *Group Processes: An Introduction to Group Dynamics,* 2nd edition. Palo Alto, CA: National Press Books.

Luft, J. and Ingram, H. (1955) *The Johari Window Model.* Western Training Laboratory Group. Los Angeles, CA: UCLA.

Lukes, S. (1974) *Power: A Radical View.* London: Macmillan.

References

Lymbery, M. (1998) 'Care management and professional autonomy: the impact of community care legislation on social work with older people', *British Journal of Social Work*, 28(6): 863–78.

Lymbery, M. (2001) 'Social Work at the Crossroads', *British Journal of Social Work*, 31(3): 369–84.

Lymbery, M. (2005) *Social Work with Older People*. London: Sage.

Macdonald, G. and Macdonald, K. (1995) 'Ethical issues in social work research', in R. Hugman and D. Smith (eds) *Ethical Issues in Social Work*. London: Routledge. pp. 46–64.

Madden, R. (2000) 'Legal content in social work education: preparing students for interprofessional practice', *Journal of Teaching in Social Work*, 20(1/2): 3–17.

Madden, R.G. and Wayne, R.H. (2003) 'Social work and the law: a therapeutic jurisprudence perspective', *Social Work*, 48(3): 338–47.

Main, M. and Solomon, J. (1986) 'Discovery of an insecure disorganised/disoriented attachment pattern: procedures, findings and implications for classification of behaviour', in M. Yogman and T.B. Brazelton (eds) *Affective Development in Infancy*. Norwood, NJ: Ablex. pp. 95–124.

Manning, N. and Shaw, I. (2000) 'Introduction: the millennium and social policy', in I. Shaw and N. Manning (eds) *New Risks, New Welfare: Signposts for Social Policy*. Oxford: Blackwell Publishing. pp. 1–11.

Manning, N., Baldock, J. and Vickerstaff, S. (2003) 'The origins, character and politics of modern social welfare systems', in J. Baldock, N. Manning, and S. Vickerstaff (eds) *Social Policy*, 2nd edition. Oxford: Oxford University Press. pp. 3–28.

Marsh, P. and Doel, M. (2005) *The Task Centred Book: Developing, Learning, Sustaining and Reviewing Task-Centred Social Work*. London: Routledge.

Marsh, P. and Fisher, M. (1992) *Good Intentions: Developing User Orientated services Under the Children and Community Care Acts*. York: Community Care/Joseph Rowntree Foundation.

Maslow, A. (1987) *Motivation and Personality*, 3rd edition. New York: Harper and Row.

Masson, J.M. (1984) *The Assault on Truth: Freud's Suppression of the Seduction Theory*. London: Faber & Faber.

Masson, J.M. (1993) *Against Therapy* (Revised). Monroe, ME: Common Courage Press.

Mauss, M. (1965) *The Gift*. London: Routledge & Kegan Paul.

Mayer, J. and Timms, N. (1970) *The Client Speaks*. London: Routledge & Kegan Paul.

McDonald, A. (2001) 'The human rights act and social work practice', *Practice*, 13(3): 5–16.

McGregor, A., Glass, A., Higgins, K., Macdougall, L. and Sutherland, V. (2003) *Developing People – Regenerating Place: Achieving Greater Integration for Local Area Regeneration*. York: Joseph Rowntree Foundation.

Mead, G.H. (1934) *Mind, Self and Society*, C.W. Morris (ed.). Chicago, IL: University of Chicago Press.

Means, R. and Smith, R. (1994) *Community Care. Policy and Practice*. London: Macmillan.

Merton, R.K. (1957) *Social Theory and Social Structure*. Glencoe, IL: The Free Press.

Midgley, J. (1997) *Social Work in a Global Context*. Thousand Oaks, CA: Sage.

Miller, W. and Rollnick. S. (eds) (1991) *Motivational Interviewing*. London: Guildford Press.

Mills, C.W. (1959) *The Power Elite*. New York: Galaxy.

Mitchell, J. (1974) *Psychoanalysis and Feminism. A Radical Reassessment of Freudian Psychoanalysis*. Harmondsworth: Penguin.

Monach, J. and Spriggs, L. (1994) 'The consumer role', in N. Malin (ed.) *Implementing Community Care*. Buckingham: Open University Press. pp. 138–53.

Montgomery General Hospital (2004) *Advanced Treatments, Enhanced Trust Annual Report*. Olney, MD: Cancercenter, Montgomery General Hospital. www.montgomerygeneral.com/programs_services/MG_CancerAR_14181_8.pdf

Morgan, A. and Swann, C. (eds) (2004) *Social Capital for Health: Issues of Definition, Measurement and Links to Health*. London: Health Development Agency.

References

Morris, J. (1991) *Pride Against Prejudice*. London: Women's Press.

Morris, J. (1998) *Still Missing? Disabled children and the Children Act*. London: The Who Cares? Trust.

Morris, J. (2000) 'The disabling society: fighting back', Talk to Joseph Rowntree Foundation Summer School, July.

Morris, P. (1969) *Put Away*. London: Routledge Kegan Paul.

Mullender, A. and Ward, D. (1991) *Self Directed Groupwork: Users Take Action for Empowerment*. London: Whiting and Birch.

Munday, B. (1990) 'Social services in the EC and the implications of 1992', in C. Cannan, L. Berry and K. Lyons (eds) *Social Work and Europe*. London: Macmillan. pp. 47–8.

Munro, E. (2004) 'The impact of audit on social work practice', *British Journal of Social Work*, 34: 1075–95.

National Association of Social Workers (NASW) (1999) *Code of Ethics*. Washington, DC: NASW. www.naswdc.org/

National Asylum Support Service (NASS) (2005) *Policy Bulletins*. www.ind.homeoffice.gov.uk/ind/en/home/applying/national_asylum_support/policy bulletin

National Mentoring Network (NMN) (2005) www.nmn.org.uk

Neugarten, B.L. and Datan, N. (1973) 'Sociological perspectives on the life cycle', in P.B. Baltes and K.W. Schaie (eds) *Life-Span Developmental Psychology: Personality and Socialization*. New York: Academic Press. pp. 53–69.

Neugarten, B.L. and Neugarten, D.A. (1986) 'Changing meanings of age in the aging society', in A. Pifer and L. Bronte (eds) *Our Aging society. Paradox and Promise*. New York: Norton. pp. 33–51.

NHS *Allied Health Professions* (AHP) (2004) www.nhscareers.nhs.uk/nhs-knowledge_base/data/4900.html

NHS Modernisation Agency (2004) *A Career Framework for the NHS*. Discussion Document – version 2, June 2004. London: DH.

The National Institute for Mental Health England (NIMHE), The Sainsbury Centre for Mental Health Joint Workforce Support Unit The NHS University (2004) *The Ten Essential Shared Capabilities for the Whole of the Mental Health Workforce*. London: DH. www.dh.gov.uk/publications

National Institute for Mental Health in England (NIMHE) (2005) www.nimhe.org.uk/

Northern Ireland Social Care Council (NISCC) (2003) *Practice Learning Requirements for the Degree in Social Work*. Belfast: NISCC.

Northern Ireland Social Care Council (NISCC) (2004) *Learning Teaching and Assessment Requirements*. Belfast: NISCC.

Northern Ireland Social Care Council (NISCC) (2005) *Explanation of Social Care Workers' Roles*. www.niscc.info/careers/faq.htm

Nursing & Midwifery Council (NMC) (2002) *Code of Professional Conduct*. London: NMC. www.nmc-uk.org/nmc/main/publications/

O'Brien, J. (1987) 'A guide to lifestyle planning', in B. Wilcox and G.T. Bellamy (eds) *A Comprehensive Guide to the Activities Catalogue. An Alternative Curriculum for Youth and Adults with Severe Disabilities*. Baltimore: Paul H. Brookes.

O'Hagan, K. (1986) *Crisis Intervention in Social Services*. London: Macmillan.

O'Hagan, K. (1991) 'Crisis intervention in social work', in J. Lishman (ed.) *A Handbook of Theory for Practice Teachers in Social Work*. London: Jessica Kingsley.

Oliver, M. (1996) *Understanding Disability. From Theory to Practice*. Basingstoke: Macmillan.

Oliver, M. and Barnes, C. (1998) *Disabled People and Social Policy*. London: Longman.

Oliver, M.J. (1983) *Social Work with Disabled People*. Basingstoke: Macmillan.

Oliver, M.J. (1989) 'The social model of disability: current reflections', in P. Carter, T. Jeffs, and M. Smith (eds) *Social Work and Social Welfare Yearbook I*. Milton Keynes: Open University. pp. 190–203.

References

Oliver, M.J. (1999) *The Disability Movement and the Professions.* Leeds: University of Leeds Centre for Disability Studies Research Archive UK. www.leeds.ac.uk/disability-studies/

Paine, T. (1995) *Collected Writings: Common Sense/The Crisis/Rights of Man/The Age of Reason/Pamphlets, Articles, and Letters.* New York: Library of America.

Parker, R. (1981) 'Tending and social care. Divisions of responsibility', in E.M. Goldberg and S. Hatch (eds) *A New Look at the Personal Social Services.* London: London Policies Institute. pp. 17–34.

Parkes, C.M. (1998) *Bereavement: Studies of Grief in Adult Life,* 3rd edition. London: Routledge.

Parsons, T. (1951) *The Social System.* Glencoe IL: The Free Press.

Parton, N. (1996) 'Social theory, social change and social work: an introduction', in N. Parton (ed.) *Social Theory, Social Change and Social Work.* London: Routledge. pp. 4–18.

Parton, N. and O'Byrne, P. (2000) *Constructive Social Work. Towards a New Practice.* Basingstoke: Macmillan.

Pascall, G. (1986) *Social Policy. A Feminist Analysis.* London: Tavistock.

Pavlov, I.P. (1927) *Conditioning Reflexes,* G.V. Anrep (trans.). New York: Liveright.

Payne, M. (1991) *Modern Social Work Theory: A Critical Introduction.* London: Macmillan.

Payne, M. (1996) *What is Professional Social Work?* Birmingham: Venture Press.

Payne, M. (2006) *Social Work Continuity and Change.* Basingstoke: Palgrave Macmillian.

Pease, B. and Fook, J. (1999) 'Introduction: Postmodern critical theory and emancipatory social work practice', in B. Pease and J. Fook (eds) *Transforming Social Work Practice: Postmodern Critical Perspectives.* London: Routledge. pp. 1–22.

Peck, E., Towell, D. and Gulliver, P. (2001) 'The meanings of "culture" in health and social care', *Journal of Inter-Professional Care,* 15(4): 319–27.

Percy-Smith, J. (2000) 'Introduction: the contours of social exclusion', in J. Percy-Smith (ed.) *Policy Responses to Social Exclusion towards Inclusion?* Buckingham: Open University Press. pp. 1–21.

Perlman, H.H. (1957) *Social Casework: A Problem Solving Process.* Chicago, IL: University of Chicago Press.

Perlman, H.H. (1979) *Relationship.* Chicago, IL: University of Chicago Press.

Phillipson, C. (1982) *Capitalism and the Construction of Old Age.* London: Macmillan.

Piaget, J. (1932) *The Moral Judgment of the Child.* New York: Macmillan.

Pierson, J. (2001) *Tackling Social Exclusion.* London: Routledge.

Pincus, A. and Minahan, A. (1973) *Social Work Practice: Model and Method.* Itasca IL: Peacock.

Pinfold, V. and Corry, P. (2003) *Who Cares?* London: Rethink.

Pinker, R. (1982) 'Appendix B An alternative view', in P. Barclay (ed.) *Social Workers. Their Roles & Tasks.* London: National Institute for Social Work Bedford Square Press/NCVO. pp. 236–62.

Pitt-Aikens, T. and Thomas Ellis, A. (1986) *Secrets of Strangers.* London: Duckworth.

Pitt-Aikens, T. and Thomas Ellis, A. (1989) *Loss of the Good Authority. The Cause of Delinquency.* London: Viking.

Powell, W. (2003) 'Doing it, artfully. Editorial comment, families in society', *The Journal of Contemporary Human Services Alliance for Children and Families,* 458(84): 457–9.

Pray, K.L.M. (1949) 'The role of professional social work in the world today', in *Social Work in a Revolutionary Age.* Philadelphia, PA: University of Pennsylvania Press. pp. 33–4.

Preston-Shoot, M. (2000) 'Making connections in the curriculum: law and professional practice', in R. Pierce and J. Weinstein (eds) *Innovative Education and Training for Care Professionals: A Providers Guide.* London: Jessica Kingsley Publishers.

Preston-Shoot, M. (2004) 'Education and training for the social care workforce', a presentation at an ippr seminar 28 June 2004, London.

Preston-Shoot, M. (2006) *Effective Groupwork.* London: Palgrave.

Prochaska, J.O. and DiClemente, C.C. (1982) 'Transtheoretical therapy: toward a more integrative model of change', *Psychotherapy: Theory, Research and Practice,* 19(3): 276–88.

References

PSE (1999) *Poverty and Social Exclusion Survey*. York: Joseph Rowntree Foundation. www.bris.ac.uk/poverty/pse/welcome.htm

Putnam, R.D. (1993) *Making Democracy Work. Civic Traditions in Modern Italy*. Princeton, NJ: Princeton University Press.

Putnam, R.D. (1995) 'Bowling alone: America's declining social capital', *Journal of Democracy*, 6(1): 65–78. http://muse.jhu.edu/demo/journal_of_democracy/v006/putnam.html

Putnam, R.D. (ed.) (2002) *Democracies in Flux: The Evolution of Social Capital in Contemporary Society*. New York: Oxford University Press.

Putnam, R.P. (2000) *Bowling Alone: The Collapse and Revival of American Community*. New York: Simon and Schuster.

Quality Assurance Agency (2000) *Social Policy and Administration and Social Work Benchmark Statements*. Gloucester: QAA.

Radtke, L. and Stam, H.J. (1994) 'Introduction', in H.L. Radtke and H.J. Stam (eds) *Power/Gender. Social Relations in Theory*. London: Sage. pp. 2–14.

Rankin, J. (2004) *Mental Health in the Mainstream. Developments and Trends in Mental Health Policy*, Working Paper One. London: ippr.

Rankin, J. and Regan, S. (2004a) 'Meeting complex needs in social care', *Housing, Care and Support*, 7(3): 3–8.

Rankin J. and Regan, S. (2004b) *Meeting Complex Needs: The Future of Social Care*. London: Institute for Public Policy Research (ippr).

Reder, P., Duncan, S. and Gray, M. (1993) *Beyond Blame: Child Abuse Tragedies Revisited*. London: Routledge.

Reid, W. and Epstein, L. (1972) *Task Centered Casework*. New York: Columbia University Press.

Reid W.J. and Shyne, A.W. (1969) *Brief and Extended Casework*. New York: Columbia University Press.

Richmond, M. (1917) *Social Diagnosis*. New York: Free Press.

Riley, M.W., Johnson, M. and Foner, A. (1972) *Aging and Society: A Sociology of Age Stratification*. New York: Russell Sage.

Roberts, A.R. (2004) *Crisis Intervention Handbook: Assessment, Treatment, and Research*, 2nd edition. Oxford: Oxford University Press.

Robertson, J. (1967–71) *Young Children in Brief Separation Series. Five Studies of the Effects of Separation on Young Children*. Ipswich: The Robertson Centre Concord Video and Film Council. www.concordvideao.co.uk

Roche, D. and Rankin, J. (2004) *Who Cares? Building the Social Care Workforce*. London: Institute for Public Policy Research (ippr). www.ippr.org

Rogers, C.R. (1961) *On Becoming a Person*. London: Constable.

Rose, A.M. (1965) 'The subculture of aging', in A. Rose and W. Peterson (eds) *Older People and Their Social World*. Philadephia: F.A. Davis. pp. 3–16.

Rosow, I. (1974) *Socialization to Old Age*. Berkeley, CA: University of California Free Press.

Rousseau, J.J. (1998) *The Social Contract: Or Principles of Political Right*. Ware: Wordsworth Edition Ltd.

Rowntree, B. Seebohm (1901) *Poverty: A Study of Town Life*. London: Macmillan.

Royal College of Nursing (RCN) (2005) *Practice Development*. www.rcn.org.uk/resources/practice development/about-pd/tools/values-clarification

Rutter, M. (1972) *Maternal Deprivation Reassessed*. Harmondsworth: Penguin.

Sainsbury, E. (1970) *Social Diagnosis in Casework*. London: Routledge & Kegan Paul.

Schon, D. (1983) *The Reflective Practitioner: How Professions Think in Action*. London: Basic Books.

Sebald, W.G. (2001) *Austerlitz*, Anthea Bell (trans.). London: Hamish Hamilton.

Seden, J. (2005) *Counselling Skills in Social Work Practice*, 2nd edition. London: Open University Press/McGraw Hill.

References

Seebohm, Sir F. (1968) *Report of the Committee on Local Authority and Allied Personal Social Services*, Command 3703. London: HMSO.

Senge, P. (1990) *The Fifth Discipline – the Art and Practice of the Learning Organisation*. London: Century Business.

Shakespeare, T.W. and Erickson, M. (2000) 'Different strokes: beyond biological essentialism and social constructionism', in S. Rose and H. Rose (eds) *Coming to Life*. New York: Little Brown. pp. 190–205.

Shakespeare, T.W. and Watson, N. (2002) 'The social model of disability: an outdated ideology?', *Research in Social Science and Disability*, 2: 9–28.

Shardlow, S. (2002) 'Values, ethics and social work', in R. Adams, L. Dominelli and M. Payne (eds) *Social Work Themes, Issues and Critical Debates*, 2nd edition. Basingstoke: Palgrave. pp. 30–40.

Shaw, I. (2000) 'Resources for social policy', in N. Manning and I. Shaw (eds) *New Risks, New Welfare: Signposts for Social Policy*. Oxford: Blackwell Publishing. pp. 24–35.

Sheldon, B. (1982) *Behaviour Modification*. London: Tavistock.

Silverman, P. (1987) 'Introduction: the life course perspective', in P. Silverman (ed.) *The Elderly as Modern Pioneers*. Bloomington, IL: Indiana University Press. pp. 1–16.

Simmons, L.W. (1945) *The Role of the Aged in Primitive Society*. New Haven, CN: Yale University Press.

Simon, S.B., Howe, L.W. and Kirschenbaum, H. (1978) *Values Clarification. A Handbook of Practical Strategies for Teachers and Students*, revised edition. New York: Hart Books, A & W Visual Library.

Sinclair, I. (1990) 'Residential care', in I. Sinclair, R. Parker, D. Leat and J. Williams (eds) *The Kaleidoscope of Care: A Review of Research on Welfare Provision for Elderly People*. London: National Institute for Social Work/HMSO.

Sinclair, I. and Payne, C. (1990) *The Consumers' Contribution*. London: DH/SSI HMSO.

Siporin, M. (1988) 'Clinical social work as an art form', *Social Casework*, 68: 177–83.

Skills for Care (2005) *The State of the Social Care Workforce 2004: The Second Skills Research & Intelligence Annual Report*. Leeds: Skills for Care.

Skinner, B.F. (1938) *The Behavior of Organism*. New York: Appleton-Century-Crofts.

Sklyarova, T.V. (2004) *Social Pedagogy and Social Work*. Moscow: St. Tikhon's Orthodox Theological Institute, Department for External Relations of the Moscow Patriarchate, Round Table Education for Change and Diaconia. www.rondtb.msk.ru/info/en/social_pedagogy_en.htm+Social+pedagogue&hl=en

Smale, G. and Tuson, G. with Biehal, N. and Marsh, P. (1993) *Empowerment, Assessment, Care Management and the Skilled Worker*. London: National Institute for Social Work Practice and Development Exchange/HMSO.

Smales, B.J. (1975) *Economic History*. London: Heinemann.

Smith, D. (2002) 'Social work with offenders', in R. Adams, L. Dominelli and M. Payne *Social Work. Themes, Issues and Critical Debates*, 2nd edition. Basingstoke: Palgrave. pp. 308–28.

Smith, M.J. (1975) *When I Say No, I Feel Guilty*. New York: Bantam Books.

Smith, M.K. (2004) *What Is Community Work? How Has it Developed in the UK? A Review and Book List*. www.infed.org/community/b-comwrk.htm

Smith, R. (2005) *Values and Practice in Children's Services*. Basingstoke: Palgrave Macmillan.

Scottish Executive (SE) (2003) SiSWE *Standards in Social Work Education. Framework for Social Work Education in Scotland*. Edinburgh: SE.

Scottish Executive (SE) (2004) *Scotland's Social Care Labour Market*. Edinburgh: SE.

Social Care Association (2005) *Definition of social care*. www.socialcaring.co.uk/

Social Care Institute for Excellence (SCIE) (2003) *Types and Quality of Knowledge in Social Care*. London: SCIE.

Social Exclusion Unit (SEU) (2004a) *Mental Health and Social Exclusion*. London: ODPM.

References

Social Exclusion Unit (SEU) (2004b) *Social Inclusion Unit Leaflet/Handbook*. London: SEU/ODPM.

Social Services Inspectorate (SSI) (2003) *Modern Social Services a Commitment to the Future. The 12th Annual Report of the Chief Inspector of Social Services 2002–2003*. London: DH.

Social Work Services Policy Division (SWSPD) (2005) *21st Century Social Work Review*. Edinburgh: SWSPD Scottish Executive. www.21csocialwork.org.uk

Solomon, B. (1976) *Black Empowerment: Social Work in Oppressed Communities*. New York: Columbia University Press.

Soydan, H. (1999) *The History of Ideas in Social Work*. Birmingham: Venture Press.

Stainton, T. (2002) 'Taking rights structurally: disability, rights and social work responses to direct payments', *British Journal of Social Work*, 32(6): 751–63.

Steiner, R. (1925) *The Story of My Life*. Herndon, VI: Steinerbooks Anthropomorphic Books.

Stevenson, O. (1989) *Age and Vulnerability*. London: Age Concern Arnold.

Stroebe, M. and Schut, H. (1999) 'The dual process model of coping with bereavement: rationale and description', *Death Studies*, 23: 197–224.

Sure Start (2000) www.surestart.gov.uk/home.cfm

Sure Start (2001) *What is Sure Start?*. www.surestart.gov.uk/aboutWhat is.cfm?section=2

Sure Start (2004) *Choice for Parents, the Best Start for Children*. London: Sure Start/DfES, London.

Szasz, T. (1960) 'The Myth of Mental Illness', *American Psychologist*, 15: 113–18.

Theorising Social Work Research (TSWR) (2000) ESRC Seminar Series Electronic Library for Social Care www.elsc.org.uk/socialcareresource/tswr/seminars.htm

Thomas, C. (1999) *Female Forms: Experiencing And Understanding Disability*. Buckingham: Open University Press.

Thomas, D. (1983) *The Making of Community*. London: George Allen and Unwin.

Thompson N. (2001) *Anti-Discriminatory Practice*, 3rd edition. London: Palgrave.

Timms, N. and Timms, R. (1977) *Perspectives in Social Work*. London: Routledge & Kegan Paul.

Titmuss, R.M. (1950) *Problems of Social Policy*. London: Longmans, Green and Co.

Titmuss, R.M. (1970) *The Gift Relationship From Human Blood to Social Policy*. New York: The New Press.

Titmuss, R.M. (1976) *Commitment to Welfare*, 2nd edition. London: Allen and Unwin.

Tolson, E., Reid, W.J. and Garvin, G. (1994) *Task-centered Practice: A Generalist Approach*. New York: Columbia University Press.

Topss England Training Organisation for Social Care (2000) *Modernising the Social Care Workforce – the First National Training Strategy for England*. Leeds: Topss England.

Topss England Training Organisation for Social Care (2003) *The first Annual Report of the Topss England Workforce Intelligence Unit (Eborall, C.)*, vols 1–3. Leeds: Topss England.

Topss England Training Organisation for Social Care (2004) *Registered Managers Award*. Leeds: Topss England.

Topss UK Partnership (2001) *International Definition of Social Work* (International Association of Schools of Social Work, International Federation of Social Workers) in *National Occupational Standards for Social Work*. Leeds: Topss UK Partnership.

Topss UK Partnership/Skills for Care (2002) *National Occupational Standards for Social Work and Statement of Expectations*. Leeds: Topss Training Organisation for Social Care England. www.topss.org.uk/pdf/purpose_roles_unit_elements.pdf

Tossell, D. and Webb, R. (1994) *Inside the Caring Services*, 2nd edition. London: Hodder Arnold.

Townsend, P. (1962) *The Last Refuge*. London: Routledge & Kegan Paul.

Townsend, P. (1981) 'The structured dependency of the elderly: the creation of social policy in the twentieth century', *Ageing and Society*, 1(1): 5–28.

References

Townsend, P. (1986) 'Ageism and social policy', in C. Phillipson and A. Walker (eds) *Ageing and Social Policy*. Aldershot: Gower. pp. 15–44.

Townsend, P. and Abel-Smith, B. (1965) *The Poor and the Poorest: A New Analysis of the Ministry of Labour's Family Expenditure Surveys of 1953–4 and 1960*. London: Bell.

Tregenna-Piggott, A. and Daly, C. (2001) *ChildRight* 181, pp. 8–9.

Turner, M. and Evans, C. (2004) 'Users influencing the management of practice', in D. Statham (ed.) *Managing Front Line Practice in Social Care* Number 40 in the Research Highlights in Social Work series. London: Jessica Kingsley.

Twining, W. (1967) 'Pericles and the plumber', *Law Quarterly Review*, 83: 396.

UK Bright Life (2004) *Mail Order Leaflet*. Liverpool: UK BrightLife.

Utting, W. (1991) *Children in the Public Care: A Review of Residential Child Care*. London: HMSO.

Vernon, S. (2004) *Social Work and the Law*, 3rd edition. Oxford: Oxford University Press.

Vickerstaff, S.A. (1999) 'Work, employment and the production of welfare', in J. Baldock, N. Manning, S. Miller and S.A. Vickerstaff (eds) *Social Policy*. Oxford: Oxford University Press.

Victor, C. (1994) *Old Age in Modern Society*, 2nd edition. London: Chapman Hall.

Voltaire (1994) *A Treatise on Toleration and Other Essays*. Amherst, NY: Prometheus Books.

Waddilove, D. (2004) *Redesigned and Redrawn – Developing New Roles in Social Care*. Leeds: Topps England.

Wagner, G. (1988) *A Positive Choice: Report of an Independent Review of Residential Care*. London: HMSO.

Walker, A. (1980) 'The social creation of poverty and dependency in old age', *Journal of Social Policy*, 9(1): 45–75.

Walker, A. (1981) 'Towards a political economy of old age', *Ageing and Society*, 1(1): 73–94.

Walker, A. (1983) 'Social policy and elderly people in Great Britain: the construction of dependent social and economic status in old age', in A.M. Guillemard (ed.) *Old Age and the Welfare State*. London: Sage. pp. 143–67.

Walker, A. (1991) 'The social construction of dependency in old age', in M. Loney, R. Bocock, J. Clarke, A. Cochrane, P. Graham and M. Wilson (eds) *The State of the Market*. London: Sage. pp. 41–57

Ward, A. and Mullender, A. (1993) 'Empowerment and oppression: an indissoluble pairing for contemporary social work', in J. Walmesley, J. Reynolds, P. Shakespeare and R. Woolfe (eds) *Health, Welfare and Practice: Reflecting on Roles and Relationships*. London: Sage. pp. 147–53.

Warner, N. (1992) *Choosing with Care: The Report of the Committee of Inquiry into the Selection, Development and Management of Staff in Children's Homes*. London: DH.

Washington, A. (2004) 'The role of information giving in head injury', unpublished draft thesis Graduate School for Business, Law, and Social Sciences, Nottingham Trent University, Nottingham.

Weber, M. (1958) *The Protestant Ethic and the Spirit of Capitalism*. New York: Scribners.

Weiss, I. (2005) 'Is there a global common core to social work? A cross-national comparative study of BSW graduate students', *Social Work*, 50(2): 101–10.

Werner, E.E. (1989) 'Children of the garden island', *Scientific American*, 260: 106–11.

Werner, E.E. and Smith, R.S. (1982) *Vulnerable but Invincible: A Longitudinal Study of Resilient Children and Youth*. New York: McGraw-Hill.

Whittaker, J.K. and Tracy, E.M. (1989) *Social Treatment. An Introduction to Interpersonal Helping in Social Work Practice*, 2nd edition. New York: Aldine de Gruyter.

Willcocks, D., Peace, S. and Kellaher, L. (1987) *Private Lives in Public Places*. London: Tavistock.

Williams, F. (1996) 'Postmodernism, feminism and the question of difference', in N. Parton (ed.) *Social Theory, Social Change and Social Work*. London: Routledge. pp. 61–76.

Williams, J. (1993) 'What is a profession? Experience versus expertise', in J. Walmsley, J. Reynolds, P. Shakespeare, R. Woolfe, *Health Welfare & Practice. Reflecting on Roles and Relationships*. London: Open University/Sage. pp. 8–15.

References

Williamson, M. (1966) 'Poverty in the United States', in M. Webb (ed.) *Wealth and Want in One World.* New York: Friendship Press. pp. 23–40.

Wing, J.K. (1978) 'Medical and social science and medical and social care', in J. Barnes and N. Connelly (eds) *Social Care Research.* London: Policy Studies Institute Bedford Square Press. pp. 123–38.

Wolfensburger, W. (1982) *The Principle of Normalization in Human Services.* Toronto: National Institute of Mental Retardation.

Wolfensberger,W. (1992) *A Brief Introduction to Social Role Valorization as a high-order Concept for Structuring Human Services* (2nd revised edition.) Syracuse, NY: Training Institute for Human Service Planning, Leadership and Change Agentry (Syracuse University).

Worden, J.W. (1991) *Grief Counselling and Grief Therapy: A Handbook for the Mental Health Professional.* London: Routledge.

The World Bank (WB) (1999) 'What is social capital?'. *PovertyNet.* www.worldbank.org/poverty/scapital/whatsc.htm

Yalom, I. (1985) *The Theory and Practice of Group Psychotherapy.* New York: Basic Books.

Yeates, N. (2001) *Globalization and Social Policy.* London: Sage.

Younghusband, E. (1951) *Social Work in Britain.* London: Carnegie UK Trust.

Younghusband, E. (1959) *Report of the Working Party on Social Workers in the Local Authority Health and Welfare Services.* London: HMSO.

Younghusband, E. (1978) *Social Work in Britain, 1950–1975: A Follow-up Study.* London: Allen and Unwin.

Younghusband, E. (1981) *The Newest Profession: A Short History of Social Work.* Sutton: Community Care.

Youth Justice Board (YJB) (2003) *ASSET Young Offenders Assessment.* London: YJB. www.youth-justice-board.gov.uk

Youth Justice Board (YJB) (2004) Youth Justice Board/Youth Offending Teams 14 October 2004. www.youth-justice-board.gov.uk/

INDEX

Index

Index

Index

Index

Social Services Inspectorate (SSI), 69
social skills training, 101–2, 191
social welfare, 56–9
    international models of, 75
social work
    criticisms of, 21–2
    definitions of, 4–5, 7–11, 18–20, 26–8, 79, 202, 137
    as a protected title, 1, 14, 142, 201
social work process (SWP), 180, 192, 196–7
socialisation, 156
socio-educational work, 77
Soloman, J., 159
Solomon, Barbara, 134–5
Soydan, H., 20
special educational needs, 170
specialisms in social work, 103–4
staged learning, 43–4
stakeholders, 41, 97, 107, 149
Stam, H.J., 89–90
Statham, D., 44
Steiner, Rudolf, 77
stereotyping, negative, 157
strange situation experiment, 159
Stroebe, M., 161
structured dependency, 155
subsidiarity, 75
super ego, 87
supervision, 37, 50, 88, 142, 144, 178, 198, 200
Sure Start, 22, 46, 76, 78–9, 100, 106–7, 110, 160, 173
sustainable environments, 65
synchronic perspective on human development,
        151, 154, 157–8
systematic thinking, 196
systems theory, 192
Szasz, T., 167

targeting of interventions, 66
task-centred practice, 192
Thatcherite policies, 58
Theorising Social Work Research initiative, 12
Third Way policies, 60–1, 66, 73
Thomas Ellis, Alice, 161–2
Thomas, D., 93
Thompson, N., 131–2
time, dimensions of, 158
time management, 32
Timms, N., 19, 21
Titmuss, R.M., 62
tokenism, 134
Tolson, E., 192
Townsend, P., 21, 60, 155
Tracy, E.M., 83, 90, 98, 101, 108–9
training for social work, 16, 105, 108
    see also continuing professional development

transactional analysis, 88, 191
transferable skills, 29, 177, 196
transference, 88
Turkey, 160–1
Turning Point, 105
Twining, W., 97

unconscious mind, 87–8, 188
United States, 8–10, 20–1, 103, 107, 130

values in social work, 112–15, 121, 125–6, 144–5, 176, 201
    in community care, 127–8
    emancipatory, 136–8, 147
    permeation across social care, 130
    structural, 130–1
values clarification, 123–4
values consensus, 84
values dilemmas, 140, 142
village communities, 77
voice, 135, 139
Voltaire, 57
voluntary sector, 45, 166, 185

Wagner Report (1988), 126–9
Wales, 41
    see also Care Council for Wales
Walker, A., 66
Warner Report (1992), 49
Waterhouse Report (2000), 68
Watson, N., 169
Webb, Beatrice and Sidney, 57
Weber, M., 89
Weiss, I., 26–7
welfare mix model, 79–80
welfare state, 5, 58–62, 66
Werner, E.E., 163
Whittaker, J.K., 83, 90, 98, 101, 108–9
whole system thinking, 80, 201
Williams, F., 50, 87, 196
Wing, J.K., 16
Wolfensberger, W., 127–9
Worden, J.W., 161
workforce intelligence, 16, 67–8
workhouses, 20
World Commission on the Environment, 65

Yeates, N., 73
young carers, 173–4
Younghusband, E., 90, 92–3
Youth Justice Board (YJB), 6, 100, 173, 181, 198
youth offending teams (Yots), 6–7, 100, 110, 173, 197–8
youth work, 171